PRAISE FOR *ARCT...*

T0246810

"Michael Engelhard shows us what ı ... Arctic's
sights, sounds, and smells . . . the nature of memory and mortality."
—SUSAN SOMMER, editor of *Alaska* magazine

"Engelhard is a writer who knows wilderness as well as he knows himself."
—PETE FROMM, author of *The Names of the Stars*

". . . timeless storytelling. *Arctic Traverse* shimmers with
caring, connection, and poetic prose."
—HANK LENTFER, author of *Raven's Witness*

". . . captures the vastness and beauty of the Brooks Range."
—KENNETH BROWER, author of *Earth and the Great Weather*

"Engelhard weaves rich human and natural history into lyrical prose . . ."
—ROMAN DIAL, author of *The Adventurer's Son*

"Lovers of far-north lands shouldn't miss this elegy
to one of the world's last great wildernesses."
—SHANNON POLSON, author of *The Grit Factor*

"Grizzly encounters and brutal tundra slogs are punctuated by side
treks into natural and human history and philosophical musings spiced
with humor and literary wit . . . a true adventure of the human spirit."
—NICK JANS, writer and longtime Brooks Range resident

"A great read for armchair adventurers, full of insights for those with
a passion for that ineffable place and state of mind we call wilderness."
—PETER STARK, author of *Last Empty Places*

"The closest thing to lacing up your boots and opening your heart to one of
America's last great wildernesses."
—KARSTEN HEUER, author of *Being Caribou*

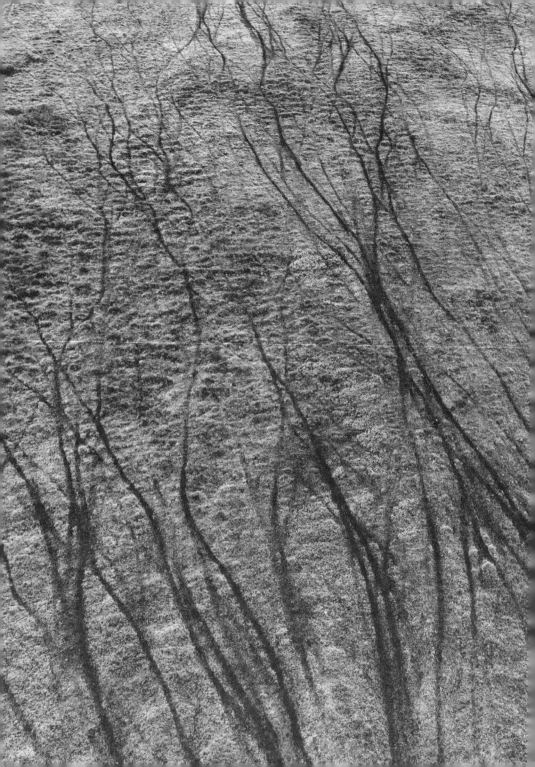

ARCTIC TRAVERSE

A THOUSAND-MILE SUMMER *of* TREKKING *the* BROOKS RANGE

MICHAEL ENGELHARD

MOUNTAINEERS
BOOKS

MOUNTAINEERS BOOKS is dedicated to the exploration, preservation, and enjoyment of outdoor and wilderness areas.

1001 SW Klickitat Way, Suite 201, Seattle, WA 98134
800-553-4453, www.mountaineersbooks.org

Printed in the United States of America
27 26 25 24   1 2 3 4 5

Design and layout: Kim Thwaits
Cartographer: Lohnes+Wright
Cover photographs: front, *Backpacker in the Arctic National Wildlife Refuge* (Photo by Michael Engelhard); back, *Caribou of the Porcupine herd in the Arctic Refuge* (Danielle Brigida, US Fish and Wildlife Service)
Frontispiece: *Caribou trails in the northern foothills of the Brooks Range* (Photo by Lisa Hupp, US Fish and Wildlife Service)

Library of Congress Cataloging-in-Publication Data is available at https://lccn.loc.gov/2023034459. The LC ebook record is available at https://lccn.loc.gov/2023034460.

Mountaineers Books titles may be purchased for corporate, educational, or other promotional sales, and our authors are available for a wide range of events. For information on special discounts or booking an author, contact our customer service at 800-553-4453 or mbooks@mountaineersbooks.org.

 Printed on FSC®-certified and 30% recycled materials

MIX
Paper from responsible sources
FSC® C005010

ISBN (paperback): 978-1-68051-678-4
ISBN (ebook): 978-1-68051-679-1

An independent nonprofit publisher since 1960

To my father—
who exposed me to the outdoors early on
and thus helped to shape the man I have become.

A journey is of no merit unless it has tested you.
—**TAHIR SHAH**, *In Search of King Solomon's Mines*

Glorious it is
To see long-haired winter caribous
Returning to the forests.
Fearfully they watch
For the little people,
While the herd follows the ebb-mark of the sea
With a storm of clattering hooves.
Glorious it is
When wandering time is come.
Yayai-ya-yiya.
—**NETSIT**, of the Umingmaqtormiut (the Muskox People),
lyrics recorded by Knud Rasmussen in the 1920s

Perhaps when we hike we do so by necessity, as we trace
the invisible songlines of our genome.
—**RICHARD LOUV**, *The Nature Principle*

CONTENTS

III. GATES

IV. RIVER

V. STRAIT

AUTHOR'S NOTE:
ON LANGUAGE AND LAND

While the colonial baggage of *Eskimo* ("netter of snowshoes" in the neighboring Innu's Cree language) has rendered the term offensive in Greenland and Canada as well as in some parts of the US, Alaska's Inupiaq speakers, especially of the older generation, still widely embrace it. Most do not self-identify as Inuit, and it remains part of names of organizations and events like the Alaska Eskimo Whaling Commission and the World Eskimo-Indian Olympics as well as of US federal statutes and offices. The same holds true for *Indians*, among them Athabaskans of the Interior and Cook Inlet, related to the lower forty-eight states' Apache and Navajo speakers. The suffix *-miut* ("people of") serves to distinguish Eskimo subdivisions as part of their names for themselves.

Less than three miles from the cabin we rent, the University of Alaska Fairbanks (UAF) sits on a height that after 1917 was commonly known as College Hill, and when I studied there, West Ridge. From a pullout above a sledding slope on its south side, on clear days now exceedingly rare because of wildfires and ice fog, you can see the Tanana Flats and the Alaska Range with Denali, North America's tallest peak. Bones, charcoal, and stone tools from the UAF Campus site, discovered in 1933 and recognized for its archaeological importance, are at least three thousand years old. That's twelve times the age of these United States. The region's Kokht'ana (Lower Tanana Athabaskans in the anthropologists' tongue) call the hill Troth Yeddah', "Wild Potato Ridge," for the edible tuber growing there. In 2013, the USGS Board on Geographic Names approved a proposal to restore the landmark's original name.

I humbly and gratefully acknowledge that the woods that became my home were home first to the Kokht'ana and their predecessors. Those include two ice age girl infants who died about 11,500 years ago in a camp on another ridge, fifty miles to the south, above the Tth'itu' ("Straight Water," the newcomers' Tanana River). Their skeletons, covered in red ochre, adjacent to gifts of stone spear points and incised antler foreshafts, are the oldest human remains so far found on the American side of Beringia. Despite this and much more physical and oral proof of the depth and breadth of Indigenous tenancy, the State of Alaska took sixty-three years, until 2022, to formally recognize Alaska's 229 tribes.

I hereby also grant that the resource extraction I condemn enables my lifestyle and standard of living. "If one were trying to live sustainably, one couldn't live in Alaska," I often say. Or in few places at all, it seems. The following pages owe much to the fact that nature, culture, and history have shaped each other ever since humans stepped into the scene. Ethnicity and economies merely provide the varied conduits through which such energies flow.

PROLOGUE:
GEOGRAPHY OF DESIRE

Summoning my life's longest, most formative journey, I sometimes put the maps of my arctic traverse end to end. When I do, all the wilderness I could ever want spreads across my living room floor, a smorgasbord of possibilities. "You must walk like a camel," Thoreau counseled, "which is said to be the only beast which ruminates when walking." And I did.

Riven by glacial valleys, shoaled by the coastal plain, Alaska's largely treeless Brooks Range spans the state's entire width, arcing east to west, a thousand miles scaled down to just thirteen feet. The dot-and-dash line of the Continental Divide, which I crossed numerous times, squirms on the mountainous spine, splitting waters headed north to the Arctic Ocean from those southbound for the Bering Strait. To save weight on my fifty-eight-day venture, I kept a journal on the maps' backs and in their margins. It was a quest whose magnitude I'd desired yet dreaded for decades and that I had finally planned throughout one year.

I first set foot in that country in 1990, as a University of Alaska anthropology student doing graduate research. The National Park Service wanted to know which areas of Kobuk Valley and Gates of the Arctic National Parks Eskimo and Athabaskan hunters and gatherers had used in the past. If those groups could establish prior claims, they would be entitled to forever hunt, trap, and fish in those preserves. I learned much about the region's topography from Inupiaq elders north of the Arctic Circle. For my unfinished dissertation, I studied how a boreal people, the Gwich'in, who until recently had led nomadic subsistence lives, construe place, how maps form in their minds, and if landscapes forge personalities.

From early adulthood, I'd shared those northerners' peripatetic streak and love for stark country. In lieu of their guidance, maps and books had fostered my independence, nudging me into new terrain. Too much Jack London at a susceptible age perhaps. I've based many life choices on scenery and concomitant open space, which has not always panned out. After only six years, I quit anthropology, in part because, like the cultural critic and English professor Marie Louise Pratt, I couldn't stomach that with too few exceptions, such interesting folks doing such interesting things wrote such boring books. I neither could handle postmodern constructs then in vogue that diluted the rich flavors of reality, even nature's importance, in so many vertiginous words. Still, my academic training and interests have informed my nonfiction writing and wilderness guiding, careers short on pay raises and promotions that I've stuck with for more than two decades.

The maps are frayed, taped at the folds, as I consulted them often, frequently in a drizzle, seeking guidance from a two-dimensional oracle. The occasional bloodstain or squashed mosquito proves that my words did not come easily but had to be earned. All formerly blank spaces now crawl with my cursive script, with life transposed into text, the work of a nature accountant or ambulant graphomaniac. The map panels, too, are annotated, with my symbols for caches, campsites, and the airstrips' lifeline to civilization—and my route worming into the wildlands.

Following map contours step by laborious step, I'd quickly wised up to the cartographers' code. Bunched chocolate-brown lines meant steep climbs or descents; hedgehog marks promised squelchy swamps; robin's-egg blue stood for lakes, ponds and rivers, or, finely striated, for snowfields and glaciers; that same hue spelled wet crossings, creekside coffee breaks, slippery footing.

What the ten US Geological Survey quadrangles fail to show: tussocks, the knee-high vegetation humps taxing my knees, ankles, and spirit; the bushwhack up Ekokpuk Creek, the trip's worst section, not even hinted at by the usual mint-green patches on the map; the vigor of streams I forded that made hiking poles thrum; veils of mosquitos that shadowed me, eager for a meal; grizzlies that circled downwind for a rank whiff of me, which normally but not always sent them bolting. Though I did not mark wolf encounters on these sheets, I can to this day pinpoint each one to within a mile, even without my dense notes.

The maps do not hold the metal taste of springwater so cold it induced ice cream headaches. They do not carry the perfume of crushed heather or Labrador tea, the soughing of breezes or the tang of August blueberries. They omit the fog that blotted out Peregrine Pass, the wind gusting in Noatak Valley, the rain that soaked me for thirty consecutive days. You will not find in them, either, the image of me afterward, reduced by twenty-five pounds yet refined somehow, distilled to a new essence, with mental dross and routines stripped away. Six hundred miles walking and four hundred rowing the Noatak River, all by myself, had reopened my eyes to nature's small, quiet wonders.

The blue swath on my westernmost map—the Bering Strait, terminus of my traverse—stretches south to encompass my onetime hometown, Nome. Now residing roughly a hundred miles from the Arctic Circle, in the state's center, its Golden Heart City, Fairbanks, I keep feeling close to the Brooks Range, locus of my desire. In this world, I realize once again, there are no topographic margins. Unlike a sphere rendered in two dimensions, a Mercator projection, Earth has no here or there, no beginning or end. Like the segments arrayed on my floor, maps and dreams and the worlds maps encrypt are connected.

THE BROOKS RANGE

Utqiagvik (Barrow)

Teshekpuk Lake

Utukok River

National Petroleum Reserve in Alaska

Kokolik River

Colville River

Chukchi Sea

Alaska Maritime NWR

De Long Mountains

Chandler River

Noatak River

Noatak NP

B R O O K S

Chandler Lake

Kivalina

Cape Krusenstern NM

Noatak

Baird Mountains

Gates of the Arctic NP&R

Cape Krusenstern

Kiana

Kobuk Valley NP

Schwatka Mountains

John R.

Alatna River

Arctic Circle

Kotzebue

Ambler

Kobuk

Bering Strait

Ending point

Kobuk River

Shungnak

Alatna

Allakaket

Bering Land Bridge NP

ALASKA

Seward Peninsula

Koyukuk River

Nome

Yukon River

Norton Sound

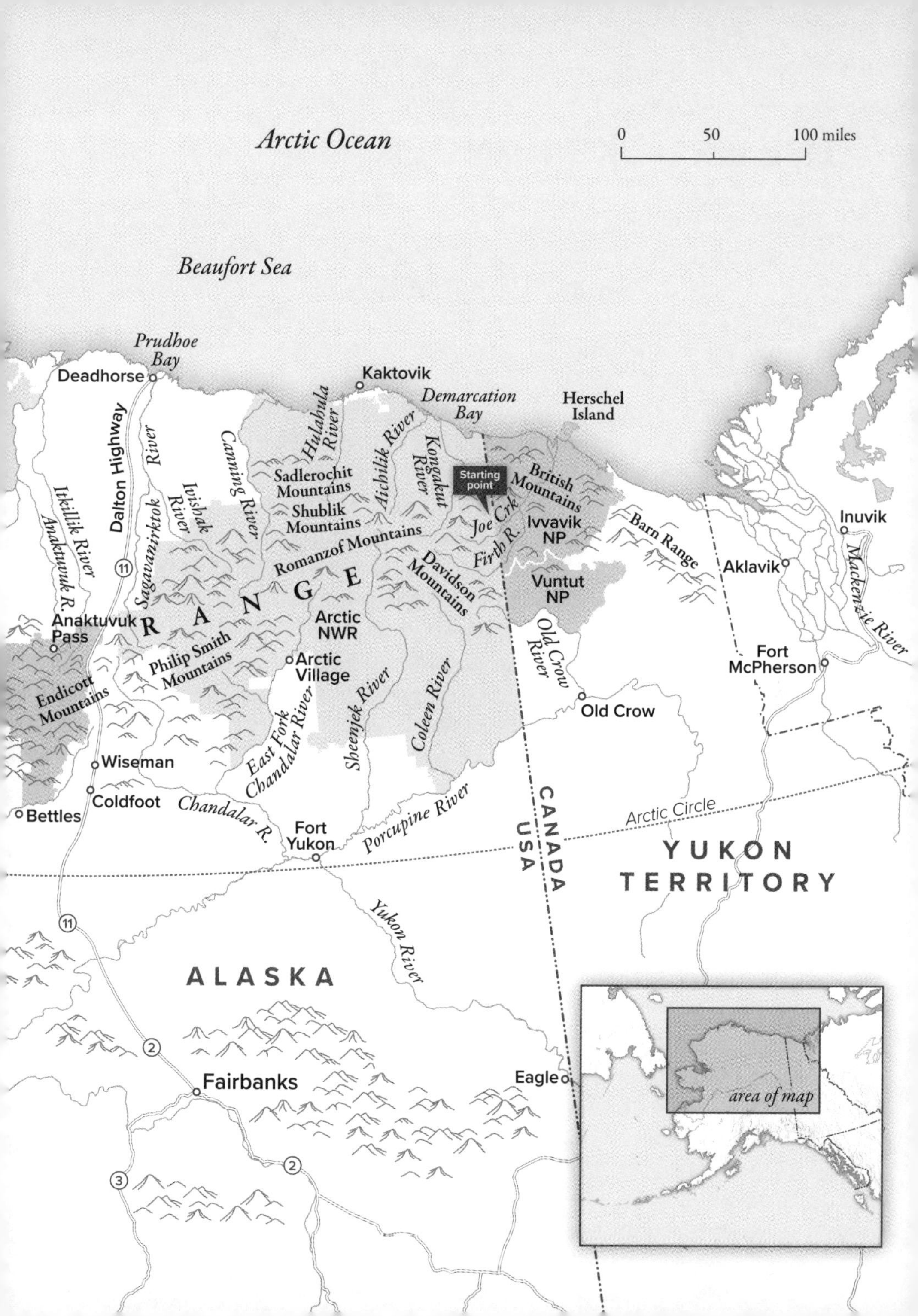
Arctic Ocean
0
50
100 miles
Beaufort Sea
Prudhoe Bay
Deadhorse
Kaktovik
Demarcation Bay
Herschel Island
Dalton Highway
Sagavanirktok River
Canning River
Hulahula River
Aichilik River
Kongakut River
Starting point
British Mountains
Sadlerochit Mountains
Shublik Mountains
Ivishak River
Itkillik River
Anaktuvuk River
Joe Crk
Firth R.
Ivvavik NP
Barn Range
Inuvik
Romanzof Mountains
Davidson Mountains
Aklavik
Mackenzie River
Vuntut NP
R A N G E
Anaktuvuk R.
Anaktuvuk Pass
Arctic NWR
Philip Smith Mountains
Arctic Village
Old Crow River
Fort McPherson
Endicott Mountains
Sheenjek River
Coleen River
Old Crow
East Fork Chandalar River
Wiseman
Coldfoot
Bettles
Chandalar R.
Porcupine River
Fort Yukon
Arctic Circle
CANADA
USA
YUKON TERRITORY
Yukon River
ALASKA
Fairbanks
Eagle
area of map
11
2
3

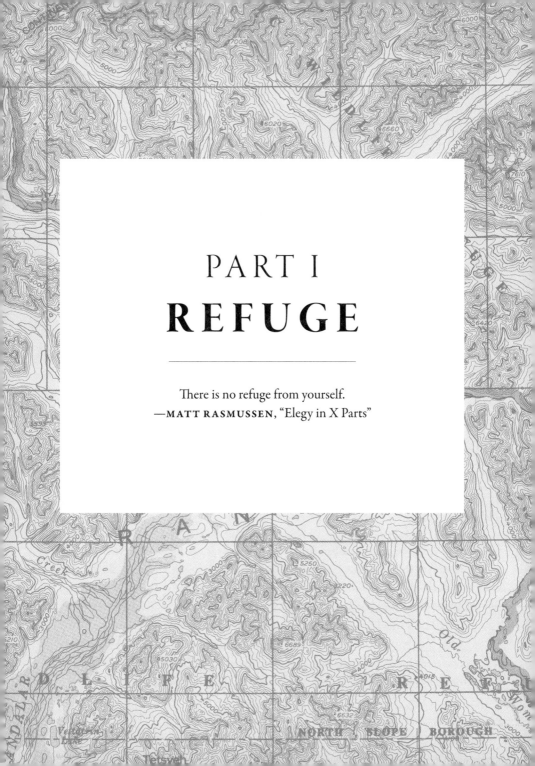

PART I
REFUGE

There is no refuge from yourself.
—MATT RASMUSSEN, "Elegy in X Parts"

A WARM WELCOME

DAY 1 (7 MILES)
QUAD: TABLE MOUNTAIN

Some element of fear probably lies at the root of every substantial challenge.
And it makes no difference at all whether the challenge is to your mind or to your
body, or whether—with richer promise than either, alone—it embraces both.
—COLIN FLETCHER, *The Man Who Walked Through Time*

I arrive at Joe Creek in the far eastern Brooks Range one month before
Independence Day, still beholden to clock time, at five in the afternoon. The sun
hangs high in the northwestern quadrant, two weeks from its tipping point back
into winter. Caribou graze placidly, scattered across the tundra. When the pro-
peller has stuttered to a standstill, I unlatch the door and step out of the fat-tired
Cessna and receive my gear, which I drop beside the runway. Before Kirk Sweetsir
climbs back in to disappear, the suave, gray-haired, clean-shaven owner-operator
of Yukon Air Service warns me that Joe Creek is "bear-y."

Don't I know it.

On a previous trip, I laid over with three clients in Joe Creek, which trends
westward from the Canada border 170 miles above the Arctic Circle. We'd struck
out bright and early to bag one of the unnamed peaks crowding it, or rather, to
succumb to the view from the top of range upon range marching toward the
horizon. While we were crunching on gravel past willow hedgerows, I chatted
with the group strung out behind me in the wash. Near a brace of gray-faced
limestone bluffs, belligerent coughing interrupted our footsteps and conversation.
Bull caribou, I thought as I scanned the slopes for movement.

For days, we had tracked caribou along the traces they twine into marshland, over passes, down broken defiles, fording streams fat with boulders, waist deep in snowmelt or up to our kneecaps in mop-headed tundra, trying to get within optimal camera range, which meant close enough to hear the herd's voice—its grunts, bleats, and snorts a parody of an old folks' home—or closer still, what sounded like knuckle cracking: the tendons in feet that plied scree and *aufeis*, riverine "ice on top," and smoothly as pistons postholed the boggy pits that separate tussocks. The voices we heard were all female; bulls vocalize only in a huff, during the rut.

In the migration's wake we had stalked wildness. Next thing we knew, it came barreling down at us from that ridge at the pace of a cantering horse, bellowing gruffly, just once, more of a snarl, really, jaws clacking, ears flattened.

"Cub and two sows," I called out to my clients. My mind somersaulted, scrambling language, and I used terms I normally don't. (More on that later.) A female grizzly, a blond bulge of fur and muscle, rippled downhill with twin teddies in tow.

Following my lead, my trio scuttled up the far embankment, determined not to panic or turn their backs to the bear. We then stood and faced carnivorous anger. The clients hung back, perhaps thinking that I got paid and should therefore take the brunt or that I had experience with this. I did not. My prior bear encounters never had been that stressful.

As I fumbled with the pepper spray's safety clip, I understood hermit crabs caught switching shells. My soft body's every fiber itched to turn and run or at least curl into the fetal position before impact.

The bear reached the creek bed sixty feet from us.

To everybody's surprise, she stalled as if she had hit an electric fence. It must have been a lingering trace of our odors. In one fluid motion she pivoted, disciplined one overeager fuzz ball at her heels with a plate-size paw, and blustered up the wash, the cubs bouncing as if rubber bound them to her.

Shaken, we tried to coax our heart rates back to normal. The tundra was awash with adrenaline, abuzz with color and detail. Soldiers after combat report this "ecstasy of survival" against which everything pales and that thenceforth they crave. We flopped down and decompressed, our voices overlapping in disbelief. I suddenly remembered hearing clicks behind me while the bear charged. Incredibly,

Steve, on "burst mode," had taken several pictures during the brouhaha. "That's what I came here for," he said. I was on burst mode myself.

Any attempt to fit the scuffle into a quotidian frame of reference failed. We had teetered at the brink. We had passed through moments in which nerves and ligaments could have torn, life trajectories could have changed.

After fifteen minutes—long enough for the bear to traverse several ridges and valleys if she chose to—we continued our hike. Each rock bear on the hillside looked ready to roll. Around the next bend I spotted her again. She was contouring a slope high above. But no, that one looked different. Its legs were the color of freshly cut peat, darker than the body; its size and shoulder hump declared it to be a male. The bear paid us no attention. He ambled through talus to a razorback ridge, where mountain debris swallowed him.

We replayed both sightings out loud, sifting through apparent randomness for clues to a larger plot.

Most likely, the female had first scrapped with the male. Male grizzlies routinely kill offspring their rivals sired, and perhaps even their own. She must have been riled up already when she heard us in the wash. Poor-sighted like all bears, she then rushed the new aggressors to protect her cubs. As soon as she realized her mistake, she fled in terror, as most grizzlies will upon getting a whiff of people.

By fitting the pieces together, we made sense of the experience. We would revisit it for years to come—embellished, refined, acted out on other trips or on paper—whenever bear behavior cropped up as a topic. In the retelling, we construed meaning, and the emphasis slowly shifted from personal, localized lore to link with larger, older mythologies.

That day had not yet spent its powder.

We did not let the encounter deflect us from our goal. Hours later we summited, and the view was everything we had hoped for. I chose a different route on the descent back to camp, wanting to avoid the bears if they were still hanging out on that slope, but also because I like to see new country whenever possible. Near the base of the mountain, we dropped into a drainage that quickly narrowed into a small gorge. Willows crowded the streambed, reducing visibility. I felt uneasy, preferring high ground with a view as a safety precaution. So, we climbed from the defile and stayed on the level slightly above its rim, on the mountain's flank.

The going was awkward, hard on the feet—off-trail sidehilling is no fun—but I felt better about this route.

Validating my gut feeling, not ten minutes later we noticed another bear. He lay on the far side of the gorge, napping close to the rim. If we had followed the bottom, we would have marched by right below him, and our footfalls no doubt would have awakened him. Instead, we tiptoed past on the safer side, and he never so much as lifted his head.

The Joe Creek episode has a postscript. I stayed in touch with Steve, actually guiding him on another backpacking trip. He sent me the photos he'd snapped behind my back. The bear looked small and far away in them, not at all threatening, like a golden retriever fetching a ball. "Please don't show these to anybody," I wrote. "They don't do our experience justice. They don't match the story I have been telling."

So, yes, Joe Creek *is* bear-y.

Within minutes of landing at the start of my traverse, the first bruin pops up at the airstrip. I'm still fiddling with my pack, transferring enough provisions from my bearproof food barrel for a day's hike east to the Canada border. He rears for a better view, catches my scent, and scoots. I leave the barrel at the strip to lighten my load, planning to get it upon my return. In an arcane calculus of pack weight, finances, caloric needs, and the nature of the terrain, I determined that I'll need six caches along my planned route to Kotzebue. Each holds supplies for roughly nine days, except for the final, river one, which should last for two weeks.

A total of seven bears, counting cubs, cross my path within the next four hours. Number five gallops up to me from the stream bottom, curious and confident, looking very excited. I unholster my spray can, the fastest gun in the North, before this sub-adult turns and flees. Another bear spooks some caribou cooling off on the aufeis, the stream's shield of frozen overflow layers that might linger all summer. I tread on mats of tiny pink stars and white mini-urns, alpine azalea and bearberries—it can't be avoided. I'll see the latter fruit into purplish-black spheres among scarlet leaves, if I live long enough.

This is my first multiday backcountry journey after six months of hibernation in Nome and another slush month of *breakup* (when the ice vanishes from the rivers and the Bering Strait). Therefore, my skills, body, and tolerance for risk and ambiguity all have weakened. Before my departure from Fairbanks, I sacrificed to the voyaging gods not a white goat but my shoulder-length, then still-blond ponytail, betokening the beginning. I also knew that short hair would be low maintenance, with no need for shampoo or a brush. Now I feel naked, and the buzz cut alone is not to blame.

As far as bears go, my arsenal holds the usual low-key devices: pepper spray and a whistle, along with one tool I've never tried: a handheld marine signal flare guaranteed to burn sixty seconds at 15,000 candlepower to deter any busybody who hangs around or approaches camp. Ecotourism guides on the Katmai coast swear by these. I decided against a pistol, because they are heavy and cumbersome and a charging bear is no easy target. A wounded one is even more trouble than one who's pissed off. Statistics show properly sprayed bear repellent is almost always effective, whereas armed hunters have been mauled or killed. A gun makes you cocky—never a good stance in bear country. Also, I'm a visitor to their home, and it would be rude to shoot the owner.

Generally, a functioning brain is your best weapon to avoid confrontations in the first place, though staying alert and keeping your cool is sometimes easier said than done. Mind a few simple precautions. Holler and blow your whistle long before you plunge into thickets that congest ravines or while you thread through the belts of riparian willows and alders. Or sing; nobody will judge your performance out here. Watch for bear diggings, scat, and tracks. Camp away from game trails, and maintain a clean camp, which is why I did not bring fishing gear. Don't hike by yourself if possible.

Passing through Bear's world is a humbling that reminds us of our place in the food chain; we're not always top dog. Who spots whom first in this setting becomes a matter of safety. Vision, hearing, and smelling have been refined in the tundra's denizens to various degrees to ensure survival of the most sentient. Exposure and this landscape's spare natural soundtrack awaken instincts long dulled. With an awareness thus sharpened, you notice nonessentials that enrich your stay. As much as bears can cause stress, a place without them or other alpha predators is poor indeed. In their presence, you feel fully, if at times frightfully, alive.

After dinner, pulling out the antenna, angling it for the optimal triangulating signals from satellites that hold me in their invisible web, I try to call my girlfriend, Melissa, in Nome from the hillside above my tent. An outfitter friend in Kaktovik, the Inupiaq Eskimo activist Robert Thompson, lent me the phone. Little do I know at this point that it will become a source of agitation, while simultaneously saving my bacon when resupply problems crop up. Required to carry one on the job for emergencies and evacuations, I don't on private adventures, as phones give a false sense of security and make bailing out far too easy. The safety margin with satellite phones does not increase. Trusting that rescue always is close at hand, people take greater risks.

Each call, whether social or logistical, is a regrown umbilicus. It links you with the world of mundane comforts, the one some people insist is the real world, the one I strive to leave behind. "Don't you know you cannot escape your life?" a hiking partner glued to his inReach needled me once. I do, but I'd like to take breaks from it and revert to an older, elemental mode of existence, one closer to the land and farther from the clanging of civilization. "Why should a man be scorned if, finding himself in prison, he tries to get out and go home? The world outside has not become less real because the prisoner cannot see it," I could have riposted with Tolkien. By cutting through digital ties as I would a Gordian knot, I feel, perhaps foolishly, that I am moving *toward* life. When the going gets tough, the tough go camping.

I get Melissa's answering machine. She must be out after work, hiking, on this beautiful summer evening. Somehow, the message I leave feels like a goodbye. I'm afraid I won't survive the night. None of my friends or acquaintances could muster enough vacation, or motivation, to accompany me on this two-month quest. And I was not about to throw in my lot with a stranger, someone I might have met through a social app had I even known how to use one. So, here I am going alone. Wildlife experts advise against solo travel in bear country, and admittedly, there is some safety in numbers. But I did not want to put my desire forever on hold.

Though I've been smitten with bears for decades, I don't want to be smitten *by* one. I'm already stamped with their mark, a paw print tattooed on my thigh. Down in Tucson, twenty-some years ago, cooped up in a ranch job, I tried to invoke wildness with this ink-stencil totem. I've had a bearish streak since childhood, bearish moods and bearish manners, combined with a thick skull, that only worsen with age. If you've seen male grizzlies out and about after six months of denning, you know what I mean. My hair is gray now; I could pass for a silvertip. But my beard, though bushy, is only a five-o'clock shadow of grizzly hirsuteness. My sense of the land pales next to theirs. I regret not speaking their language, not smelling what they smell, not knowing what they dream about in the winter. I rate my trips by how many bears we encounter and eagerly scan the country, trying to get clients their money's worth.

Technically, a bear sighting differs from an encounter. But the first, which I prefer, can transmogrify into the second the moment you are noticed. I always hope for a bear early in the trip, which will put my clients on guard. They'll instantly understand that the safety talk back at the outfitter's Fairbanks warehouse was not just a formality. If that first grizzly is a relaxed one, unaware of our presence, so much the better. People realize then that bears can be awesome fun.

But that's not my current frame of mind. I go to sleep with a folding knife next to me, bought as an afterthought at a Fred Meyer where a friend stopped before driving me to the airfield. If a bear slices into my flimsy makeshift cave, I mean to put up a fight, though one pocketknife blade won't be a match for ten four-inch claws and an appetite.

And to think they named a pastry after those lethal tools.

DIVIDING THE INDIVISIBLE

DAY 2 (4 MILES)
QUAD: TABLE MOUNTAIN

Cloudless. Two more bears along the way, a female and yearling, pay me no attention. As members of the order Carnivora, bears are much more closely related to seals, dogs, and weasels than to swine. I therefore avoid "boar" and "sow" as labels for the male and female, which is also the custom among wildlife biologists.

Deciding spontaneously that I don't really need to toe the international line on this fine day, I climb a peak near the border instead. I am eager to return to the airstrip and begin my westward journey. It seems nonsensical to add six round-trip miles when one thousand await me in the opposite direction.

The boundary, which forms the country's longest straight line where it matches the 141st meridian west for nearly seven hundred miles, runs from Demarcation Point, forty-five miles north of where I stand, south to Mount Saint Elias, before it jigs east into the Alaska panhandle's littoral. Crews with choppers and chainsaws faithfully groom the scar of this recent historical break—visible proof of two nations' failure to understand and acknowledge a region's natural flow.

Starting in 1904, engineers, astronomers, and surveyors from both countries "in a spirit of hearty co-operation" ventured into "a paradise for all kinds of insects" that never left the men alone. Sweating, bleeding, fraying pant legs and holing boots, hoping clouds would dissipate, they plunged into crevasses; lined, portaged, and capsized canoes; maneuvered through brash ice; packboarded supplies; and cursed devil's club, stubborn nags, and each other. All the while they cemented monument bases, felled tree giants blocking vistas, aimed theodolites (tools for measuring angles) from eagle-roost peaks, and, harnessed like mules on sand flats, hauled "overland rafts": barrel-wheeled carts. They dropped shreds of playing cards in fog thick as gruel to be able to retrace their steps.

On some, it sleeted and rained for forty-two days in a row. Horses skidded on glaciers, slopped through bogs under special mosquito blankets and hoods, and pulled freight across mud holes and snow bridges. One chap, lacking kitchenware, cooked marmot in a coffee pot. One French-Canadian crew boss was a self-professed "son of beech." Only three "boundary hunters" died in accidents—astounding, given the odds the crews faced. That number proves the surveyors' utter competence.

A 1906 crew determined Boundary on the Yukon—the meridian's ground zero, a lone fixed point that anchored the line, which modern river runners there pass—and then leapfrogged northward. Six summers later, two parties fixed the Demarcation Bay terminus. US Boundary Survey Chief Thomas Riggs Jr. and his Canadian counterpart hoisted flags and alma mater pennants before taking a dip among arctic floes. Riggs, a onetime prospector in Dawson and Nome, would spend eight summers, his life's happiest, pegging the nation's back-of-beyond. "The surveyor," he wrote, "dreads the day when he shall have thrown his last diamond hitch, broken his last camp, and, from the deck of a homeward-bound steamer, have watched a free life fade away in the mist with the distant hills."

Among two hundred cairn waypoints to a polar sea that the men erected in cement along the cleared international corridor were fifty-five-pound aluminum-bronze obelisks. Streams cross this cartographic construct, as do snow geese, moose, and caribou, flowing undeterred between winter and summer ranges. I heard from a resurveyor who helicopters to the line's peaks that a smart gopher lives in a burrow beneath one of the monuments. Poised for unilateral crises, it has dug exits to both sides, oblivious of passport requirements.

When the first boundary surveyors of both nations saddled up, a mere one-fifth of Alaska had been mapped, by "a few carefully chosen men," as the US Geological Survey (USGS) branch head Alfred Hulse Brooks, for whom the range is named, put it. This geologist, also honored with Hulsite, a mineral with the sheen of fresh asphalt, decided that the range was structurally distinct from the Rocky Mountains. Those were uplifted 35 to 135 million years later, 65 million years ago. Brooks proposed the unwieldy "Arctic Mountain System," which luckily never caught on.

Despite the USGS crews' efforts—six major Brooks Range reconnaissance missions by 1911—as recently as 1951 blank space terminated streams and contour lines on the 1:250,000 Demarcation Point map quadrangle east of the Kongakut, west of the Turner, and south of Beaufort Lagoon. Roughly two thousand square miles at that point in time still slumbered unsurveyed, most likely the nation's last off-grid quarter. That graphic fog blotted out a swath of caribou calving grounds, so life roiled below it.

To Thomas Riggs, who became the territory's appointed governor during the Spanish flu epidemic, "The vast solitudes, uninhabited and lonely" had an "irresistible call." Resources beckoned then as they do today. But the country he surveyed was far from unpeopled.

Bessie John, an Upper Tanana elder from Beaver Creek, a border crossing on the ALCAN Highway roughly five hundred miles south of the line's endpoint in the Arctic, recalled her grandfather's brush with the bug-bitten government trailblazers. He'd been camping, probably fishing or hunting: "They say, 'Could you move? Your tent gonna be cut. You gonna be Alaskan, you gonna be Yukon?'"

More Beckettian nonsense ensued when in 1981 Canadian custom agents seized funeral-potlatch gifts from visiting Upper Tananas who could not pay import duties. Bitterness condensed into a song sung on both sides of the border. "King George got diarrhea," the translated refrain mocked—history echoes long here even without written records. The White Man's real estate dreams also severed Gwich'in homelands and bonds farther north, on the ranges of caribou feeding fifteen villages.

The land rolls away from me toward a branch of the Firth River, a supreme white-water run in two countries that ends in the Arctic Ocean. A grove of freshly leafed-out poplars among scraggly black spruce on the tundra is a pea-green island in an emerald sea. The spruce trees crowd closer together on the Canadian side. There's not a plane in the sky, not one single contrail slashing it.

I indulge in a summit nap among butterflies, cream-colored dryas, and Lapland rosebay, a fragrant, heathery bonsai-rhododendron with fuchsia blossoms and relatives in the Himalayas. What is this need for completion, the obsession with artificial boundaries? The Welshman Colin Fletcher, the granddaddy of long-distance hikers, was the first known person to traverse the Grand Canyon below the rim uninterrupted and on foot, from Hualapai Hilltop to Point Imperial, but this was before the park was expanded significantly in 1975. Does that make his feat any less impressive or memorable, or less worth doing?

Consider the photojournalist and documentary filmmaker Renan Ozturk, who, inspired perhaps by the team of the British surgeon Charles Evans on Kangchenjunga, stopped five feet below the summit of Everest, kneeled in the snow, put his hands together in a gesture of prayer, and refused to climb any higher, because he did not want to "stand on the head of the Sherpa's god." It's an old saw: the journey, not the destination, matters. Perhaps what's true for the end is true for the start.

Still, my destination, Kotzebue, matters to me. It's my gateway home, the only one through which I can pass with my head held high rather than with my tail between my legs. I'm referring to self-regard, not the opinion of others. By the time I disembark there, I will be as feral as a wolf hybrid.

To jumpstart that process, I sunbathe naked in camp.

ORIGINS

DAY 3 (12 MILES)
QUAD: TABLE MOUNTAIN

These are ways of living I have to remember each time I go to the mountains.
—KENNETH BROWER, *Earth and the Great Weather*

A screen of stratus slid in during a night without darkness, for a complete overcast. Back at the airstrip I picked up the barrel after walking right up to it with the GPS as a test. The digital display led me to within eight feet. Good enough. When I shoulder the replenished pack—a "packing system," some call it now—it nearly pulls me off balance and I grunt involuntarily. The beast weighs at least sixty pounds. I bought the biggest I could find, with a volume of ninety liters. Fully loaded, it's the size of a four-year-old child. I used to think hiking with a heavy burden would make me stronger; now I know it will cripple me. That's another drawback of soloing—you can't split group gear like the tent, stove, fuel, first aid kit, maps, and communication devices among people.

Two northern shrikes perch in a tall willow, pearl gray and white bellied, with black bandit masks and meat hook bills. These robin-size hunters are called butcher birds for their habit of dismembering voles, lemmings, sparrows, snow buntings, ptarmigan chicks, and even young ermines after snipping their spinal cord, and for impaling body parts on sharp twigs or wedging them into the forks of branches for future consumption. As many as twelve carcasses have been found cached near a single nest. Equal parts raptor and songbird, sharp-eyed shrikes catch bumblebees on the wing. They spot them from three hundred feet and de-sting them by squeezing and rubbing bee abdomens against a perch.

Even Thoreau, slightly rattled by watching a shrike "pecking to pieces a small bird" one Christmas Eve, deemed such comportment "not birdlike." An ornithology text from 1950 states, "The outstanding traits of this bloodthirsty rascal are boldness, fierceness, and savagery." Its German name, *Raubwürger*, which translates as "robber-strangler," is hardly more flattering, while Inupiaq *irirgik*—"eye extractor"—rings with the dispassion of a people who know that surviving means spilling blood. Here is another species we've given a bad rap, lumping it in with the "killer whale," the media's "orca serial killers" even. But ah, we're *Homo sapiens*, "wise man"—"wise guy," more like.

Despite an awareness that the names we give animals and the stories we tell about them say more about us than them, I hope the butchers in the bush are no omen for the day.

From here on I'll head west, west, west. "Eastward I go only by force, but west I go free," Thoreau proclaimed in his seminal essay "Walking." For Henry D. the West was "but another name for the Wild." For me, with a northward slant, it is the direction in which I felt drawn long before I managed to leave Europe for good.

The longest journey begins with a single step. One day at a time. These are clichés, to be sure. I resolve to reach the next landing strip, for which I've budgeted ten days, and to reassess there. I'm aware of how much such an easy way out differentiates my journey from a pre-1927 one. That year, Noel Wien steered a World War I biplane to Wiseman, the first flight to cross the Arctic Circle in Alaska.

Something I will learn after my trek when he emails me is that John Cantor, an Australian thru hiker, having repeatedly bailed on his traverse on a route similar to mine, succeeded only on his fourth attempt. He must have been rather driven. Only four people had traversed the range lengthwise and solo at that point, according to him. I do not know if that is true, since I have never researched those numbers.

At twenty-seven, Cantor was trying to set a record for the youngest person to complete this trek, and the first from Down Under. He left Joe Creek ten days after I did and noticed my boot prints over long stretches, he told me. Kirk, the pilot, must have let him know that I was out there ahead of him. Unlike me, Cantor updated fans through text messages posted on Facebook, and his parents tracked his progress via satellite monitor. Mine are not even aware what I'm doing this summer. I don't know if I'll ever have the money or weeks off from work to try again if I fail, or if I could scrounge up enough motivation again.

It may well earn them slots in adventure magazines and "build social media platforms," but I've never understood the frantic pursuit of records or why people brag about the miles they hike in a place or over the years. On his hardest day, the Australian, plagued by Achilles tendonitis, hiked nineteen hours with only two five-minute breaks, guzzling olive oil by the cup. He set a speed record as well, twice as fast as I would manage in the end. Kudos to this youth—my body and mind rebel if I don't get my afternoon coffee and eight hours of sleep.

Cantor is now a corporate speaker. I loved that in an interview this Aussie called bushwhacking "bush bashing"—I did my share of that during Panama, the Gulf War, and the Iraq invasion, or when Al Gore's opponent vowed to funnel royalties from drilling the refuge into conservation programs and heat for the poor.

I spy a mother and yearling, napping, two peas in a pod, a Hallmark card motif. Could they be yesterday's pair? A melting aufeis field has soaked the ground downstream of it, which makes walking difficult, squelchy. After a mile, my feet are wet. My knee-high gaiters keep bunching up around my ankles, and while they don't keep out water, they protect my feet from "trail mix," pebbles and plant debris that will wear out insoles and socks and skin on the heels. Short of rubber boots and perhaps heavy-duty alpine leather clompers, no footwear will stay dry in these conditions. The sooner you resign yourself to that, the happier you'll be. As I often tell clients, apropos of raingear also, hiking warm and wet beats hiking cold and wet, the latter a perfect combo for bringing on hypothermia.

I lug my load through a tussock field up to a saddle, mud trying to suck my boots off at each step into gunk pockets between the grass knobs. Without upper body strength and hiking poles for support, I would founder here on the Devil's slalom course. My right knee hurts, a bad sign so early. I dislocated a shoulder repeatedly years before, and eventually the pain on long hikes with heavy packs would become so strong that I had to go under the knife. But on this traverse, luckily, it never becomes a problem. I camp on a windy knoll overlooking the soggy pass, and my camp chair—my inflatable sleeping mat with a sleeve that converts it—sails off. Again luckily, it snags on a cracked boulder without getting punctured. Later: light rain.

A little to the south, I see on my easternmost map another Firth tributary, Mancha Creek. Its name was first reported by the International Boundary Commission survey in 1911. Am I engaged in some quixotic enterprise, a Draconian ordeal like theirs?

Between being stiff and sore in the morning and tired and sore in the afternoon, there usually opens a window in which the body works smoothly, efficiently, and painlessly. "For most of the time," the naturalist Ann Zwinger characterized back-packing, "one disciplines oneself to ignore the discomfort of being hot or tired or having sore hip bones or being hungry, thirsty." People have slandered this form of locomotion as the most miserable way of getting from point A to point B. Legs, on the plus side, will convey you where otherwise only a helicopter can. Now considered a sport, schlepping a knapsack over uneven terrain is humanity's oldest form of travel.

Once hooked, do backpackers have a choice? The dopamine hit that seeking produces and the opiates shed after finding rewards in beauty and awe or in shelter and food tickle our pleasure center. Dopamine "brightens the air, quickens the heart and breath with anticipation," Thad Ziolkowski writes in his memoir of surfing addiction. "Motile and restless," as in rats, it "creates focus and the will to move toward or away from something." It's a runner's high but only in small doses for slowpokes and the elderly. As with any drug, its potency wanes over time, hence the progression from day hikes to month-long ordeals. Withdrawal also explains the post-trail blues many long-distance walkers mention. Is the craving spiritual or physiological? No need to split holistic hairs.

Backpacking was my first outdoor love and, despite the forced marches of army days, remains my preferred mode of transport. It offers a sense of self-sufficiency and independence rarely experienced in a world hedged with constraints and demands. What I want is to inhabit a different, wilder world, at a minimum fleetingly. A backpack holds what I need for that. As a snail does its shell, I carry all essentials—food, shelter, and extra clothes—humbly on my back. Except for spiritual nourishment and chance-encounter miracles, I expect nothing but water from a place. Ecstasy is always welcome, a bonus.

Neither prone to consult gear lists or reviews as the faithful would scripture, nor obsessed with the weight I shoulder, I've never mastered the art of traveling light. I am rough on equipment and myself, and the weight-saving materials of most ultralight bling are too flimsy and too expensive. The pack I bought weighs close to ten pounds empty. But my body shows signs of wear and tear, the dislocated shoulder and a bum lower back that is payback for motorcycling and jumping from airplanes in my foolhardy youth. Manhandling rafts onto and off of trailers and loading and unloading the same rafts daily for weeks didn't help either. My toes and fingers creak from being immersed too often in barely liquid water. Like some shark species, I'll just have to keep moving to stay alive.

I still glissade down scree slopes like a lunatic and jump from low sandstone ledges in the canyons, even with a full pack. I finally buckled, investing in some hiking poles, which I previously considered geriatric apparel. They do make a difference for joints on the downhill, not to mention creek crossings and tussock obstacle courses. And they're handy for probing bear scat—vital information. (You probably know how to tell grizzly from black bear piles. The first contain bells of the kind hikers wear to warn bears of their approach.) An orthopedic doctor once told me that the knee should nix any belief in intelligent design. No omniscient being worth its salt would build such a shoddy joint.

My boss at Arctic Wild, a Fairbanks wilderness guiding outfit, has sold fewer backpacking trips recently, he speculates because boomers are aging out. Multisport, multidestination vacations involving paddleboards, ski kites, scuba tanks, paragliders, snowboards, or virtual reality goggles are in vogue with a younger or more affluent clientele. One of his best sellers is the Northwestern Parks Sampler, with two-day basecamp stints at the Kobuk Valley National Park sand dunes, and in Cape Krusenstern National Monument, the Bering Land Bridge National Preserve, Gates of the Arctic National Park, and the Noatak National Preserve.

Many of these preserves were designated or enlarged in 1980 under the Alaska National Interest Lands Conservation Act (ANILCA). Predictably, statewide protest erupted. Fairbanks marchers braving nearly zero-degree weather carried "Go Back to Farming, Carter" and "All I Want for Christmas Is My Future" signs and a casket with the remains of "dead Alaska." The target of citizen ire,

Jimmy Carter, remains the only president ever to set foot on any of these lands when he visited the Arctic National Wildlife Refuge in which Joe Creek lies and witnessed one hundred thousand caribou of the Porcupine herd milling about on its coastal plain. For him, it was "perhaps the most beautiful place in all the world." Obama traveled to Kotzebue and drum-danced with the Inupiat, yet his first-term administration leased more acreage nationwide for fossil fuel exploration and extraction than the following Republican one. He gave Shell final approval to resume offshore drilling in arctic Alaska for the first time since 2012, when the company lost control of an oil rig and Coast Guard divers dropped from helicopters had to rescue crewmembers. His last year in office, he scrapped the highly publicized, fiercely protested Keystone XL and Dakota Access pipelines while approving two pipelines for sending fracked gas from Texas to Mexico.

In 1959, the year of my birth and the state of Alaska's, legislation was introduced to establish the Arctic Wildlife Range, as the refuge was known then, and in 1960, against the will of Alaska's businessmen and senators, President Eisenhower signed the act. For the first time in American history, an entire ecosystem received federal protection. From the very start, the range sparked political and economic controversy. Of a total of nineteen million acres included in the refuge, only eight million were protected as wilderness. ANILCA, which created the refuge's current shape, also earmarked 1.5 million acres of the coastal plain as the 1002 ("ten-o-two") Area, mandating studies of its natural resources, especially petroleum. Congressional authorization is needed before oil drilling can proceed where the Porcupine caribou herd spends part of its summer feeding and giving birth.

Driven by oil revenues, the expectation of jobs for constituents, and ever-increasing demand for oil, Alaska's pro-development politicians repeatedly spearheaded bills to open this sanctuary to drilling. One held up a blank white poster board on the US Senate floor, a mirror image of the void that had lingered on that Demarcation Point map half a century earlier like a preterritorial ghost. "This is a picture of ANWR as it exists for about nine months of the year. . . . It's flat; it's unattractive," he said, pronouncing the acronym "an-war," as if it were the name of some exotic country we were at loggerheads with. He was trying to persuade fellow senators to open the calving grounds to extractive commerce.

One of those, parroting him, called it "empty," "ugly," "a barren wasteland," and a secretary of the interior overseeing the person who managed it saw "a flat white nothingness." They were wrong—as animal tracks in the snow, winter photography, and Alaska Native testimony demonstrate. But even if the senator's statement were true, three months of glory should be reason enough to save America's Serengeti. The word "Serengeti" may be misleading here. The Arctic *can* feel empty much of the time. But when it springs to action with a crush of panting antlered bodies, with blinding-white sheep dotting talus, with a garden of whale spouts blooming offshore, or with ranked birds undulating above, it serves up an embarrassment of riches for the attention.

On the other hand, it is easy to get the impression—from documentaries, photos, and coffee table books—that the Brooks Range is always teeming with life. Honestly, nothing could be farther from the truth. Animals can be regionally or seasonally abundant, typically in large numbers of fewer species than in the tropics, but I've guided ten-day trips during which we saw only birds and mosquitos. Much of life focuses on the coastal plain. Still, the tally for the refuge as a whole is impressive. It harbors the most wildlife species of any preserve girdling the circumpolar North. Visitors may see eagles, gyrfalcons, tundra swans, plovers, sandhill cranes, longspurs, and terns among nearly 180 bird species total, some full-time residents but mostly visitors from six continents and every US state. Forty-five mammal species, including marmots, wolverines, polar bears, and wolves, live here at least temporarily, nine of them, like the bowhead whale, offshore. Grayling, arctic char, Dolly Varden—an olive-backed pink-patterned trout named for a gaily dressed Charles Dickens coquette—thrive in refuge waters with thirty-two other fish species, most of them in the nutrient broth of river-fed coastal lagoons.

A set of interlocking ecological zones forms the grid for all this fecundity. From south to north, these comprise boreal forest or "taiga"; foothills and mountains; the coastal plain's sprawl of tundra, river deltas, and wetlands; and last, lagoons ringed with barrier islands, beaches, and spits. Smaller habitats dapple these zones, stepping-stones for life's evolving continuation.

The refuge's boundaries do not confine its biodiversity. Birds flock from around the globe to nest in the coastal plain, where food awaits them and chicks hatch before they disperse again on the winds. Habitat loss on their wintering grounds

or at stopover sites south of the Arctic Circle has triggered slumps in most populations. Oil development could push some species over the brink.

Through the lens of conventional aesthetics, the coastal plain may appear less
scenic, less stimulating, but without it, the Brooks Range would be robbed of
vitality. The mountains' relative dearth is the reason Indigenous settlement, with
the recent exception of the Nunamiut Eskimo village of Anaktuvuk Pass, stuck
to the southern foothills, western rivers, and coast.

Quick trips into arctic parks and preserves are my least favorite trips to guide,
since they involve repeated moves with piles of gear and much time spent sitting
on those, waiting for bush planes. Such three-for-ones feel rushed and superficial,
and sometimes it surprises me when clients get bored already the day after their
arrival. For these few travelers, it's as if once an item has been checked off a bucket
list, they're eager to vamoose. The late Richard Nelson, an anthropologist-turned-
nature-writer who taught at my alma mater, the University of Alaska Fairbanks,
had something to say about conspicuous geographic consumption: "There may be
more to learn by climbing the same mountain a hundred times than by climbing
a hundred different mountains." Or, as Marcel Proust put it, "The real voyage of
discovery consists not in seeking new landscapes, but in having new eyes." But then,
questioning lifestyles or acquiring a deep knowledge of places never topped our
society's list of priorities. Where a tourist wants the glittering skin, a true traveler
pines for the bones, the structure that holds all together and determines appearances.

Since my youth, my preferences have changed. I now try to heed Nelson's
advice, confining my trekking to arctic Alaska along with Utah's and Arizona's
Canyon Country. Other regions in Alaska may have more spectacular and more
challenging scenery. But besides its wildlife and solitude, its vastness and endless
daylight, this cordillera lures me with this: I can fix my eyes on any feature, barring a few summits and crags, and get there under my own power, without ropes,
crampons, or more complex gear. Grant Spearman, an anthropologist who lived
in a sod house in Anaktuvuk Pass for more than three decades, nicely captures this
physical and psychological appeal. "For all of their ruggedness," he writes, "these
mountains are neither precipitous nor overwhelming, and to those who know
them best, they are possessed of a stately but uniquely human scale." Time may
have filed down most of the fangs, but they still can deliver a bite.

Despite its long occupation, few Alaska Native names for the Brooks Range as a whole exist and the ones that do are seldom used, as if this corrugation of space in its totality were beyond contemplation, or inseparable from the valleys. A Gwich'in name reported is Gwazhał, "Place Where the Land Bulges Up." It's certainly bare-bones nomenclature, laconic in the ways of people with other than scenic priorities, people averse to grand words, loud feelings, abstractions, and sweeping gestures.

I want this 700-mile-long, 150-mile-wide upthrust not fully mapped until forty-four years after Alaska's purchase, the world's northernmost major range and largest official wilderness, to be my jagged Sand County, my bottomless Walden Pond, and my boggy Arches with bears. In that literary tradition, I try to recalibrate the perspective of clients, making them question our society's blistering pace. "While a young man fears that by going too slow he might miss something," I taunt, "an older man fears that by going too fast he will miss everything." I really talk like that sometimes; mostly though, I let the land do the talking.

I turned fifty-three a month before this traverse, about twice the Australian's age. He held his dream close for six years. I have nourished mine so much longer. On guided trips there is never time to explore each tempting vista or route, each peak, glen, or cascade the maps hint at. Chores demand my attention, and I can't ignore the rigid schedule for reaching our destinations either. (Missing connecting flights home due to weather delays in our bush pickups always galls clients.) Also, I have long felt that weekend and even weeklong trips are too short to find equilibrium. It takes days to quiet the monkey mind and tune out all concerns of the world left behind, which start to intrude again days before the end of a wilderness journey.

I want to stretch the middle part, that time of single-minded blissful presence, as much as humanly possible. I know from Outward Bound courses I have worked that somewhere beyond the two-week threshold, where resupplies are necessary if you are not in a boat, roaming will transform if not you, then the nature of the endeavor from a pastime into a primeval passage. At that point, you settle into the itinerant life as if it's the only one you've ever known. Camp chores, like locking the door of your home when you leave, no longer require conscious effort. Despite the occasional hardship, the landscape through which you move fits like a glove. Competence lies at the core, with a mental component, a confident ease that can still get you into trouble. Last, I long for a block of time with no distractions or obligations, an opening in which I can ponder my place in the great chain of being.

I desired this trial and opportunity as a fiftieth birthday present but hesitated year after year, because I earn most of my money in three months of guiding and can ill afford to take most of a summer off. And frankly, I dislike and dread logistics, which for this expedition are complex and crucial. Eventually, uncannily, three key events got my rear end into gear. They alerted me to the fact that time keeps on slipping into the future, in Steve Miller's psychedelic words, and that I will get neither younger nor fitter.

The financing, a significant hurdle, resolved itself first. The charter fare for five airdrops of caches, including the one with my boat on the upper Noatak, plus a flight for myself to Joe Creek and return ticket from Kotzebue to Nome, were big budget items. My gear had become ragged, since I use it on guiding trips and am miserly when it comes to new purchases. I needed an inflatable craft for this undertaking and had my eye on a refurbished, sixteen-foot SOAR canoe with a unique rowing setup instead of paddles—oars would really come in handy in the Noatak's mind-numbing headwinds. The manufacturer offered a 25 percent guide discount. In addition, I wanted a big lightweight Kevlar bear barrel for carrying food on the backpacking section and an ultralight double-walled tent set up with a single hiking pole that allows a 160-degree view from inside, an asset in bear country. I cannot recall the exact figure, but including the food and sundry equipment and clothing, the bill ran to somewhere north of ten grand—that's a guide's wages of fear in a below-average year.

Sitting in the lee of rafts we'd propped up with paddles as a windbreak at camp downstream from Grasser's airstrip one day, a group I guided together with Robert Thompson discussed whether the Hulahula's midsummer runoff was enough to carry us to the coast without too much struggling. We'd stuck sticks into mud by the stream's edge to gauge what the water did overnight. With weaker radiation from a lower afternoon sun melting less snow on the scrum of peaks, it had slightly dropped. We had floated there the day before after launching at Grasser's, and the run had been rocky, so we were having second thoughts. Luckily, an airstrip at East Patuk Creek, near where we were sitting, was an exit in case we decided to abort the float. (We did, though we got in a few stellar day hikes and birding, which convinced one teenage girl to become an ornithologist.)

The conversation next settled on aspirations and dream projects, as it will in such camps. When my turn came, I shared the long-held vision of an arctic traverse and the reasons I kept postponing it. "We'll make it happen. We'll get you the funds," a woman who worked for a land-conservation nonprofit promised. She was as good as her word. When the bank transfer arrived, I splurged, buying things I otherwise would not have considered. It so happened that the donation came with too many strings, to the point where I felt I was not in control anymore. Having bought the two-thousand-dollar inflatable canoe, an eighty-dollar titanium camp mug, and much else, I returned the grant with a heavy heart. Thus ended my brief experience with sponsored expeditions.

The second encounter took place on one of our outfit's High Peaks Backpacking trips, a weeklong jaunt from the upper Sheenjek across Guilbeau Pass on the Continental Divide down to Grasser's, the put-in spot on the Hulahula. It is possibly the most popular refuge hiking adventure and the only area besides the Arrigetch Peaks in Gates of the Arctic where I count on seeing other people. I was leading an unusual group: a high school teacher and her police officer sister; a same-sex couple made up of a California state wildlife biologist and her petite Dominican spouse; and a Danish woman sergeant who barely spoke English. It was a memorable trip. On the penultimate day, a vanguard of the Porcupine caribou herd numbering in the thousands engulfed our camp while we ate breakfast.

The first evening, we pitched our tents a few miles from the drop-off airstrip, on terraces overlooking a headwaters lake on the Sheenjek's West Fork. Kate, the blond middle-aged teacher, fell hard for the Brooks Range at that mountain-cupped water—the place will do that to you on a fine day. Like some celestial slide projector, a restless sun piercing clouds transmuted the lake from quicksilver to pewter to jade, with cats' paws from wind gusts randomly stirring its surface. After dinner, Kate sat for hours beside her tent, absorbing the light's changes. Her vacation had started on a hectic note. The airline had lost her luggage, and we had scrambled to get her outfitted with spare clothes from our warehouse and purchases at the Fred Meyer where at the last minute I would buy this trip's folding knife.

The morning after our arrival, Kate told me she wanted to get funding to return the following summer with valedictorian students from her college and also for the northern lights. At camp two days later, she mentioned chest pains. She had not been injured and did not have a cold, so I gave her generic painkillers, thinking she might have strained a muscle because of her heavy pack. She seemed fine the rest of the hike and her fascination with the Arctic only grew. In our conversations she revealed repeated bouts with a deeply rooted carcinoma, showing us surgical scars on her forearms. I am an incorrigible sun buff and have spent years in the desert and alpine country rarely bothering with sunglasses or sunscreen. Kate's story served as a blunt reminder, a prod with a cattle zapper, a sudden memento mori.

The final nudge came at Grasser's, on that very same trip. Leading my back-packers there for their last night out before Kirk touched down and hauled us to Arctic Village where we'd catch a regular twin-prop plane to Fairbanks, I chanced upon that mythical figure: a long-distance hiker. I surprised him while he emptied a cache for the next leg of his traverse. Unused to sudden strangers materializing, intent on sorting and packing supplies, he startled when I greeted him, though I had tried to avoid sneaking up, afraid he'd mistake me for a bear. You do not do this in the backcountry without risking a pepper blast or a bullet.

Talking to this youngster, I learned that he had a hiking partner who had already resupplied and forged ahead. Here was someone who was doing what I kept fantasizing about. Having just finished a strenuous nine-day backpacking trip, I felt like a wide-eyed tour bus guide beside him, the kind that speaks into a microphone. About twenty years younger than I, he looked fit, unsurprisingly, but not deranged or inordinately tough. I saw that he was no Superman, no Lewis or Clark, no Ernest Shackleton. He was simply a guy who had started to plan and then followed through.

The financial seed of my dream had been dropped into soil on that low-water Hulahula trip with Robert Thompson. Fording the gin-clear main channel during a day hike up West Patak Creek, I'd crossed my Rubicon, though unaware at the time. As on the bumper sticker a friend once mentioned to me, "Four out of the five voices in my head said, 'Go for it!'" So I did.

VETERAN WALKERS

DAY 4 (12 MILES)
QUAD: TABLE MOUNTAIN

Home is what you carry, not a place.
—HUGO BLICK, film director

Clouds kiting and sun, a hiker's perfect mix on my way to Kongakut headwaters shaped like a bird foot. Do the cackling, muttering, honking ravens sound different here because they talk about noncity things?

In a vale halfway between Joe Creek and the Kongakut, poplars burst with tender green. A robin, a most common and therefore underrated bird, in one tree is singing his heart out, as if to impress me.

When conditions are right, green-up in Fairbanks unfolds within a few days. Summer wastes no time where it lasts only ten weeks. In May, light-starved Alaskans on their porches lift their faces and let sunshine gently massage cheeks, brows, and closed eyelids. Arctic wildflowers even more diligently follow suit in June. Attuned to circadian rhythms, some swivel their heads, tracking the sun's 360-degree midsummer arc.

Compensating for the season's brevity, between the end of April and early August the sun never truly sets. Even as it dips below the horizon at both ends of this window, turquoise twilight suffuses the boreal forest. Here on the arctic tundra, the parentheses around summer solstice are wider still. Late August in bear country creeps me out, because darkness, long forgotten, seeps in again. Daylight offers some protection against surprises. On wilderness trips I awake periodically throughout the night and peek from the vestibule without having to exit my sleeping bag. I've spotted muskoxen that way and once a grizzly headed straight toward camp, which made me wake up the clients—you don't want to pretend no one is home when these bruisers come knocking.

Though endless summer light turns me into a hummingbird buzzing at a flower, it can trip a person up. Once, in Swedish Lapland, I was to meet a friend at a train station in the middle of nowhere for a week of backpacking. Without a watch and long having lost track of the days, I showed up at what I judged to be the right time only to sit there for hours (I still don't know how many), like Kafka waiting for a train. Sleeping in rooms bright for weeks while the sun's roulette pill spins in the sky wheel never bothered me as it does people who need curtains or melatonin or masks; but getting up in the winter for dishwater-dull days wedged between sunsets and sunrises a mere three hours apart, and popping vitamin D before breakfast, does, more every year.

After surviving yesterday's tussock testing grounds, I revel in this unnamed budding valley. I follow a worn segment of the Porcupine herd's migration route. Where it trends north, generations furrowed the tundra, thronging between winter ranges south of the tree line and their arctic nursery. The 'bou know before I do when they're about to cliff out or face deep ravines, and they cross to a valley's opposite side. I quickly learn to trust their instincts and experience.

The Inupiat's Gwich'in neighbors in Arctic Village, 110 roadless miles southwest of my current position, call themselves the Caribou People. They, as well as the residents of fourteen villages astride the US-Canada border bonded in kinship and sharing, depend on the Porcupine caribou. Those beasts of no nation provide more than half of all food for Gwich'in families plus material for tools and clothing and for stories, dances, and songs. Twice a year, slopes and flats come alive as caribou home in on their destination: summer calving and grazing ranges on the coastal plain, which the latest Republican president slated for drilling; and wintering sites in the boreal sash, Vinijáatan, where caribou, according to one elder, "settle down and lie around and just eat" because the snow between spruces is soft there, not wind packed. This herd, upward of two hundred thousand heads at last count—reminiscent of early-nineteenth-century bison abundance—pulls off the continent's largest land mammal migration and at twenty-eight hundred miles, Earth's longest. By the age of nine, an average lifespan for a caribou lucky enough to survive calfhood, a cow will have effectively circumnavigated the globe.

The villagers named the refuge's contested 1002 Area, a heartland almost as big as Delaware, Iizhik Gwats'an Gwandaii Goodlit, "the Sacred Place Where Life Begins." Their creation story reminds all Gwich'in that humans and caribou were one once, long ago. When they split, the humans kept a piece of the caribou's heart inside their own, so their fate and health will forever be linked. "We are not separate," they warn. "What happens to them happens to us. It happens to you. It happens to all of us." Caribou nourish the people, who should take no more than they need and protect the herd and its home, which also is theirs. Wasting meat is disrespectful, as is touching the living animals or causing needless suffering. Gwich'in hunters let the vanguard pass, fearing the herd could turn as these veteran caribou lead the rest between their summer and winter ranges. Their Eskimo neighbors' tradition dictated that they not butcher animals or leave bones near migration routes, from concern that this would spook any herds.

As newlyweds, the Canadian wildlife biologist Karsten Heuer and his wife, the documentary filmmaker Leanne Allison, trailed the Porcupine herd for five months, first on skis and then on foot and by canoe, across four mountain ranges, hundreds of passes, and dozens of rivers from the Yukon Territory's forests to Alaska's tundra and back to the Gwich'in village of Old Crow. A hungry, sick grizzly too weak to catch up to the herd accosted the honeymooners. At their journey's halfway point, they awoke amid hundreds of cow caribou giving birth. Not wanting to disturb the mothers' calving and grazing and the calves' suckling and first explorations of their world, the two became tentbound for several days. They watched newborns orbit around resting does, "a hundred new moons spinning around tired old suns." The land would devour twenty-five out of each hundred in their first month in a Darwinian eclipse.

In his writing, Heuer promotes connectivity, the safeguards of corridors crucial in times of climate breakdown as species ranges shift. Detached havens lose genetic diversity through inbreeding. Furthermore, as conditions within preserves change or deteriorate, mobile species find no exit routes, no access to distant sanctuaries. One of the grandest initiatives yet in North America calls for Yukon-to-Yellowstone parks linked by wildlife connectors.

A dead Dall sheep ram rests at the bottom of a scree slide: a section of spine, fur like stuffing from a ripped mattress, the skull with "broomed" curls, frayed from the abrasion on stone during his feeding. He may have descended to one of the salt licks that streams sometimes expose. I've rarely seen sheep at the river, though once in a while when we float round a blind corner, there they are. Wolf tracks zippering a nearby gully might explain the mystery of the ram's death. The Arctic's only horned ungulate besides the muskox, this snow-white athlete was named for William Healey Dall, who conducted the first surveys of coastal Alaska and the Aleutians after the land transfer in 1867.

Each mountain pass is a portal offering a glimpse of a new world; each ptarmigan flushed from bushes is a near heart attack. It will take me a while to regain the steady nerves and stamina of previous backcountry seasons, to let wilderness break me in again. I did not train for this trip. Snow in Nome is not fit for cross-country skiing—wind turns it into pavement. No longer "content to rot by inches in ignoble ease," as one former president put it, I'd gotten off my wintering couch trusting that the first fifty miles in harness would whip me into shape.

I am in illustrious company. A handful of adventurers have undertaken—and finished—Brooks Range traverses on various routes and by various means, including one that was accomplished on foot entirely. The Alaskan Dick Griffith, using pack dogs, has been credited with the first documented though abridged crossing, from Kaktovik to Kotzebue, in two separate expeditions in 1959 and 1977. When a partner dropped out with an overtaxed Achilles tendon, Griffith cut their shelter in half and sewed it into "a very miserable one-man tent." Low on food, he survived on dog-meat jerky. He also skied alone through the Northwest Passage and bragged that his only gear sponsor was the Salvation Army. "I have discovered that you must be alone with yourself and like the company you keep in the empty moments," Griffith confided in his exploration journals.

Some of the early questers required decades, pressed into work lives or owing to other factors. Dennis Schmitt takes the prize in that regard, needing thirty-five years for the first full-length traverse of the range from Point Hope, Alaska, to the Mackenzie River, Northwest Territories.

My favorite is Keith Nyitray, a New York–born Alaskan homesteader who had worked in North Cascades National Park as a porter and later became an organic farmer in Sitka, in Southeast Alaska's panhandle. "Doing this the old way as much as possible" in 1989, the year I moved north, he set out from Fort McPherson in Canada's Northwest Territories with his wolf dog, Smoke, and another friend, Paul "Pappy" Lowe. After a six-and-a-half-week slog through deep snow, the two-legged companion quit at Old Crow. Traveling 1,450 miles in 303 days, sledding, snowshoeing, rafting, canoeing, and walking with Smoke, Nyitray got frostbite at 60-below temperatures. The thirty-one-year-old carried neither a tent nor a stove. He slept under a tarp and burned willows or grass for warmth. He bartered for some supplies and built his snowshoes and raft from local materials. The kids at Noatak called him Walkman. His eleven grizzly encounters, given the length of his trek, do not seem like much. But then, he was moving largely when they were hibernating. Starving, he hacked dead salmon from river ice to which he was led by fox tracks. Once, he cooked soup from the feet, feathers, and scraps of raptor-killed ptarmigan. Smoke was packing forty pounds of his own food that at one point his master was reduced to sharing in.

Nyitray finished in 1990 in Kotzebue, and his was the first *continuous* passage through the entire range. During his journey, *Exxon Valdez* rammed Bligh Reef, tanks rolled into Tiananmen Square, and the Berlin Wall became rubble. His once-in-a-lifetime experience, resounding thirty-odd years later yet, changed him in ways that he finds difficult to define.

Soloists fascinate me because their need to meld with a landscape, to live and survive in it by their own rules and wits, trumps their desire for fellowship and the safety net it entails. The records these predecessors set, impressive as they may be, do not concern me much. If not the slowest, I can perhaps become the oldest person to ever have done this. I am looking forward to an open-ended journey, one not bound by the deadline of a charter plane touching down.

Tussocks again, after lunch. Formerly maligned as *têtes de femmes* ("women's heads") or sometimes, still, even worse, with a racist slur, they remind me of guiding my brother and his betrothed on their honeymoon on the John River. As we hiked southwest from Anaktuvuk Pass into Gates of the Arctic National Park, at one point she sat down on a hummock and cried. "I want trails. I want trees. I had no idea what wilderness means." Most Europeans don't and, frankly, neither do many Americans. A New Yorker once asked me what the stuff on the black spruces was. I had no idea what he meant until he pointed to it: sap. Another client could not understand my excitement about the "porcupine herd." (For the record, you'll never see more than three porcupines in any one place.) Not all were babes on the tundra. One of four Caltech postdocs who ate as if they had hollow legs wired a boot sole to a toecap when it came unglued at Guilbeau Pass. A diabetic backpacker bound for Demarcation Bay regularly checked his blood sugar levels and injected himself.

Negotiating tussocks, also known as doing the tussock two-step, is a full-contact sport that combines aspects of mudwrestling and tae kwon do. Step on the grassy columns, a balancing act upon camel humps, as they bend underfoot, and you may twist an ankle. Step between them, *scrunch*, and their mushrooming caps entrap your foot. Pulling out, *slurp*, takes as much effort as freeing your boot from the morass the hollows often contain. To one Canadian naturalist, fields growing this crop exclusively are "almost as regular as textured wallpaper." Why do these speed bumps slow you always at the end of the day, when you're fried and pining for a dry, level campsite—surprisingly rare in such wide, open country?

Tussocks benefit if not us then other organisms at least. Catching spring sunshine, each forms a miniature greenhouse above frozen ground, hosting plants that colonize it—dryas, or cottongrass sedges soon topped with white pompoms—for an early, snow-free shot at budding. As miniature compost heaps, tussocks recycle decaying matter ten times faster than the surrounding substrate does. Their origins remain unknown. Moss cushions erupting from damp soil, ice nuclei expanding underground, or meltwater eroding and rounding surfaces sectioned by polygonal networks of frost cracks have been proposed as mechanisms. Hate them or don't, but just as mosquitos fill birds' bellies and pollinate flowers, tussocks prop up arctic ecosystems.

I close my eyes as I write this and they stipple my vision again as they did my dreams during the traverse.

Slogging across aufeis soft in the afternoon near the ankle of the bird foot's trio of Kongakut tributaries, today's destination. A traveling bear smells me from half a mile away and bolts. I must be doubly stinky at this stage. What is it about human odor? Is it simply alien, wrong to their noses, broadcasting a potential for cruelty unmatched in nature, or perhaps its novelty? Wolves and wolverines react similarly to it. These bears could not have learned to fear this scent, I believe. For starters, there aren't enough of us out here—thankfully—and few grizzlies confronted by hunters live to pass on any aversion to cubs. We puny humans scare the crap out of these bundles of brawn and attitude, sometimes literally. Fellow bears being their most common enemies, they may mistake us for ones standing on hind legs.

Bears at ease follow their nose to a buffet of grasses, roots, herbs, flowers, fungi, willow shoots, tubers, berries, eggs, insects, lemmings, ground squirrels, and salmon, to carrion and the occasional caribou. Conveying further facts obscured to us, glands in their paws cue fellow passersby with an acuity shaming hounds. Expert pheromone sniffers, polar bear males thus latch onto receptive females in sea-ice expanses. Their inland cousins "stomp-walk," especially in the breeding months, pissing purposely and then grinding their urine into the earth, as if squashing bugs or foes. Such "mark trails" integrate prominent trees or boulders against which bears rub not to scratch but to impart skin odors and anal secretions, olfactory fingerprints. Notes combining twenty distinct perfume compounds on such message boards curb bear brawling by establishing hierarchies. The where, when, how much, and how often of chemical Post-Its with aromas far from subtle differ according to sex and age.

Grizzlies have favorite rubbing stations, chat rooms where ranges overlap. They mangle trees along travel corridors too. Trunks fiercely bitten bleed sap. Curved claws scar them with hormonal graffiti. "I'm yea tall, sucker!" the glyphs proclaim not just to wary backpackers but to conspecifics as well. In addition, they might be waypoints by which bears orient themselves, milestones in unfamiliar country.

Though bear agendas web wilderness largely unseen, evidence helps you dodge trouble: a field cratered not by backhoe or carpet-bombing but by grizzlies craving ground-squirrel snacks; dung like a horse's, unmistakably coarse with caribou hair or grass roughage or pebbled and purpled by berries, depending on the season. Its freshness dates a bear's passage. Do not camp anywhere near if it's soft as dough. Alaskan male coastal brown bears can weigh fifteen hundred pounds because of a richer habitat. That's what makes their five-hundred-pound Brooks Range kin so edgy. Arctic grizzlies *always* are hungry. While I perk up at bear sign, it jolts me with unease. Still, a playing deck lacking carnivore aces—or omnivore ones in the grizzly's case—makes for a rigged game experientially and ecologically. They are beautiful, at a safe distance, gravitas turned into muscle, superbly tuned eating machines, their shiny coats jiggling with every move.

Some people smell bears hidden in bushes. I am not so lucky, less well equipped. Aware of bears nosing about, I choose a cooking area (the "kitchen") away from my tent to avoid tainting that with attractive odors. In addition, I whizz onto rocks near my bedroom before turning in, creating a force field in lieu of an electric fence that, I hope, will deflect intruders.

Out of weight considerations, I carry only one book, written by a solo canoeist who retraced the 1834 voyage of British Navy Captain George Back through the barrens of the Canadian tundra. "When I walk into a house for the night, my conversation with the sky ends," the author, Robert Perkins, muses. "To wake up in a house is to find the next day has begun without me." Physical separation indoors is just the beginning of alienation from nature. As the eco-Marxist critic Andreas Malm observes, our getting lost in the media hall of mirrors, a "virtual cocoon," blinds us to the matrix of life and the biocide under way.

It is different in my little pyramid of a tent. Sandpiper and rushing-water music lulls me to sleep, yet I'm always two-minded about camping too close to streams, as they mask an approaching bear's footfalls. Flowers perfume my sleep like potpourris in Scheherazade's tales. A mozzie drizzle ticks against the rain fly onto which midnight sunshine casts the insects' silhouettes. With the low-angle light, I can sunbathe inside the tent when it's too buggy. The earth also reminds me of its existence each time I camp upon lichen crunchy as cornflakes or on moss that makes my sleeping mat redundant and gives springily when I crawl inside the tent.

While it's nice to avoid screens other than protective mesh temporarily, I consider reading material important during lengthy wilderness trips. I'd rather skimp on food or gear, or electronic equipment, if I can pack *War and Peace* or *Moby-Dick* instead. When I don't carry books, the silent conversations they instigate are what I miss first. I sometimes burn the spent pages in camp, though the daily weight savings are ridiculous. Books out here compensate for the lack of human company.

They console me on listless tentbound days—during one forty-eight-hour storm on Denali, with the fly whopping too loudly to converse, my climbing partner and I got so desperate we read the medication guides for our high-altitude prescription drugs. Vicariously sharing the hardships of travelers past or present may strengthen your own resolve by putting suffering into perspective: If they endured, so can I. Last, a good read sparks reflection, as does journaling, both of which come easily here, going solo. In my transitional state, to borrow again from Ziolkowski, "New thoughts well up, changes of life direction are contemplated." As I move through this forest-tundra ecotone and borderlands between the Inupiat and Gwich'in, lands both groups frequented, my identity becomes fluid, less clearly defined.

There are as many reasons for expeditioning on your own as there are against it. A partner can add safety in tight spots, advising, warning, or opining about a route. Instead, I bought and brought a GPS thingamajig as a navigational backup. Four sharp eyes detect bears better than two, and a second pair of hands can administer first aid and help with an evacuation. Conversely, backcountry buddies may distract you from your surroundings. Or, under stress, fall apart or morph into antagonists. I've observed cliques forming in larger groups, and conversations drifting toward movies, restaurants, sports, office gossip, or the latest in gear.

I have an evening visitor in my camp at the Kongakut's northward hook. Fiddling with the GPS in front of my tent, I'm engrossed, still perplexed by its buttons and functions. When I look up, a bear forty yards away, as surprised as I, gets a beady eye on me. Mentally flinching, I call out "Whoa, buster," raising my arms as if surrendering or showing that I'm unarmed. It's a gesture and tone I cultivated working with skittish horses and which now is instinctual. Caught with his paw in the cookie jar, or at least near it, the bear saunters off.

Let them know you are human, different from what they normally eat.

Beliefs circulated from Greenland to Siberia that in a mythical distant time, a time before we had fallen from grace, animals lived in societies that mirrored those of humans and could communicate with us. Sometimes animals that wanted to talk to you pushed their muzzles or beaks aside as if they were masks. A humanoid face would show—the Inupiat's *inua*, symbolic of the animal's sentient nature. Miniature carved *inua* faces often peep at the observer from modern animal sculptures, homunculi embedded in walrus ivory, soapstone, or wood. In Indigenous minds, bears mediate between this world and the spirit world, between nature and culture, which are Western dichotomies. The high latitudes' twilight, with storms or sea-ice mirages blurring horizons, dissolve long-held certainties about earth, sky, ocean, and those with whom we share this planet.

Boundaries separating humans from other-than-humans were thought to be permeable. Shape-shifting commonly bespoke power and warned against snap judgments. It acknowledged atavistic drives. Modern sculptors carve shamans that incarnate as bears from soapstone or walrus ivory. In Eskimo thought, the visual media expert and anthropologist Edmund Carpenter wrote, the "lines between species and classes, even between man and animal, are lines of fusion, not fission."

While possible, unions of people and bears always spelled danger. The two species' physical and behavioral resemblances suggested such "promiscuity," which germinated a shared ancestry many myths detail. Of twin brothers born to a woman, one could be a cub and the other a child. The sole offspring of a human couple could be a bear. In one Inupiaq story providing a mythological explanation for three species' commonality, a woman gives birth to a polar bear and a grizzly.

Gwich'in women, seldom approached or attacked, addressed grizzlies as "brother-in-law," reminding them "It's your sister here." Speaking to bears invokes this ancient kinship, and it's a credit to their race that they normally listen to us. Hunters avoided bragging about kills they expected to make when they went searching for dens and in low tones uttered circumlocutions, oblique references instead of the bear's name, because one might overhear them. They knew that "even if he is sleeping, he knows you are talking about him." Gwich'in elders admonished their young men "not to bother it, but just to talk to it and to tell them to go away." Bears were powerful, physically and spiritually, so ritual gestures of respect appeased them. In the hunt, the proper tools had to be sharp and well cared for, and no blood or waste was left around for a person to walk through. The forest and tundra had ears and eyes that constantly monitored human behavior.

Wildlife biologists corroborating ancient approaches recommend talking calmly to a bear while also avoiding eye contact, which the bear might interpret as aggression. That is, if you find yourself the target of a "defensive attack." What may sound like an oxymoron describes a provoked charge, a response in which a surprised bear defends her cub, food cache, or personal space upon which a hiker has infringed. The other, scarier kind, a "predatory attack" by a prowling bear, requires you to fight for survival instead of playing dead or otherwise trying to deescalate moments that raise the hair at the back of your head literally, moments that can feel like hours.

Back to scrutinizing my GPS after the interruption, I do not yet know that I will encounter a grizzly on average every other day, enough to put together three football teams.

KING OF THE KONG

DAY 5 (11 MILES)
QUAD: TABLE MOUNTAIN

Barely a day passes without some graphic reminder of mortality, whether close bear encounters or bones scattered on the tundra—a skull, scapula, vertebrae, or mummified leg with hoof attached. On a gray morning, while I cross aufeis strangely radiant, as if it were collecting what little light there remains, a shred of blue above and ahead feels ethereal, like a window onto the afterlife. Unlike on other outings, I have blebs not on my feet, which stay wet more often than not, but on my hands, from my tussock crutches. My hands are soft, a milquetoast writer's, not callused as usual at this time of year from days at the oars already.

Woolly louseworts in bloom evoke strawberry ice-cream cones. It is too early in the trip for such cravings.

I reach the Kongakut near its elbow, the first familiar landmark since Joe Creek. Memories flood in, of Drain Creek, Whale Mountain, Icy Reef. River trips launch in this vicinity, and I did on my first arctic float as a rafting guide. An Australian couple in a basecamp I pitched at Caribou Pass donated a thermal underwear top and bottom, as I'd been woefully unprepared for a cold front sliding in from the Arctic Ocean. I really needed it on the following hike to the coast with a different pair of people, along the Clarence River to Demarcation Bay, the boundary survey party's icy infinity pool. My hikers had vowed they too would take a dip once we got there, for bragging rights. After testing the water with a finger, they'd changed their minds. They always do.

The Kongakut, easternmost of popular North Slope rivers, throws gnarly rapids at boaters. The biggest one killed two Californian women paddlers on a guided trip. When disaster strikes wilderness enthusiasts, I often hear, "At least they died doing what they loved doing," as if that were consolation. Taking their last breath, pale with terror, blue with regret, the doomed may have hated what they were doing. They certainly would have preferred to keep doing just about anything.

A different, less hairy beast on its milder stretches, "the Kong" boasts good fishing holes, sail-finned grayling, and five-pound arctic char.

What is this need to abbreviate? "The Kong," "the Hula" (Hulahula) . . . more than three syllables seem a bother. Some writers refer to "the Brooks," omitting the most important part: the range. We also clip syllables elsewhere: "Flag" for Flagstaff, "Frisco" for San Francisco. My wife says frequent flyers pronounce abbreviations on luggage tags instead of their destination's name. Hence, "AKP" for Anaktuvuk Pass, "NUI" for Nuiqsut, "KOTZ" for Kotzebue. Otto von, the old Baltic globe circumnavigator serving Tsar Alexander I, would have been indignant. Named after him, the Bering Sea burg is the intended terminus of my traverse, bookend to Joe Creek and forty-five jet minutes from Nome, so I have a certain fondness for it. The casual language, I suppose, projects familiarity with the subject, distinguishing speakers as insiders, whether or not they have earned that status.

I'm easily entertained, admittedly, and out here, aside from the antics of wild-life, have to find amusement in myself.

From the heights, I see a huge aufeis field and large inky stretches of open Kongakut. Willow flats sprawl where the current changed channels and unburdened itself of trainloads of gravel. Dwarf birch covers the bluffs I walk without undue effort toward my crossing.

Vegetation in part determined the course of this traverse. Forest and thickets of alder and willow, despite spilling over the Brooks Range where they infiltrate sheltering draws, foremost cling to its southern slopes. Global heating's greening of the Arctic is changing that fast. Still, I chose a southerly route. At this time of year, south-facing passes and slopes should largely be free of snow, in theory. This, however, puts me in brush more often than a walk on the coastal side of the divide would. Having traveled the middle and lower reaches of the region's major north-south trending rivers during my ethnographic fieldwork and on private trips and those I have guided, I know I must cross as near to their sources as possible to avoid the deep, raging currents June snowmelt feeds into them. I did not bring a flotation device for crossings so will have to make all of them by wading. Though a few valleys run east to west, the majority of my planned route goes against the landscape's grain, requiring that I scale dozens of passes. I will loosely stick to the Continental Divide. In the Rockies' northern tail, the great watershed separates the Arctic Ocean's Beaufort and Chukchi Sea drainages from the Pacific's Bering Sea drainage. There, the dot-and-dash line doglegs from north to south into east to west, yet another trick of plate tectonics, and I shall vault it repeatedly.

Thumps of aufeis shelves collapsing into the Kongakut herald summer. Boaters in early June scout the moribund ice because streams sapping it sometimes flow underneath. In 2003, a father and son on the North Fork of the Koyukuk in Gates of the Arctic got stranded for four days in T-shirts and with one pair of boots when their raft hit an aufeis shelf, tossing them into the drink. The current dragged them under it for a hundred yards before spitting them out at the far end. An air pocket where they briefly clung to the ceiling saved them from drowning, but they got scraped up badly and lost everything but one lighter. Cautious guides on early-season river trips carry ice screws and lines to quickly anchor their boat to a wall should they round a bend only to face a cold, dark maw.

I think of Edward Abbey, a writing influence early in my career. For him, who never much liked Alaska, it was "our biggest, buggiest, boggiest state." At that stage in his life, he wrote on assignment for glossy men's magazines, all expenses paid, a far cry from the dirtbag or pre-*Desert Solitaire* days. He felt out of his element here, and professional guides led both of his Alaska excursions.

Despite his yearning to experience nature at its wildest and woolliest, Abbey never saw a brown bear, not even at the Tucson zoo, where one hid in its den on the day he visited. His friend "Grizzly Man" Doug Peacock, the model for Hayduke in Abbey's *The Monkey Wrench Gang*, carried an eight-foot homemade Inuit-style spear once as a security guard on a Canadian arctic expedition. Even Peacock could not get the familiar Montana bears to show themselves to his pal Ed.

Debbie Miller, an author and former Arctic Village teacher who lunched, fished, and birded with Jimmy Carter and his wife, Rosalynn, during their stay at her Okpilak River camp, also met Abbey, in Kaktovik. "He had just floated the Kongakut River," she recalls, and "perhaps what surprised him most was an

American robin that perched near his tent, singing its joyful song in an arctic gale." The robin, which Abbey knew from his Tucson backyard, impressed him as living evidence of an epic unrest. Like all migrants, it combines here and there in one body. Yet in his essay about the adventure, the man receptive to nature described Barter Island, the home of three hundred Inupiat, as "the most dismal, desperate, degraded rathole in the world." On a clear fall day, the Brooks Range scrimshaws Kaktovik's southern horizon—snowy, majestic, above a powder-blue piedmont. The embittered writer coming down with the flu called the bear "the hypothetical grizzly." "I have seen but little of the real North," he confessed at the end of "Gather at the River," "and of that little understood less."

Upon reinspection, hero bronzes on pedestals sometimes have clay feet. Sledgehammer them at the knees so you can stand eye to eye.

More birds enliven the Kongakut than anywhere else on my route thus far: gulls, loons, ducks, tree and white-crowned sparrows, and jaegers—buoyant, yelping gulls with hooked bills and tails one could take for long stingers. Unlike ravens, white-crowns speak different tongues. Bird repertoires stay fixed neither geographically nor historically. Singing cultures like the white-crowns innovate. Males conspicuous on the highest branches stake claims and announce their mate qualities in dialect. Musical cliques inhabiting segmented landscapes may evolve into new species. Sonograms allow visual and computer comparisons of their vocal styles, and those of other singers, thereby revealing population sizes, their relatedness, and environmental shifts.

Before the trip's end, my notes in the map margins will spill over onto the backs of six four-square-foot map sheets, cluttering them with the tiny, curlicued extracts of my days. I realize how much richer the hours have been here than in town, how much life can be packed into mere minutes. My attention is keener, less scattered, yet paradoxically wider, more open than in the humdrum boxes of urban routines.

My script crowds expanses on the maps as the waypoints of explorers once did, possibilities turned into facts, at least, if not certainties. The small tent-shape triangles with which I mark campsites align into a string of prayer beads that shield me from a harsh world. Each one signifies a sweet home away from home.

Writing and travel in their linearity and directedness overlap. Putting the first sentence on a page can petrify you; so can first steps into the unknown, and you don't know where either will lead. Places fantasized about before with the help of these maps now cohere. First, they become reality, and too soon will exist for me only as memories. What from an airplane perspective resembled a hostile rucked labyrinth has started to feel like boots broken in well.

FLOWERS FOR THE AGES

DAY 6 (10.5 MILES)
QUAD: TABLE MOUNTAIN

Overcast. Focusing attention is a necessity, a prerequisite for survival. Breakfast bearanoia grips me with suffocating paws as something big and brown moves toward camp. It becomes a caribou partway concealed by brush. Wolf paws the size of my palms imprint black sand at a ditch between vegetation clumps. The hiking improves on drier ground after lunch.

Bell heather, unlike sun-tracking dryas and arctic poppies, but like Cassandra, bog rosemary, and various berry bushes, droops tiny heads. The heather, however, also faces east to greet dawn. All danglers in fact cup the warmth rising from soil as the day gets under way. The father of modern biological taxonomy and first European to grow a banana, Carl Linnaeus, upon being ennobled in 1757, adopted the twinflower (*Linnaea borealis*), among the most graceful of the inverted miniature vases, as his coat of arms. Pink-and-white trumpet duos arcing from a single forked stem make this circumpolar honeysuckle a fairy lantern. It remains the only plant named for the ruddy "Pliny of the North" who honed his science in Lapland before sending "apostles"—a "brotherhood of the butterfly net"—on globe-spanning collecting trips. Fame, to him "flowering but for a brief time," mirrors the brocade of arctic blooming. That includes this Swede's favorite, "lowly, insignificant" *Linnaea borealis*. He signed, "From Linnaeus, who resembles it."

These are autumn thoughts, though, not musings for summer's spry prime.

Because the sun has broken through, I camp early, on a Kongakut gravel bar, and brew afternoon coffee, a rare treat. My mind unearths a memory from another arctic solo on which I forgot to bring my reusable coffee filter. Craving my fix, I improvised with a spare sock—there is a thing called a tea sock, right? The taste did not satisfy me. Hesitating only briefly, I then cut a patch from my tent's mesh screen, which worked splendidly. The resulting bug bites were worth the kick my coffee delivered.

Suffering separation pangs I will need to wean myself from if I'm to enjoy this trip fully, I feel tempted to call Melissa all the time, especially at camp in the evenings. But satellite minutes are expensive, and I should conserve my batteries.

Out here, too, I realize, looking over my notes, some days are fuller than others.

THE FAT OF THE LAND

DAY 7 (1.5 MILES)
QUAD: TABLE MOUNTAIN

During the night a wind sprang up and this morning sodden sky clamps onto the earth. No longer immune to afternoon caffeine, I did not sleep well so decide on a short day, as I'm close to the Sheenjek cache with days of food to spare. No use throwing it away or hauling extra pounds on the next leg. As the trip wears on, I will run low before each resupply and my body will start to consume itself, fat reserves first, muscle mass later. Calories matter on expeditions, but I can't be bothered with counting them or with weighing my daily rations beforehand. I don't carry much fat on my six-foot frame and not in my pack either. Soon, a lack of fat in my diet will tell, through belly growls and the fit of my hiking pants.

I've put a plastic jar of sunflower butter and some salami into every other resupply. Cheese and butter would spoil on a trip this long, melting inside black barrels by the airstrips, as I cannot expect the pilots to store my perishables in their fridges. And I did not think of olive oil, the Australian's magic potion, which gives you the biggest caloric bang for your buck by volume and weight. You would not need to guzzle it neat like he did but could add a few glugs to each dinner. I carefully ration dark mini peanut butter cups instead, allotting a few as my nightly dessert.

The rest of the fare is spartan: pilot bread—round crackers, classic Alaskan backcountry fare, two or three make a lunch; instant oatmeal and sauces; dried fruits and nuts; parboiled rice, couscous, and ramen; jerky; and dehydrated veggies. Hot chocolate and cider hit the spot before bedtime. I draw the line at having just energy bars for breakfast, though I packed dozens. To jump-start the engine I need coffee, which, paired with hot cereal, makes all the difference on a nippy morning. I'm not picky about dinners, just grab a prepacked ziplock and boil its contents. The menu repeats itself at every cache. I've not come here to eat fancy food, though any gratifies immensely, something to look forward to in the tussock arena.

Friends whom I told about my project asked if fishing and hunting would support me along the way. Some people assume you can live off the land on such a journey. Not in the Brooks Range, not if you want to cross the length of it in one summer or less. I could supplement my diet with grayling if I had brought a fishing line and hook; but the smell of fish scales and slime on my hands, pants, and cooking utensils would be a dinner bell to the bears.

Before I leave camp, while I'm breaking stuff down, two packrafters bob past without noticing me. Not drawing their attention leaves them their solitude and me mine.

A semipalmated plover does her broken-wing routine to distract me from her nest. The short-necked wader with the conspicuous black collar scuttles low to the ground for a few yards and then stops to let me catch up. Each time I do, she repeats her ruse till I'm far enough from her clutch, when at last she flies off and circles back to tend it again. We Alaskans think of these birds as foreigners, short-term visitors, even though they hatch here. Which raises a question of interest to me: Are you from where you were born or from where you spend most of your life? (I have lived longer in the US than in my native country.) This South American migrant, like other snowbirds, times her arrival so that chicks, independent from the moment they hatch, can harvest the new mosquito crop. With summer starting earlier now and bugs out sooner, timings fine-tuned over centuries have been unbalanced, especially damaging to species that depend on the larval insect stage.

Victims as much as vehicles, migrating birds for the first time have brought avian flu in their bloodstream, which in Alaska kills gulls, shorebirds, eagles, and waterfowl. Infected mosquitos, by biting and perhaps by being eaten, spread West Nile virus among birds. While mosquitos have tested positive for the lethal form of bird flu, it remains unclear yet if they transmit it to birds. As a further piece in this disconcerting scenario, with the Arctic cooking, mosquitos hatch earlier, in greater numbers, grow faster, and live longer, with consequences also for caribou.

Wading its widest, shallowest channels, I cross the Kongakut without trouble: Hydrology 101. Clouds climb the slopes. Dwarf lupines glow in the incipient sun.

The longevity of their seeds, even next to other equally tough legumes, is legendary. They've survived inside lemming burrows, frozen in sediment fifteen feet deep and ten thousand years old. They don't need a "doomsday vault" like Svalbard's, which stores almost one million important seeds—important, that is, to humanity.

I find a sweet dryas camp, in both senses of that modifier. This fragrant rose-family member loves well-drained gravel benches with thin soil and a veneer of heather or lichen. As do I. A favorite caribou nibble, perennial dryas can outlive a century, weaving leathery arrowhead leaves into carpets whose buds and seeds feed pikas and ptarmigans. Before long, each of hundreds of flowers at my tent site will wilt and twist into silvery conical plumes. These will unfurl, mini feather dusters with seed to be borne on breezes like dandelion or fireweed down.

Dryas claims land right after glaciers vacate it and lent its name to a cold spell between the end of the Pleistocene and the start of the Holocene, the era of stable climate that birthed and braced civilization, until now. The Younger Dryas, between 12,900 and 11,700 BCE, allowed crossings via Beringia, the continent cold exposed when it bound seawater in glaciers. First Americans on the Brooks Range north flank left more than seventy leaf-shaped flaked-stone projectile points on a mesa-shaped ridge that served as a hunting lookout. Around the time these Paleoindians departed their roost, with temperatures climbing, the ice sheets melted and Bering Sea levels rose, flooding the path to the New World. Except for those who traveled in skin boats, like the Inupiat's ancestors.

The periodic abundance of dryas deep within lake sediments speaks volumes about Earth systems, about the dusk of epochs past and the dawn of coming ones. Dryas, for me, is the Arctic's signature flower, defiance wrapped inside delicate tissue.

As I climb a long, serene ridge to the north of my camp, the world opens up more, step by step, surprising even in this treeless country. Five clusters of wolf droppings string me along, desiccated and white with caribou hair and bone splinters. In the absence of movies, human music, or books, shit becomes entertainment. Thus, I revert to my childhood.

When I top out, the sun splits the sky's scrim above glaciers that melt into the river. It spotlights two rams bedded down on an outcrop not far below as if pointing them out. One rakes his back with a horn. I feel that lazy Sunday morning vibe but have no idea what day it is other than its place in my running count. It has been a week already, which seems like a month. On weekend excursions into wilderness, you rarely enter the zone of "being there," in the crystalline present, at least not dependably or extensively. The first day, you still sway under the workweek's burden, while on the last you already mull things that await you, tasks that can't be avoided. Around day ten of a longer trip, kinks have been straightened out—or they won't be, fine either way. Worries have been cast off or at least superseded by more immediate ones: bears, the weather and route, where to camp. Decisions overall become simple, though repercussions may be dramatic. This lets your brain grapple with other, important matters. You have slowed down enough to open yourself to a place and its myriad tales. Abbey—he grasped many issues despite his biases—believed that it could and should take a human lifetime to understand the story of one single gnarled juniper.

Above the sheep but below me, a golden eagle gyres, wings locked. It's not often that you can watch one from this vantage. Her broad back flexes as she trims wings on the air currents in a balance of strength and elegance. The configuration of sheep, bird, river, and mountains is perfect, a reward for three days of ankle busting. I've seen enough beauty for several lifetimes in one. Got to get Melissa out here. Sharing can make an experience all the sweeter—one boon of matrimony and wilderness guiding.

This is my Mowat moment. Caribou on the march, out of nowhere, walk right through the camp, some as close as between my kitchen and tent. I first smell their musk on the wind while sunbathing nude. Luckily, I did not bring a camera, which would tempt me to try freeze-framing their urgency, an impossible undertaking. The moment approximates that grand *Never Cry Wolf* scene, minus the hunting wolves. In the Disney adaptation of Farley Mowat's memoir, the rookie biologist, having taken a dip in a lake, lies on the tundra to let a breeze dry him off. Out of nowhere, migrating caribou crowd around him. They panic when a pack closes in. Caught up in the melee, trying to keep pace, to prolong the rush, to witness it all, reduced to instinct and quivering flesh, the biologist runs with the bucks as buck naked as on the day he was born, as his ancestors might have. Shedding society's wrappings, he has progressed to an older self.

"In solitude you strip yourself bare, you rest your mind on what is essential and true," one of my favorite authors, the late desert rat and philosopher-clown Ellen Meloy wrote. She meant nudity as a metaphor, surely.

I normally cannot undress like this, not with clients watching, not without risking complaints to my boss. The willows around my tent wear socks, which I wash every evening to prevent blisters.

This day has shaped up nicely, as days here will, always springing surprises. A lost calf visits, approaching me on the off chance that I am her mother. Poor thing. The idea of wildlife-watching must be revised on this tundra. It seldom is passive observation. Animals might check you out as insistently or impertinently as you do them. From the calf to the feigning plover, from the jaegers' dives to the haughty headmistress glances of sheep—not to mention the hungry probing mosquitos and bears—you are routinely engaged, without an escape, always part of the social fabric, never truly alone. Which can be a kind of solace for a solo hiker also guilty of furthering their world's diminishment.

We evolved amid wildlife on the savannah, an environment in many ways similar to the Arctic Coastal Plain. Biologists like E. O. Wilson claim that this heritage still lies in our genes, that we prefer landscapes similar to our ancestral home. Animals made us human. They clothed and armed us. They taught us to hunt and to sing, to escape and to blend in. They imbued art and religion and metaphor as their tracks did narration and proactive reasoning. They also warn us that we neglect our bonds to the natural world at a high cost, which entails social dysfunction. Wilderness remains critical for the well-being of wildlife and people, in their completeness of plants and stone; its preservation therefore becomes a moral imperative. Its significance is symbolic as much as it is ecological. "While thousands have visited the refuge," a US Fish and Wildlife Service (USFWS) former deputy manager said, "millions more who will never come find satisfaction, inspiration, and hope in just knowing it is there." It is foremost the animals' refuge, but we need it as badly.

One of several human cognitive biases—brain fogs, if you will—is prognostic myopia: the distant future means zilch to us. Scenarios we imagine for hazy years beyond the next election don't carry the same emotional weight as those staring us in the face. Beringia's gradual inundation at the end of the Pleistocene (which observant hunter-gatherers drinking from a fount of knowledge that drew on ancestral generations surely noticed) paled versus the cave lion pouncing from a water hole's reeds. By extension, our hunger *right now*, whether for donuts or fossil fuels and their concomitant entertainments, shapes our decisions in the present. It's not an inability to anticipate far-off feelings or needs that trips us up but rather that those are less meaningful, less pressing than our current preoccupations.

After dinner, with oblique light etching copperplate mountains, I listen to complementary voices: the creek purling next to my campsite and the wind-in-the-trees soughing of the Kongakut slipping past gravel bars. Sun firing through gaps between clouds on a conveyor belt sends spokes of a heavenly wheel marching across velvet slopes, spotlights upon an archaic stage.

Other writers have tried to preserve this Brooks Range light. "The long low rays sculpt and gild, so that each ridge, each rock and scarp stands brilliant in its own dimensionality," wrote John M. Kauffmann, a former chief planner for Gates of the Arctic and Noatak National Preserve. "The smallest plant turns vibrant and luminous." Kauffmann, a colleague of the travel writer John McPhee while both taught at Princeton, germinated the idea for McPhee's Alaska classic *Coming into the Country*. His final recommendation for what Gates of the Arctic administrators should do regarding development was: nothing.

BONES ON THE BLOSSOMING ARCTIC SPINE

DAY 8 (4.5 MILES)
QUAD: TABLE MOUNTAIN

Sunny with clouds. The first plane since I started buzzes overhead, perhaps a chartered Cessna going to Drain Creek north of here, or to the coast to pick up floaters. I am moving camp only a little, to gorge on some excellent day hiking. The best route between two points is not always the most direct line. I won't say "straight," because this country abhors such geometry. As the raven roves is not as the hiker hikes. Absent roses, I stop and smell the medicinal spice of crushed Labrador tea's pine-needle-like leaves. Even as someone lacking roots in these mountains, I cannot walk ten miles in them without tripping over some story, human or otherwise. One lies in a double sweep of bull caribou antlers strong as a recurved bow that bleaches on the tundra. The skullcap with a fur patch is attached, so it can't be a castoff.

To build headgear weighing one-tenth of his body's heft fast—up to thirty-five pounds in less than four months, adding half an inch daily—this bull pilfered minerals from his skeleton. His ribs, but not weight-bearing bones, became brittle plywood slats. He would have restored his strength pre-rut with feeding frenzies. In the caribou arms race, his cranial grandeur touted health, seniority, dominance, the smarts to dodge predators, and the balls to sire hale calves, all turn-ons for the cows. In September, the spongy limbs hardened; itchy, mangling willows, he would have stripped his prongs of their velvet—dun, chocolate-brown, or black skin laced with nerves and arteries, a cornucopia for mosquitos. Sparring with scrub, prepping for courtship with antlers stained crimson, he must have been a sight: crazed, a tad ragged, festooned with gory pennants. Brilliant arsenal ready, he awaited autumn's contests, a jousting without much muscle put into it yet, while drifting up to fifty miles south every day. When push finally came to shove among bulls, the odd bleary-eyed bout would end with both combatants starving to death, tines interlocked. Still, his were not purposely fatal duels, no gladiator trident fights but arm-wrestling matches.

In the years preceding his death, he discarded the unwieldy weapons every November when bone-eating cells eroded the basal burrs. Come winter, non-pregnant cows would have surrendered much shorter, slenderer, less ornate rigs. Budding resumed weeks after their sore knobs had healed. Expectant mothers fully racked since September, keeping theirs into June, bested rivals at snow they cratered with saucer-size hoofs to reach lichen and deterred summer wolves circling the nurseries. After birthing, they dropped their antlers, rerouting calcium instead into milk. Theirs and the bulls' castoff "sheds" gathered moss and soon showed gnaw marks of vole, wolf, or other caribou, who cycled nutrients in their scat back into caribou forage. Bones, flowers, and birds too joined in this energetic carousel: skeleton parts and lone boulders make excellent tundra perches, and the bird droppings fertilizer.

I wonder about the stories these wrist-thick bone brackets do not tell, the ones exceeding such generic details. This bull, more than Abbey's Methuselah juniper, had a personality, an individual history. My journey pales next to the total of his, but I know his must have been as unique. In life, his ossified pride shone like buffed mahogany. Human hunters have worshipped the caribou since cave art premiered. The documentary filmmaker and photographer Sumner MacLeish described the flare of caribou antlers as "movement, caught and stilled." This bull's movement, like Yorick's, has been stilled forever. He was once what I still am, and I shall be what he is now. "If we relish the artifacts of death / it's for a sign that life goes on / without us," Robert Wrigley writes in "The Skull of a Snowshoe Hare."

Paths the bull's fellow travelers incised thread the tightening valley I follow. Lineaments of a seasonal urge, they pull summer and winter together. Single lanes seam the hillsides with foot-wide benches, my highways. The onset of cold, or a snowstorm, likely triggers the caribou's southbound push. They may share a built-in compass with migratory birds since they sometimes bridge areas unfamiliar to them before reaching the calving grounds.

The lush green throat of a canyon gapes before me. In places, the creek fills it wall to wall, forming watery narrows. Dryas that honey the breeze fleck a slope. Summer's hold on the tundra is a short, brilliant florescence. Arctic perennials bud just before winter slams the door, then power up and unfold as soon as temperatures climb again in the spring; some take a decade to mature. How much nectar they produce depends on the sunshine they receive. These dainty creations love south-facing slopes, though all yield less than their austral kin. Waxy leaves the size of ladybug wings hug the earth, ducking winds, their smallness and coating slowing evaporation. A few species screen their reproductive goods, pollen, from rain. Under gathering clouds, arctic gentian's porcelain petals, ribbed and spattered with royal blue, close within minutes to keep its nectar undiluted.

Hardier, dwarf species or subspecies evolved in harsh environments with shorter growing seasons and skinflint soils. For instance, take two of the refuge's magenta marvels: Lapland rosebay and purple saxifrage, "stone breaker," a cluster more flower than leaf named for the power of its roots to drill into rock and split it, or for its ability to crack kidney stones. This saxifrage is the world's northernmost flower, a holdfast in Ultima Thule, northern Greenland, the closest land to the pole. A plant of such brittle beauty, so terminal—it busts my heart.

Two ewes, white sphinxes, recline on a mountainside as if on the softest of beds. Clouds ripple like sand on a beach: undulatus. Mares' tails (cirrus) brush the blue in a different quarter, pregnant with ice crystals, forecasting snow or rain in a day or so. I must learn to get better at identifying different forms and what weather they bring. Or does it bring them? Mares' tails should not be confused with fibratus or Father Christmas's beard, *The Cloud Collector's Handbook* informs me. These wisp scraps tell its author nothing about weather in store. "Perhaps they are there just to look nice," he thinks. For the longest time, I did not care much about clouds. I'm too busy with my eyes, nose, and ears at ground level to study celestial matters; astronomy is another example. But guides like to know what's what out there. Natural history interpretation is part of our job. Curiosity is in our nature. Weather affects us. As Rebecca

Solnit, with whom I once floated a river, remarks, "There's an art of attending to weather, to the route you take."

Speaking of beaches and sand—where is the ocean, anyway? Still eighty eagle miles from here in one direction, and roughly five hundred daunting ones in the direction I'm headed—but also underfoot, as fossilized corals, mollusk shells, and segments of crinoid or "sea lily" stems looking like Polo mints. They rest in a Lisburne limestone matrix, one of the Brooks Range's most noticeable geological layers. The limestone itself was built from tiny exoskeletons settling at the bottom of a waist-deep Permian Sea that later fused under pressure. It resists erosion in the cold, dry arctic climate, forming two-thousand-foot cliffs near Atigun Gorge, where the Dalton Highway climbs and cleaves the range. (The Dalton Highway or Haul Road is the dusty gravel track paralleling the pipeline that connects Fairbanks to Prudhoe Bay's oilfields on the Beaufort Sea shore. Motorists consider driving its four hundred miles an adventure, and on a stormy gray day at Atigun Pass, one is bound to agree.)

The frozen monster wave I try to ride is young, relatively speaking, coterminous with the first flowering plants and 100 million years younger than the Grand Canyon's uppermost layer, composed of another limestone. Melissa, a seasoned Grand Canyon hiker, calls it a baby range—for its age, not its size. It is the result of the Pacific and North American plates plowing into each other at a snail's pace, starting about 145 million years ago. This oceanic and continental crust pileup set the heroic slant of its rock tiers, vertical in locations like Thunder Valley, near the Itkillik headwaters. Seafloor thrust up in the collision has yielded treasure far more ancient than the range. In scree sloping at Atigun, a geology student from Barrow found an imprint of a buzz saw shark's pearly whites. With teeth on a whorl partly embedded in its lower jaw, twenty-foot-long *Helicoprion* roamed Permian Seas more than 270 million years ago. The rock chunk, which went missing for almost thirty years, is the only known trace of it in Alaska.

The range that keeps giving still rises incrementally and culminates in a clutch of four peaks almost nine thousand feet high north of my current position. Quartzite, limestone, and metamorphic rock make up their spiny crest, and much younger sandstone, shale, and conglomerate their aprons. John McPhee compared the range's complexity to a driftwood heap; the bands and lobes of geological zones coloring maps of it also share aspects with the fronts and pressure systems on weather maps.

After dropping camp a few miles south of snowfields that are the Aichilik's source, I go on an afternoon hike, a bonus of short-distance days. Part of this trek's raison d'être, after all, is that I never get to explore at my leisure when guiding clients, or not enough. There are always meals to be fixed, needs to be attended to, and I do not want my hikers groggy for the days following.

I almost stomp rock jasmine, a white delicate face on a single stem. How can something so small smell so intensely good? To put its scent in perspective, imagine eight months without outdoor odors (except in the outhouse), because nothing greens, nothing blooms, nothing decays, and the air is too dry and the particles are not volatile and your nostrils freeze shut half of the time. Breathing on the jasmine humidifies its scent molecules, which swell inside my brain.

Next, an explosion of pink draws my eyes. A favorite of mine, Alaska moss campion. It's the Mr. Freeze of floral cold adaptation—unsurprisingly, garlands from blossoms of a related species crowned antiquity's champions. Individual plants grow up to two feet in diameter over the course of three centuries at 6,600 feet. Moss campion pillows in densely packed greenery saying "moss" but sprouts spangled splendor. It loves dry gravelly spots, rocky ridges, and scree, fell fields some people think of as barren. Lodging in cracks where few things dare to, this stunted carnation buffers meat-locker conditions, nursing other plants in and around it. It migrated south along Pleistocene ice edges, and when those retreated clung to alpine refugia in Wyoming, Colorado, even Arizona, pockets much like its original habitat. Cushioning, a trait it shares with creeping phlox and arctic forget-me-not, lets this relict hoard moisture from flurries and fog. It also gleans minerals from blown silt and its own leaf litter caught in the verdant matt. The hedgehog silhouette combines the largest photosynthetic surface with the least exposure, the lowest risk of damage. Air flowing over the domes as over a plane wing traps warmth underneath.

Ah, warmth. Golden blessing.

Moss campion channels it into segmented blushing, erupting in a gorgeous south-side rash first while pea green still mantles its shaded half—hence its second moniker: compass plant. Its duotone contrast outshines sandworts, equally shrunken white, grounded star showers. Sometimes, at their peak, campion florets hiding foliage tint an entire hemisphere.

Alas, as with porches or tanning beds, too much of a good thing can cause harm. Expanding in mild years, moss campion contracts during the hottest, which now march in lockstep. This is troubling Lower Forty-Eight holdouts especially, as, shifting upward, they'll run out of mountain at last.

I climb a peak near camp whenever I can, not just for aesthetic and spiritual uplift or from any excess of energy but also to scout the next day's route and terrain. As I check the landscape against my map from this perspective, the larger layout crystallizes, revealing its logic. Individual mountains grow into ranges that bunch rambling creeks into watersheds. One of these peaks, snow flecked in the distance, marks my first resupply, on the Sheenjek, three days out.

I can barely spot my tent's gray-green shell from up here. It looks tiny and fragile, sitting in the valley like a plover egg, offering not that much in the way of protection. But it truly is home for the time being, an impromptu twenty-six-square foot cocoon, a membrane that stakes out my personal sphere. In little more than a week, I've developed a habit of thanking each campsite silently, sometimes wordlessly, for harboring me, before I walk into the morning. There's a sense that the land that could crush me in an instant is watching over me.

As the mares' tails foretold, big-bellied clouds have barreled in. The sky's canopy now is the color of rubble on the mountaintop where I stand.

I stuff myself with spaghetti Alfredo and compote from dried apples I soaked during my preprandial hike, with a mug of hot chocolate to finish. I am full as a bloated tick and struggle to walk uphill from the kitchen to the tent. All my food tastes delicious in the outdoors and assumes meaning beyond its sheer calories. Dinner is an occasion, ringing in the day's end and well-earned relaxation.

I called Melissa yesterday around this time. She was atop Newton Peak, on Nome's outskirts, next to the cell phone tower. We disconnected a few times, but the familiar voice still felt good. Today, she flew out to Shaktoolik as part of her Bering Strait nursing routine. She's on griddle-flat land holed with ponds, a different world, one I tend to forget, coexisting with mine.

WINTER'S SEND-OFF

DAY 9 (12 MILES)
QUAD: TABLE MOUNTAIN

Sunny but windy and cold. During breakfast I am wearing every layer I have. In the Inuit language, Inuktitut, the same word designates wind, breath, spirit, and climate—flowing air pervades everything, a fact I'll relearn later on the Noatak. This weather must have blown in from the north, straight from the pack ice, or what's left of it. We fly to the moon and drill miles into the earth, but we've never invented anything better than down feathers for warmth? Nothing artificial is as light and insulating and compressible. The only natural materials in my kit are the down in my sleeping bag; the leather in my boots; and some merino in my socks and liner gloves. I'm wearing a lot of synthesized Mesozoic sludge and acknowledge the cruel irony here in this embattled refuge.

Things have been looking up, though. Another oil company just backed out of a lease it had acquired, the third corporation to withdraw recently. Shareholders pressured five major banks in 2020 to announce commitments to finance no oil or gas ventures inside the refuge. Harvard University divested from fossil fuel industries, and other public institutions may follow its lead. Perhaps the tide has turned for good. This incomparable land once more has been granted reprieve—until it burns up or the next Republican pretender tramps in.

Already the numbers paint a grim picture. Data from Alaska and western Canada indicate that winter temperatures have risen there by as much as seven degrees Fahrenheit in the past fifty years. Snow cover has decreased about 10 percent over the past thirty years. Permafrost, which can be thousands of feet deep, warmed three to five degrees within two decades on the coastal plain.

Sea ice not only shrinking in its lateral extent but also thinning forces three times more polar bears to den and give birth on land, where seismic testing or other human activities might evict them. Midwinter icing from freezing rain and thaw episodes seals off forage for muskoxen, forcing them to burn more calories searching for it.

During the past twenty years, communities that never before saw my old acquaintance the American robin have borrowed its inland Inupiaq name: *koyapigaktoruk*. And my outfitter friend and fellow guide Robert Thompson tells me that the Porcupine herd has been crossing the mountains in late April and early May recently, perhaps chasing premature summers. Anecdotal evidence, sure, but long-term climate phenomena affecting polar bears, other fauna, and plants are well documented.

Even on my sporadic jaunts, I have noticed disturbing signs: lightning storms, cutbanks sagging atop melting permafrost, aufeis shrunk or no longer perennial, tundra as dry as AstroTurf, and ranges wrapped in the smoke of forest and tundra fires. In the new normal, more than 250 burns rage statewide during peak combustible days on which up to ten thousand lightning bolts strike.

I can't help but wonder how the refuge will change in the next fifteen, thirty, or sixty years. Will hikers have to bushwhack through willows and alders farther and farther to the north, as they already do on the south side of the range? Will lightning become a regular hazard like fording streams can be in June? Will the days be too hot to hike and heatstroke the new hypothermia? Will foxes carry rabies, and ticks Lyme disease, replacing mosquitos as our biggest bug worry, or will anthrax from thawing reindeer carcasses or some nameless superbug sicken or kill people as it did in Siberia? Already, higher soil temperatures spread a lung parasite specific to muskoxen. Will the native animals leave, die off, or lie low much of the time? And where could they go?

Flurries drop flakes onto rotting snow patches as I trudge through a plain east of the Sheenjek, about to cross to the divide's south side for the first time on this trip. Strange to think that tomorrow's creeks drain into the Bering Strait not far from home. Winter has not had its last say just yet. It can snow any month of the year in arctic Alaska.

Forget-me-nots, the state flower, the prettiest blue, so delicious I want to spoon it up, are especially welcome on a day that has grayed into gruel. They're bits of heaven, each with its own cheerful sun at the center.

Three squatting lakes perhaps supplying two different seas make me think of watersheds and their protection and of the importance of potable water. Mined like fossil fuels from aquifers or captured in withering reservoirs, it is a precious commodity in the drought-choked West. You cannot tell where city water originates, beyond a spigot or reservoir. Waterborne diseases in human, animal, and chemical waste account for 80 percent of illnesses in developing countries. One-fifth of the world drinks water that kills or gives people the runs, while another fifth sells water in designer bottles labeled Fountain of Youth for four bucks a pop or hawks thousand-year-old "100 percent natural" glacier cubes for your cocktails—get them while you can. Record droughts now also rack central Europe, depleting rivers and exposing "hunger stones," engraved hydrological markers warning of bad harvests and famines. "If you see me, cry," one from 1616 on the banks of the Elbe reads. "When this stone sinks," a more optimistic one promises, "life will become more colorful again." They were bulletins addressed to the future. What words will we carve for the yet unborn?

On my trek through the land of snowfield milk and honey I don't even carry a purifier, though I've had giardia twice, from stagnant water. Alaska's most hated backcountry bug (besides the miasmal mosquito) causes "beaver fever"—it lives in their feces and in those of bears and off-grid campers. I'm careful at popular sites, like airstrips and the put-ins for river trips. But we're in serious trouble if we can no longer drink the water in a refuge.

Reading Robert Perkins does not perk me up today: "Ever since the idea of compromise was embraced, every power under the sun has been used to ensure that the rights of people are protected and the rights of every other creature are compromised." It is high time we give rivers and mountains their due.

The year's first golden plover does buoy me, matching the forget-me-nots in refinement. A bold white stripe in the breeding plumage curves around the face to end abruptly at the upper chest, which is charcoal, as is his entire front. From the side, he appears to wear a powdered wig. Gold spangles his cap and whole back. He makes me chuckle. He races a few steps like a windup toy and then stops, *wheetle-wheetle*, before another burst. Unsurprisingly given his splendor, the species is still rebounding from last century's millinery fad; now pesticides, wind farms, and habitat loss along its flyways have replaced the threat that those who hunted quills for ladies' hats posed.

The first jet overflight since I started the hike. I mistake it for the wind initially. Cannot find a good tent site, so I lumber all the way to the Sheenjek, about a mile short of cache number one. How rare good sites can be, even in this treeless expanse! Cottongrass tufts signal level but boggy camping from a distance. Ground near game trails should be taboo, since bears may commute there. Lakeshores can suck, and I always prod their turf with a finger to test for wetness under the surface. This time, I have to take a subpar spot that willow thickets border, the stream's greenbelt.

Glaciers encasing the heart of the Romanzof Mountains feed the Gwich'in's "Dog Salmon River," the Sheenjek, which hurries south for two hundred miles to join the Porcupine—namesake of the caribou herd—and afterward, a sweep of the rolling Yukon. Open white spruce stands have infiltrated this valley from the south since the Pleistocene ice in the Brooks Range receded. More June rain and rising temperatures now boost the timberline's vanguard, whose outliers take a century to grow to a man's height.

A plain wooden cross leans silvered with age amid white spruce near the Sheenjek airstrip. In the early 1980s, refuge staff flew several Gwich'in elders from Arctic Village there to map cultural sites. One of them died during this walk down memory lane, and the party buried him, with the Reverend Trimble Gilbert, who grew up hunting and trapping in these parts and had come along, officiating. They left a jar with the man's name and some papers in it, Kirk told me. I never saw that, perhaps because it had deteriorated or moss swallowed it. Who's to say the elder wasn't right where he wanted to be when his time was up?

The sun lost, moisture moves in, so I rush dinner and retire early to my bedchamber. I'm not anywhere near the Sheenjek's source, so I worry about tomorrow's fording. The Forest Service, summarizing the region's precipitation patterns, writes, "Drainage is rapid due to the area's steep slopes and the low holding capacity of its soils." Random facts loom above you as portents when you're unmoored from the cushions of home. If it rains more tonight and the river rises, the thirteenth (a Friday?) could be exciting in all the wrong ways.

THE ONLY GOOD BEAR
IS A DEAD BEAR

DAY 10 (2.5 MILES)
QUAD: TABLE MOUNTAIN
CACHE #1

Morning reveals a snow dusting on peaks, which brings out their texture and adds depth to the scene. It highlights their sharp forbiddingness. The sun battles with cloud rags. I'm headed for my resupply on the other side.

My resolve is not the only thing stiffening, after being tested in my stumbling through vegetation. I start each day with a locked lower back, bent over like an octogenarian stonemason. By the time I have broken camp and hiked a mile or two, despite the load my spine has straightened out. When the engine cools, even during a fifteen-minute break, it again seizes up and has to be lubricated with motion.

"Michael chooses to live in pain," a couple on that bear-y Joe Creek hike needled when I confessed that I hate yoga or similar limbering exercises. It's an old aversion, grounded in army calisthenics and Outward Bound stretch circles. The latter preceded breakfast and finished with instructors and students plunging from a cliff into the Colorado. (Need I say I don't like morning showers either?)

I am out of reading matter already. *I should have put some into the caches.* I mull over what I read last night, chewing my thought cud—plenty of time for that. Robert Perkins wrote, "Civilization is an experiment that has failed; only technology keeps it limping along." But this shows a limited understanding of technology, which begins with two sticks really: the ability to start a fire. Athabaskans and Inupiat formerly traveled light. Nomadic hunter-gatherers carry technology in their heads in the form of skills acquired over generations. They fashion implements as needed from local resources. The land provides wood, stone, bone, antler, and animal skins if you know where to look.

Kirk left the first cache with a hunting outfit camped at the Sheenjek airstrip, a tundra runway on slightly slanted hardpan that pilots cleaned of rocks. Some strips situated on river islands or near-shore gravel bars come and go as the water shifts course and erodes shores, or snowmelt floods low-lying areas. This one, higher up on the mountains' apron, remains intact.

The crossing is easier than expected, though water in the deepest channel surges up to my waist. Thankfully, the hiking poles offer extra stability. Why was I worried about this?

Soaked, still dripping, I must be a sight. When I walk up to the kitchen tent, two men sit on folding chairs, yakking. The one I assume to be the client has a black eye. Their friendly demeanor rules out a fistfight as the cause.

The guide, Dave Marsh, a shorter, bespectacled Tim Robbins with a camouflage shirt and a pink hippie bandana around his head, could be a character from *The Deer Hunter*. He's clearly secure in his manhood, this choice of headwear shows. Dave is from Lexington, Kentucky, and his client, Kevin, from Pennsylvania. In front of their kitchen tent, spread out to dry, sprawls the salted hide of a grizzly they killed two days ago. Dave seems like a nice guy who cares about wildlife and the upper Sheenjek, though he admits to a sense of ownership alloyed with a dash of stewardship. Trophy outfitting *is* a competitive market. We know some people in common and have read some of the same books.

Dave generously shares splashes of a smooth bourbon and for my Perkins trades me the account of a British travel writer who searched for King Solomon's gold mines in Ethiopia—life always delivers, and not just for hunter-gatherers. It is strange reading matter for the Arctic, though the tundra and desert share similarities: open space, the quality of the light; the relative absence of people, the earthiness of the ones you do meet; a feeling of timelessness. Kevin, a pleasant guy, mostly listens to our Alaska tall tales. Dave insists on calling what he does for a living "killing," not "taking" or the bureaucrats' "harvesting," to drive home the seriousness of the act.

Still, their hunt, utilizing an airplane and high-powered rifles and spotting scopes, is a walk in the park next to the traditional forms. Koyukon Indians in the southern foothills and Inupiat in the Brooks Range killed bears in close combat. One hunter might poke a denning animal while another waited outside, poised with his spear's butt lodged in the ground and its tip slanted forward. A charging bear blind with rage would impale itself. A man out of sight also could goad the prey, raising a fist like a hand puppet slightly above a hillock and imitating a ground squirrel's *chit, chit*. I try to imagine luring a bear by impersonating food. Is there a Nunamiut word for "ballsy," or was such behavior all in a day's work?

In the winter, grizzlies sometimes go on short walks and bathe in warm-spring pools along rivers before rolling in gravel or sand. Should we really doubt that they do, or that they shake snow from their fur before they den up, to cover their tracks? The bear in the flesh and of legend thus merge, which, believe me, face-offs guarantee. Water freezing in the insomniacs' coat girds them against lance or arrow. Such bears, before the advent of firearms, had to be snared. In 2008, a Gwich'in hunter killed a polar bear a record 250 miles from the Beaufort Sea, south of Arctic Village near Fort Yukon, where it devoured lynx carcasses set out as trapping bait. One of the hunters, unfamiliar with this coastal species, mistook the animal for an "ice bear"—a frosted grizzly. Some of those roam all winter, the elders say, feeding on black bears they pull from their dens and dismember. Their ice armor clinks when these white walkers move, and you can kill them only with a shot in the eye, into a neck fold, or under their arms where the ice is thinner.

The traditional hunt was for bear grease and meat, not for inflating men's egos. "You just can't shoot a bear and just take the skin and leave the meat," Gwich'in old-timers agree. I have had my share of trophy hunting. Almost thirty years ago, still new to Alaska, I worked two springs as a packer and assistant guide, a human mule for big game outfits on Kodiak Island and on the Alaska Peninsula, near Aniakchak National Monument, Alaska's version of Tanzania's Ngorongoro Crater, which boasts one of the state's highest concentrations of brown bear dens. The gig, I thought, would be a great way to get into shape for climbing Denali that summer (it was) and to walk some pretty country on the cheap (I did) and to meet some interesting people (most were not).

Outsiders who want to hunt in Alaska need to go through a licensed outfitter. Outfitters submit a prospectus in competition for prime hunting areas, a bid without money in principle, in which they demonstrate how they'll take care of the place and their clients. Substantial state revenues accrue as the hunters buy tags for different game animals. Hunting inside a wildlife refuge seems contradictory but can be done sustainably, and Indigenous hunters have done so for millennia—though they also wiped out the North Slope's muskoxen after Yankee whalers introduced Winchester rifles.

There's a status hierarchy for wild sheep, I learn from Dave, determined by the region and population size, that is, their rareness and the cost involved in hunting them. The ascending order is Dall, Stone (named for A. J. Stone, another nineteenth-century naturalist), Rocky Mountain bighorn, and, most coveted, desert bighorn.

I learn, too, about the origin of Kevin's shiner. In his excitement at the crucial moment, he put his right eye against the scope, forgetting about recoil. Rookie mistake.

After three hours or thereabouts of socializing, I resupply and the two accompany me for a mile to some canyon they want to check out that lies on my route. Dave grabs his rifle, and we briefly stop at the naked carcass, maroon, muscular, marbled with white. He wants to ensure that I will not run into trouble there with another bear scavenging the remains.

I pitch camp on a bench near that canyon and we part. It is my last contact with people until I walk onto the Dalton Highway three weeks later.

Resembling a person, the bear corpse haunts me still. Shot through with ivory fat and our world's ambivalence. We spend thousands of dollars to come here and see bears; and we spend thousands of dollars to come here and kill them. Facing the remains, "strange sympathies" moved me, as they did Emerson at the Paris Muséum Nationale d'Histoire Naturelle. Why should these be peculiar, though?

Our innate fascination, which according to E. O. Wilson can flip-flop into a hatred of The Others, is rooted in the twilight of human time. Early Europeans emblazoned walls in the Chauvet-Pont-d'Arc Cave with the red profiles of bears next to an ibex and spotted panthers; real bears completed the art by pawing and scratching it. A skull altar there is at least twenty-six thousand years old.

Brushes with Europe's cave bears and Alaska's short-faced bears provided the raw stuff for some of those continents' earliest stories. They awed people as easily as they caused sweaty palms. They rendered existence sublime, vesting it with more than the nuts and bolts of staying alive.

Intensive management and predator control measures at the other end of the spectrum allow the hunting of mother bears and their cubs inside dens even in national preserves. Alaska bears can be legally snared, shot from helicopters, and baited with popcorn, donuts, and other junk, which habituates them to human food and may get them killed in other contexts also. Wolves in this state get an equally raw deal.

The bugs have finally caught up with me. I was expecting blisters on my feet, but so far they are fine. Instead, my fingertips have cracks from doing dishes and washing socks in icy water each day, as have the insides of both thumbs from the hiking sticks. Band-Aids don't last, so I seal these small, painful wounds every few days with the repair kit's Shoe Goo. Improvisation, far from a sign of poor planning, is key to adept wilderness travel.

In my tent's vicinity, delicate ladies greet me. Where moss campion squats, nodding arctic poppies thrust up thready stems. Their chalices, diaphanous sulphur butterflies, tremble in tundra northerlies. Parabolic reflectors track the sun full circle, gathering light, creating interiors up to forty degrees warmer than the ambient air. This heliotropism, known to the ancient sun-worshipping Greeks, observed too in young sunflowers and cream-colored, velvety dryas, quickens fly pollinators and attracts heat-seeking mosquitos while incubating the pollen through rays bundled onto the center's pistils.

Why don't the rubbernecking beauties twist their own heads off? Differences in the pressure of the fluids in the stalks' cells cause the craning most evident in time-lapse footage. Cells elongate less—that is, grow more slowly—on the sunward side, because sunlight curbs the production of hormones responsible for the poppies' vertical striving. Upward bound, they bow synced to our lodestar's rounds, except on gusty or overcast days.

In Ovid's *Metamorphoses*, the sun god Sol spurns a water nymph that, jealous of her sister, wastes away and becomes the first heliotrope, the Middle English "turnsole" whose pigment illumed medieval parchments. Pinkish globe clusters of mountain heliotrope, an Alaskan member of her valerian clan, with age blanch in bogs and river flats.

How fitting that the Brooks Range and Earth's original flowers rose toward light at about the same time! I am told there are folks who unlike poppies and me shun our main energy source, men and women who hole up in bars, wear shades, or lower blinds, cave dwellers dismissing and missing out on the heliocentric life.

For many years, risking cataracts, I pooh-poohed sunglasses as a filter between the world and myself. Late on this day, looking out through the tent's mesh screen at heath drenched with tangerine midnight sun, it hits me how never before have I seen land so unadulterated this clearly.

GRAUPELED

DAY 11 (7 MILES)
QUAD: TABLE MOUNTAIN

This mid-June day is cloudless. I hike up a pretty, narrow canyon north of Double Mountain. No bugs either today. Do the gray jays in the bushes warn me of some predator in the willows, or warn it of me? A yellowlegs feeds near the creek bank, stirring shallows for worms, fry, and insects as if she has lost something. My load is heavy again but will lighten day by day, at least until cache number two. And I should get stronger, in theory.

It turns into a hard day of walking on wobbly rocks, with many creek crossings, up one narrow valley, down another, and up a third. I make camp in a bowl on a saddle between two upper Sheenjek forks. Clouds fledged from chicks into Jersey Giants spit graupel while I set up the tent. Would you like some graupel with your tea? (In case you wonder, it's a loanword from German: "small hulled grain," a despised soup ingredient in my childhood, barley perhaps.) The pellets of soft hail tick like mosquitos as they hit the fly.

Wish I had some barley juice right now.

IN THE FOOTSTEPS
OF ANCESTORS

DAY 12 (LOST TRACK OF MILES)
QUAD: ARCTIC

Cloudless morning; ice glazes the pond of snowmelt in the bowl. *How about some ice cream?* I'm premiering my bug shirt, which is light and airy with its mesh fabric panels but will probably rip on the first bushwhacking stretch. The mosquitos in concert with tussocks keep travelers from swamping this landscape, though traffic has picked up recently.

The first White man to reach the upper Noatak River, Samuel B. McLenegan in the late nineteenth century, remarked how "after the rain myriads of mosquitos came out of the swampy lands, and our lives were made miserable by these pests. A slight relief was obtained by covering all exposed parts of the body with a thick varnish made of tar, gum Arabic, and olive oil; but even with this disagreeable preventive our sufferings were simply indescribable." Olive oil—who would have thought? A substance of unorthodox uses.

Swarms at their worst have been described as "suffocating." They stampede caribou, which flee onto aufeis. Village dogs sleep with front paws over their eyes, tails between their legs. One moose stood for days in the breeze of a building's exhaust fan at the Sag River Alaska Department of Transportation (DOT) camp off the Dalton Highway, unafraid of humans. Another, foregoing feeding, whiled away entire days neck deep in Toolik Lake, near the Institute of Arctic Biology's North Slope field station. A Depression-era photo shows a Brooks Range geologist with a horse mosquito-proofed in a hood and blankets, looking like a jousting steed.

A UAF entomologist calculated Alaska's mosquito biomass to be ninety-six million pounds. That's roughly seventeen trillion (17,000,000,000,000) beasties or eight trillion, five hundred billion (8,500,000,000,000) females lusting after your blood. Another estimate, if you prefer handier numbers, is five million adults per acre, which makes every homesteader a billionaire. Males do not bite, but the females need a warm meal to produce eggs. The females of "snow mosquito" species live almost a year, overwintering and laying eggs in meltwater pools in the spring. With global heating and extra moisture, mosquitos proliferate. Through self-experimentation and mathematical calculations that fill half a book page, scientists have also determined that it would take eleven hours for a naked person standing—or more likely, running crazed—on the tundra at peak-bug time to become quite anemic and another eleven to be bled dry. The formula does not account for drastic immune responses.

This is what scientists do.

On prime 90-degree days, I raise mosquitos while galumphing through tussocks, finding no resting place for the soles of my feet, like the cursed in the Bible. On blustery days, attacks come from the body's calm, lee side, and when wind grounds mosquitos they crawl toward their destination, ghouls sprung from their graves. It helps somewhat to remember that Satan's spawn sustains fishes and thousands of shorebirds and their chicks, either in its airborne incarnation or as tiny question marks wriggling in ponds. The males, sipping wildflower nectar exclusively, pollinate blueberry bushes, rare bog orchids, and my beloved forget-me-nots in a region with few bee and butterfly species.

The infernal host steals all the limelight in the Arctic, though there are plenty of other insects, such as blackflies, whose larvae darkly fur rocks in many a stream. Cemented to stone, they filter-feed with their mouthparts, swaying back and forth, ecstatic worshippers the currents synchronize.

Up the broad valley of the Sheenjek's West Fork, I walk where some of my heroes have walked. Clouds pile against the Continental Divide to the north like tumbleweeds caught in a fence. Atop the mountains, they look almost solid, a second formidable barrier. Another front might be moving in.

In 1956, three years before I was born, a woman slightly older than I am while on my traverse reconnoitered the upper Sheenjek with her husband. Their probe led to Eisenhower signing the Arctic Wildlife Range bill. She was Margaret "Mardy" Murie, born Margaret Thomas in 1902 in Seattle. At the age of nine, she moved with her mother to Fairbanks to join her stepfather. During a fire, she urged him and other men there to burn the town's bacon as fuel for the steam-powered water pump. In a two-room log cabin by the Tanana River, she learned to use wood stoves, to dry winter laundry inside, and, walking through town, to long-leash her dog, which guarded her against strays. Visiting her biological father in Juneau, she fell in love with nature, an infatuation that lasted a lifetime. "I wonder if we have enough reverence for life to concede to wilderness the right to live on," she wrote years later. It would cheer her to hear that Australia's Yarra, New Zealand's Whanganui, and Quebec's Magpie River or Muteshekau-shipu, all of which Whites now too regard as living entities, have been granted legal personhood.

Through a friend, Mardy in 1921 met Olaus, handsome, blue eyed, cut like a burled hiking staff. The field biologist and alumnus of Oregon's Pacific University had responded to an ad for a caribou researcher's job in Alaska. Dinners at Mardy's family home whenever her beau was in town sowed requited endearment that soon blossomed into more. But with him tracking caribou in Mount McKinley (now Denali) National Park and her being schooled in Boston, these two appeared to be star crossed. They finally married in August 1924 after Mardy had transferred and with a business administration degree became the first woman to graduate from the Alaska Agricultural College and School of Mines, now UAF. Their 3:00 a.m sunrise wedding took place in a candle-lit chapel in Anvik, on the lower Yukon River, where Olaus was birding for work. Their life together was to be "one long field trip," Mardy realized.

Olaus could coyote-howl, call down redpoll flocks, and improvise a mousetrap from a whalebone corset stay. A Fairbanks acquaintance considering him to be "half caribou" wondered how Mardy would keep up with that pace.

During their three-month honeymoon, the lovebirds boated and dogsledded 550 miles up the Koyukuk, into the Endicott Mountains. Olaus, a watercolorist, sketched, painted, and collected bird and mammal specimens. Mardy set rabbit snares, jigged for grayling, and siwashed—that is, camped without a tent, in a lean-to of spruce boughs that reflected a campfire's heat. She learned to drive a team in conditions "so snappily cold that it was joy to run behind the sled all day, to keep warm." "I shall never want to ride in a dogsled anyway," she wrote in her journal thirty miles north of Wiseman in late October. "It would be like being demoted from first mate to mere passenger. More fun to hold to the ends of the handlebars and pad along." Mushing up the Koyukuk North Fork, they "found water too easily—ominous, black slits where it boiled too blackly, rapids, the last to be smothered by winter." On glare ice sections she "stood with both feet on the brake, and its big steel teeth only made pretty scratches on the ice as around we went in a flash and came up against a snowbank."

An old photo shows Mardy cutting wood at camp somewhere above the tree line with a saw as big as she. The following year, Olaus embarked on the border-defying Old Crow River, the Porcupine herd's wintering grounds. Mardy bundled up their infant son, Martin, and joined him. Festooning willows with diapers laundered in an old gas can and cradling the babe in a tented wood box on their scow, she embraced the leisurely pace of freedom the current provided. She posed for another shot there, hair bobbed sensibly, with Martin, a mammoth tusk, Olaus, and the friend who'd introduced them. After living with the Old Crow in all its moods, she wrote, "It was good to know that the river began in beauty and flowed through miles of clean gravel and airy open space."

In 1927, the pair relocated to Jackson Hole, Wyoming, where Olaus studied elk. They lived together there for almost forty years. "I managed the money, I bought most of his clothes . . . it was I who remembered the names of people. Olaus remembered the names of the birds and mammals," Mardy listed their respective strengths. Alaska had hooked both of them deeply, and they'd often return, as they did for the Sheenjek. Humble, and gracious even toward people with whom she disagreed, Mardy served cookies and tea to some of the nation's most prominent environmentalists on the porch of her ranch home, where together they drafted wilderness legislation.

After Olaus's death, with the wildlife range designated, Mardy worked cease-lessly to save further wildlands. The couple's efforts had sped up passage of the groundbreaking 1964 Wilderness Act. The gentle, middle-aged activist kept traveling around the new state of Alaska, identifying and advocating for places worthy of protection. "Beauty is a resource in and of itself," she insisted. President Carter's act more than doubled the newly minted Arctic National

Wildlife Refuge. "I am testifying as an emotional woman," Mardy had lobbied Congress, "and I would like to ask you, gentlemen, what's wrong with emotion?"

Through Jackson Hole's Teton Science Schools, the matriarch instilled care and respect for the outdoors in younger generations. Touring for speaking engagements, writing three books, and hailed by John Denver in song, the stout, silver-haired "Grandmother of the Conservation Movement" received the Audubon Medal and the Sierra Club's John Muir Award (like Olaus), the Wilderness Society's Robert Marshall Award, and the Presidential Medal of Freedom. "The Muries pick up where John Muir left off," a docent at the ranch summed up their legacy.

Mardy sorely missed her longtime companion, even in her dreams. Still, in a 1983 interview the mother of three, grandmother of ten, and great-grandmother of two said that "to live a full life, you must have something beyond your household, beyond your family, to broaden your existence." She continued their noble pursuit another four decades as a widow, never remarrying, dying at their rustic Wyoming home at the age of 101.

On the Muries' Sheenjek expedition, a stripling accompanied them: George Schaller. The German-born biologist, blond, slim—they're all slim in those pictures—had earned a degree at UAF the year before. He would become a renowned mammologist and a conservationist, emulating the Muries. Schaller gave the commencement speech at my graduation from that school, the only one he ever gave. Had I heard him speak before that day, I might have gone into his field, not the one I chose, anthropology.

"Those who want to destroy that lovely region should be named again and again," he wrote me in an email regarding the Arctic refuge he'd helped to establish. I choose not to name them, as their names would defile these pages. You know who they are if you follow the news. Victims, not perpetrators, deserve the most ink.

Aufeis carapaces the uppermost Sheenjek reaches. Runoff runnels and crevices texture a surface whose turquoise puddles soak my boots. Ice is bridging the water that has carved grottos that glow blue, looking synthetic. I once guided an older gent on a hike out of Anaktuvuk Pass, and trying to cross that river's ice gully found that its sweating, massive walls offered few exits. We eventually found one only where collapsed shelves formed a ramp. Here on the Sheenjek, shelves ten feet thick, sooty with grit and silt, contrast with the virginal hue of alcoves the current polishes. In the day's warmth, diamonds drip from the brinks and freshets curtain where the snowmelt on top channels. Walking is tiresome on ice the sun has turned into slush. Candle ice tinkles under my footfalls, which dislodge its shards, glassy upright little daggers. They also fall in undisturbed ranks when warmth weakens their cohesion. "I listened to the chiming of the ice," the biologist Douglas Chadwick writes in *The Wolverine Way*. "It was just a moment in the mountains, but enough moments add up to a life." Calling this "rotten ice" is like calling a chandelier a "lamp," an insult to the frost giants.

Hanshan, a Taoist wandering recluse during Europe's Dark Ages, wrote poems on rocks on the Cold Mountain that was his home and his name. "For an image of life and death, consider ice and water," he advised. Nowhere else is this image clearer to me than in the dyad of aufeis and river, the yin and yang of inertia and liveliness.

Water freezes into ice
ice melts back into water
what dies must live again
what lives is bound to die.

I pitch my tent on the shoulder of a hill above a lake, the same lake we camped at the previous year on my all-women trip. What joy to see a familiar landmark, a friend's face in a crowd of strangers, an island of comfort in a foreign sea! A golden eagle this time is the welcome committee. I won't need a map to travel tomorrow. One's perspective shifts in oxymoronic cozy wilderness. I get an inkling of what it meant to the roaming Gwich'in and Nunamiut: home, not a waste fit for savages and devil beasts or a playground or outdoor museum or virgin country.

Weather has pulled blinds across the sky again, but the bugs are in hiding. It rains short and hard around dinnertime. Luckily, I'm all set up, gear squared away, and so dive into the tent to wait and fix supper later, when it clears.

It does, and idling in my camp chair, I indulge in Pleistocene pleasures. The lake constantly changes, from ruffled to polished to hammered, from dove-gray to aqua to silver. Puffs of air crimp its surface. In calm moments, it's an unblinking blue eye. Shadows glide across slopes like a haunting by dragons. Wind pushing clouds creates this effect, which showcases single ground features.

Brushing against ghosts in this place, I wonder how Kate is doing, if she is alive.

In the fall, after I return from this ambitious endeavor, my boss will tell me that Kate died two months after our trip last summer. A doctor she consulted about the chest pain I had tried to alleviate diagnosed lung cancer, inoperable. Her death will come as a shock to me. The dead are as much part of a landscape as the living, and in my memory, this heavenly tarn on the upper Sheenjek will always be Kate's Lake.

BLOOD OF THE MOUNTAINS

DAY 13 (11.5 MILES)
QUAD: ARCTIC

Cloudless again at breakfast. The lake holds mountains this morning, like a portal to some upside-down world. While I'd like to think that each day is a new beginning, there often is residue from the previous one: a night of bad sleep, sore muscles, damp clothing, swirl of weather, a worry, a train of thought left unfinished . . .

I crunch for miles across aufeis on the East Fork of the Chandalar now, the river that would lead me to Arctic Village if I were to head south. Firm footing alternates with sumps where I walk as if in sand. In the calm, I'm roasting with glare off the ice—better wear sunglasses. Up in side valleys south of me, snowfields and pocket glaciers tumble from sharp peaks unnamed on my map. An armada of Maynard Dixon clouds with flat keels and billowing tops plies the sea above. Iron oxide has daubed entire mountain flanks reddish-ochre. The Inupiat stained wooden masks, boxes, bows, snow goggles, and wolverine hides with this mineral, and the name Ivishak—a river along my route a few days hence—refers to the sanguine pigment. Long ago, Eagle Mother found out that humans were lonely because they did not know how to sing and dance. She taught the Inupiat how to drum and host the Messenger Feast. Invitations went out in the form of "asking sticks" painted with red ochre rings. It's the color that binds us all, regardless of the tint of our skin. That truth is inescapable here, where your background doesn't matter.

Good walking on dryas benches. I camp on a carpet electrified by mixed flowers, if a bit rocky. During my evening stroll some caribou jump straight up, coltishly, as if zapped by a live wire when my scent hits them. Old boot and wolf prints stamp an apron of wet river sand. Running water always draws living beings, everywhere, especially river guides.

False alert back at camp. What I think is a white wolf is a caribou calf. A red fox briefly visits. Theirs is the largest geographic range of any living carnivore, spanning the entire mainland in the Northern Hemisphere. On the heels of Anglo miners and settlers who butchered their canine competition and nemeses, they expanded their reach ever northward, clashing with the smaller arctic foxes, at least one of which they cannibalized in Prudhoe Bay's oilfields. What is next? Coyotes? They're already here, although rare, first noted in the early 1900s in mainland Southeast Alaska. Today they roam the Interior up to the south side of the Brooks Range, major predators of Dall sheep lambs in the Alaska Range.

Evening drizzle.

Much later: Rainbow and dramatic light, thick and orange, pouring out from between gray battleship clouds. Rain briefly drums on the tent, on amphetamines, a tattoo deafening. The dryas twitching in the wind in droves makes the ground shiver.

BROTHER AND SISTER BEAR

DAY 14 (4 MILES)
QUAD: ARCTIC

Overcast this morning with cerulean sky to the south limning the edge of this low-pressure front.

I normally turn north at the first valley along my way, for the guided High Peaks hikes across Guilbeau Pass, the Continental Divide. On the one with Kate, her sister, the sergeant, and the couple, we camped on a wide gravel outwash plain before the ascent. That night a wolf pack we never saw serenaded us.

Guilbeau Pass, plateauing four miles beyond that camp, bears the stamp of another tragedy. The name of this gateway to the Hulahula commemorates the twenty-six-year-old son of a Black pastor and scout leader, a geology student who died on a solo trek from Arctic Village to Barter Island, an intended north-south traverse of the refuge. Originally from Hartford, Connecticut, Samuel Furmon Guilbeau had enrolled as a graduate student at the California Institute of Technology, Caltech. He went missing in the summer of 1972; a party of climbers found him four years later on a glacier on the far side of Mount Michelson, twenty-five miles north of the pass. They stumbled upon a grisly scene—skeletal remains and those of a backpack. A later effort retrieved pages from a spiral-bound notebook that chronicle Guilbeau's trek, including his final week.

Before his attempt, Guilbeau had kayaked down the Pelly River in Canada's Yukon Territory. He was giving himself seven weeks for the Arctic Village to Kaktovik stretch, with plenty of time to explore and to climb Mount Michelson; the University of Alaska operated a research camp at McCall Glacier there. Supported by Fort Yukon Air Service, Guilbeau placed several caches along his route, also mountaineering equipment and skis. He carried a shotgun and rifle and supplemented his provisions with porcupine and with strips of caribou he dried on rocks. He scraped and saved two pieces of a bull's skin to be made into mittens or caps for his parents. A bear most likely had busted cardboard boxes and waterproof bags in his second cache and scattered ammunition and mosquito repellent, though his soy flour, sugar, peanuts, and powdered milk remained usable. He removed matches and other "alien matter" from this mess. The mixture, his notes say, was "very tasty and nutritious, and it would be a good main food."

Two days before his entries stop, Guilbeau packed winter clothing and supplies for six days for tackling Mount Michelson, at 8,852 feet the fourth highest Brooks Range peak. The following day, after hours of hard hiking, his final line tells us, he went to sleep at 8:30 p.m.

With Guilbeau a week overdue, a search was launched, though Caltech geology professor Robert P. Sharp acknowledged, "This is difficult country, and it's virtually impossible to travel according to a predetermined schedule." "Sam is a very strong fellow," he added encouragingly. "If it's just a matter of endurance, he can do it." Still, the route Guilbeau had drawn on his map beforehand in many places could not be hiked.

The cramped, largely illegible journal ends after August 19, with the rest of the last page an enigma, a drama not witnessed. I don't know if a forensic inquiry was ever conducted or if one unveiled the cause of death. Guilbeau has joined the shadows that wander a landscape now unpeopled.

Dr. Clair C. Patterson, another Caltech professor, who camped with him in the Sierra Nevada during a summer field geology program, considered the NSF trainee a friend and "a fine young man." In a condolence letter to Sam's parents, he wanted them to remember that "he lost his life in a place that was desirable and beautiful to him. . . . He wanted these challenges, and I think he would want us to understand that and appreciate it, rather than lament it."

Before I knew about him and his fate, I once tackled Guilbeau's route as a ski trip in March with a partner. The timing was unfortunate, since a minus-35 cold snap had been gripping the land. Leaving Arctic Village, we could not pick up the firmly packed snowmachine trail and instead wallowed thigh deep in powder on the Chandalar's loops. Losing my cool, bulling through a willow belt, I'd broken the metal-pole harness of my *pulk*, a Scandinavian-style sled shaped like a skiff, for pulling loads, including evacuees. The temperatures had shrunk the rubber gasket in the pump of my cooking stove. When I pressurized and lit it the first night, leaking gas set the whole thing on fire. To make matters worse, my partner had not brought any mittens. A parsimonious type, he carried some fleece, planning to sew a pair "along the way." Calling this off was a no-brainer; continuing would have been suicidal, yet Carl suggested we go on. Feeling that I had more experience than he, I refused. It was one of those cases in which a second brain on an outdoor pursuit did not improve safety. Back at Arctic Village, my old Gwich'in teacher Lillian Garnett kindly let us crash at her place. That failed south-to-north Brooks Range traverse was the last time I went winter camping.

Alaskans love to deride adventurers from the Lower Forty-Eight who arrive here to take on wilderness and come to grief. Such chauvinism fails to acknowledge that many follow the same siren call we residents did. Anyone who hankers for a full roster of wildlife, who craves solitude, a certain quality of light, as well as stillness at his or her core, and who above all treads lightly upon this land to me is a kindred spirit.

One definition of wilderness is "a place where you can disappear," temporarily or forever. Despite the heartbreak involved, it is good to know such black holes in this country exist outside of prisons, homeless camps, and detention centers.

Vetches and scorpion weed, and pink plumes like Pepto-Bismol bottlebrushes. I deviate from my route, dodging boreal forest that encroaches up-valley toward Double Mountain, a prow where Sheenjek arms join, only to run into a grizzly parked in my direction of travel. There's no way to sneak past him. So I sit and for about half an hour watch him root around on the hillside for edibles. Then the wind shifts, and he senses me and takes off. Everything in this country—bears, foxes, caribou, and even ground squirrels—outruns a human. The bear probably burned more calories in his dash than he got from a whole morning of foraging. A rough-legged hawk reconnoiters a mountain flank with a wound of purple shale. You know that it's quiet when the loudest noise is your belly rumbling.

I run into the same bear in the afternoon but pass downslope of him without stopping, unnoticed because he has his snout in the dirt again. He's still compensating for the weight he lost hibernating. In the fall, he'll be fueling up twenty hours a day for his long, dreamless rest. Alaska's Koyukon Athabaskans considered bears among the most powerful animals spiritually and treated them thus, with utmost respect. Bears would give themselves to the hunter and his family if they observed taboos. Upper Koyukuk River people made no use of the bearskin at all because it still carried part of the animal's life force, which could be dangerous. They instead hung it up near where they'd butchered the bear so chickadees could peck at it. Killing denning black bears remains a way to get fresh meat when game is scarce.

The traits bears and humans share without doubt account in part for the attraction I, my clients, scores of biologists and conservationists, and perhaps even hunters like Dave Marsh and Kevin feel. Among these biological contact points, the physical and behavioral similarities between them and us, is the fact that in the Arctic only humans, wolves, and bears hunt caribou. And bears are the only creatures to sometimes kill humans there. Among the grizzly's characteristics, the upright posture of inquisitive ones or of fighting males might be the most impressive. In the Northern Hemisphere, where apes were unknown, bipedalism is otherwise found only in lemmings, ermines, ground squirrels, marmots, and owls, to all of which the Inupiat ascribed human qualities also. The sexes in both species differ in size: male adult grizzlies can weigh twice as much as breeding females, while in humans, the difference is normally less pronounced. Europeans for a long time even thought that bears mate in the missionary position. "The female is said to be more lustful than the male," the eighteenth-century French naturalist Georges-Louis Leclerc, Comte de Buffon, wrote. "Some claim that, in order to receive him, she lies on her back, embraces him, holds him fast, etc."

The bear, a plantigrade walker, places its entire sole on the ground, as do we, and prints from the hind feet in particular resemble barefoot persons' tracks. Bears' eyes are aligned in a nearly frontal plane. Visual acuity, a keen sense of hearing and smell, dexterity, and a broad range of vocalizations further strengthen the likeness. Inupiaq hunters believe that bears vary in personality. I agree wholeheartedly. Some are aggressive, others are timid, some are extremely curious, and yet others blasé, at least in their dealings with me. Mothers are protective, while teenagers often test boundaries. Bears and ravens are thought to possess what the Inuit call *isuma*—the ability to reason—and both ceaselessly investigate their surroundings.

Ursus arctos of the subspecies *horribilis* (that name is another dis, really) is an opportunistic feeder whose appetite rivals its curiosity. Sound familiar? Bears dig out from subterranean dwellings in the spring, as did old-time Inupiat, and roam all summer searching for food. And while bears are loners, they sometimes gather at river bars to snag spawning salmon or char, a red-bellied cousin of trout that makes anglers swoon.

The grizzly's mothering grabs us as does her fitness as a forager. Dens are very clean, as the female stops eating and defecating before giving birth. The newborns—pink, helpless, thinly haired—suggest our babies, just as a skinned adult bear does a naked human adult. Bear mothers bond strongly with their offspring but also discipline them with a cuff or growl. They generally nurse in a sitting posture, with one or two cubs on their chest. The young emerging in April slide down snowy slopes, wrestle, and torture their caretakers as many of us have.

Last, like us, grizzlies are blessed with a relatively long lifespan, more than twenty years in the wild and forty years in captivity.

Up a steep saddle—beautiful view, but I can't find the way over to Red Sheep Creek. I briefly wonder about the story behind that name. Do they rub against the iron oxide? Back home, I'll find out that indeed is the case and that Gwich'in hunters before the era of firearms built a tree-stump fence there to snare sheep. The valley I chose in order to avoid forest only to bump into the bear, anonymous on my map, is Tsaihnjik, Ochre River. People gathered this mineral for paint to decorate sleds, snowshoe frames, caribou-skin tents, trousers and tunics, and warriors for striping their faces. On ceremonial occasions men also mixed it with grease and coiffed their hair, which they then sprinkled with down. Fort McPherson elders say local ochre is the blood of a shaman who long ago, grappling with enemies, fell off a cliff and pulled two of them with him into death. Mining this *tsaih*, the life essence of a powerful person, one had to leave a small offering or else a storm might descend upon the offender.

Each drop-in option for Red Sheep looks formidable, too steep, boulder strewn, intimidating. My GPS is no help on this detour as it only shows the straight-arrow direction to my next waypoint and if I get closer or farther away. I finally locate a drainage that should deliver me safely to Red Sheep. Two live sheep, plus a dead one melting back into the landscape. Distant thunder grumbles, a rare occurrence in prior years in this arctic range.

The canyon twists, rocky, narrow, and willowy and now my heart skips a beat. Another bear, sixty yards ahead, half concealed by a rise. I stand transfixed. A minute or two later, she catches a whiff of me, scrams. Only then do I see her two cubs, this year's, trailing like black dogs after her. She is strawberry blond. This could have ended badly, a situation with all the red flags raised: a female and cubs surprised at a kill. Five minutes later they're way up the mountainside as if trying for the summit. Unbelievable. She's not even taking the easiest route. Good mom! I've had more trouble with males, especially teenagers that are just plain obnoxious and perhaps need to prove themselves for future combat. When I recommence hiking, I find the family was feeding on scraps of yet another sheep. Hardly enough to be worth defending, I think. I was lucky I spotted her when I did. Any closer might have flipped her "fight" instead of her "flight" switch.

There, I'm saying it: I'm afraid of trees. But, as a cousin quoted Theodore Roosevelt, "Many things I feared, but by acting as if I was not afraid, I was not afraid."

I end up pitching my tent in a hard rain and then dive inside. It's been the longest, most tiring day yet, and I covered only four miles. All that to avoid spruces near Double Mountain. What did I dread beyond that tousled tree line? Bad visibility hiding a different surprise bear? Brushier walking? It's psychological, this dendrophobia, a yin to agoraphobia's yang. (And not to be confused with claustrophobia, an indoor affliction.)

Even barrenlands caribou wintering in the forest seek out frozen lakes to rest and chew their cud away from trees that may screen the approach of wolves. White folks in Nome—which lies on the same latitude as Fairbanks but west of the tree line—don't understand this. They'll drive two hours to look at big arboreal pipe cleaners. In January they transplant browned Christmas runts onto sea ice, creating a "Nome National Forest." Melissa laughs when in Fairbanks I complain about "too many trees." "Woodland immersion" or "forest bathing" is a recent fad. It bathes me in cold sweat.

Though we lived in boreal forest for many years and in Cordova, among conifers more picturesque and impressive, after only two weeks on the tundra

I feel safer, more comfortable. I've preferred sparse vegetation and loooong sightlines ever since falling in love with Canyon Country four decades ago. It's an aesthetic attraction but also a safety issue. In that, I side with the Inupiat, not the Athabaskans, who welcomed a ubiquitous resource. A true forest people, the Koyukon built spruce deadfall and basket fish traps, boats, houses, caches on stilts, tent frames, sleds, and bows, and burned the wood as fuel. Pitch made great chewing gum and canoe caulking. The clear sap healed sores, while an infusion from the needles was thought to cure kidney problems and to transfer the evergreen's spirit power. Boughs covered tent floors and roofed summer huts, while bark yielded shingles. The cambium, a layer between heartwood and bark, could be ground up into survival rations. (I've tried "bark bread"; it made my throat scratchy.) Roots became tightly coiled baskets or thread for joining birch bark sheets into canoes. Spruce nourished the spirit as well. Like a maypole or Lakota Sun Dance pole, an adorned trunk allied villagers at the Stick Dance, a potlatch that honored the dead.

Historically, Athabaskan-Inupiat relations encompassed trade, feasting, and cultural borrowing along with adoption, intermarriage—sometimes by raiding for wives—and sporadic warfare. Hostilities entailed long-range forays in the fall that Rachel Attituq Qitsualik sees as targeting "elusive, and therefore grossly misunderstood, tree line peoples," though taiga "always acted as a sort of fence." The woodland Indian name *Eskimantsik* ("eaters of raw meat"), which morphed into *Eskimo*, referred not solely to their marine mammal diet. Conversely, Inuit dreaded the "cannibal" *iqiliit*-infested forests. During my fieldwork, an Inupiaq elder talked about invisible Indians throwing pebbles and sticks at him when he'd traveled through unfamiliar country. Technologies and survival techniques adapted to their respective home environment reinforced fish-out-of water discomfort in both groups.

Many Koyukon still prefer moose while Nunamiut relish caribou simply because of the two species' spatial distribution. That does not mean Robert Thompson would pass up any moose stew, and I once delivered a parcel of *muktuk* (bowhead whale blubber and skin) to Trimble Gilbert, Robert's Gwich'in friend in Arctic Village, a renowned old-time fiddler. I studied such intertribal patterns for my master's thesis in the twin communities of Alatna (Inupiaq) and Allakaket (Koyukon), which face each other across the Alatna River west from here and which I should reach in another month or so. Except for the raiding and wife stealing, these cross-ethnic bonds endure in the present. In part because of those conflicts, coastal Inupiat felt more secure on the open tundra while Athabaskans did in the black-spruce belt. With the influx of traders, missionaries, and miners, the old animosities withered as people mingled in new settlements, churches, and trading posts.

Europeans and Anglo-Americans reared amid forests and warmed by firewood, not blubber or willow shrubs, shared a sylvan fondness with the Koyukon. In 1905, Nome's most acclaimed visitor, the Norwegian Roald Amundsen (not to shortchange Wyatt Earp, the photographer Edward Sheriff Curtis, and four-time Iditarod winner Susan Butcher), broke a long-dreaded barrier. On the seventy-foot whaling sloop *Gjøa*, he exited the pack ice on the American side, having been frozen fast off and on, and drifted finally through the long-sought Northwest Passage between Greenland and Alaska, a labyrinthine maw that had claimed numerous lives. The crew, lacking a Christmas tree, decked candelabras.

Squeezed in winter's vise for the third year, before his reception in Nome Amundsen sledded five hundred miles from Herschel Island up the Firth River valley to Eagle City on the Yukon and back. His push all but completed, he was "wild with eagerness" to get to a telegraph office and send news to the world. A shipwrecked American whaling captain somewhat scornful of explorers was allegedly well content to huddle in furs on the sled while Amundsen broke trail on snowshoes ahead of the dogs. The first stunted spruce elicited a "wonderful sensation" in Amundsen, proof, "hanging out of a crevice," that he was now "out of Polar regions and on more homely human ground," though the Inuuk guide couple must have felt differently. Amundsen landed at Eagle City in tatters, he said in an interview with a tad too much swagger, "with a 60 below temperature . . . and but one board [of firewood] left." His cable was almost a thousand words.

The hissing of my white gas cooking stove, the only unnatural noise within miles, drowns out any animal sounds. Still, on days like today especially, with the dinner dishes rinsed in cold water, I welcome the portable ember, a one-person hearth whose foil windbreak I cup to thaw numb fingers. Even the cornflower corona of its flame cheers me. Hot drinks on the house! And a toast to Amundsen, that leathery, crotchety, garrulous buzzard.

THE ELUSIVE RED SHEEP

DAY 15 (7 MILES)
QUAD: ARCTIC

I'm still one mile short of Red Sheep. It took me a long time to fall asleep last night, not too surprising after the hard hiking and excitement. Feeling inexplicably gloomy this morning despite the day's radiance. The walking is good on the slopes of a lovely valley I ascend. A bear on the opposite side travels parallel to me for a while, but I eventually pass him because he's checking out crannies and nooks while I'm booking it to leave him behind. It's just better, in case he looks up and gets any ideas. Arctic poppy. Cinquefoil, a shrub in the rose family with flowers like buttercups.

The GPS alerts me to a navigation error and saves my ass. I've been moving *away* from my next waypoint, which after my detour lies straight ahead. I preset a few of those cruxes in addition to the coordinates of caches stashed at the airstrips. It turns out I am not at all where I thought I was, based on the map, last night at camp. I must have dropped into the wrong drainage from the saddle yesterday afternoon. Easy enough to do, because when I changed my route to dodge the trees, I did not have the 1:63,360 scale map for this torqued section, only the 1:250,000. In the ink line on the map that charts my course from Joe Creek, this blunder forms a rhino horn pointed north.

There are no shortcuts in life, it has been said. But there are countless reroutings. I'm baffled how sometimes our notions make the landscape in which we walk conform to landmarks on a map, how we shape reality to fit a figment of our imagination, or worse, wishful thinking. Perhaps something in me sensed being errant this morning when I felt doom. As soon as we pinpoint our true position in such situations, things snap into place with an almost audible *click* and all is right with the world again. That relief is worth all the gold in King Solomon's mines.

I climb another saddle and am back on track. Another bear. Have to circle around it. Seeing several in one day is not unusual; neither is going a few days without any. But you can't let your guard down. Ever.

Camp on a nice gravel bar at Red Sheep, one with pea pebbles and sand, the first afternoon since Joe Creek that I'm spared rain showers, even clouds. And there are hardly any bugs. Small things make a difference out here. I take advantage of the weather and do laundry and wash up. It feels great to lounge au naturel in the sun again. That's what summer should be about. What a contrast to last night.

After dinner, lying on a hill, I listen to dueling robins, losing myself in bottomless blue. They sound incongruous here since I think of them as suburban birds, earthworm pullers extraordinaire on manicured lawns. Flocks numbering over a million blanket the New Jersey sky on a single weekend. In central New York, fooled by artificial light, they pour out their throaty chants during hours of darkness. They're among North America's most successful birds, benefiting from invasive species and landscape development, but have done so for only two hundred years. Their confiding and confident manner helped them adapt to humans. They seem "almost to thrust themselves upon our attentions and demand a sense of interaction," the English ornithologist Mark Cocker writes. The Arctic's robins have been migrating there from Mexico for millennia, possibly. Since I've fallen silent, their song has grown in importance, as if it could yield a key to this land if only I could grasp its inflections.

Before the pioneer of biological cold adaptation research Laurence Irving was appointed the first director of UAF's Institute of Arctic Biology, he spent a season at Anaktuvuk comparing the English and Inupiaq names for 103 bird species he recorded there. Contemplating the robin's well-organized migrating flocks, he remarked that we find "familiar sympathy" for it because of its "aggressive and demonstrative concern" for its own social pattern. Birds of a feather love each other . . .

As much as I value streamside camps, the water blots out other sounds. It's the auditory equivalent of sleeping with a mask on, which I don't, since summer's light deluge becomes normal (to me, at least). A stream can muffle sounds of a bear's rooting around a camp like earplugs do a burglary. Also, riparian willows, while good windbreaks, reduce visibility compared to a tundra bench. I can't shake that pig-in-a-down-blanket feeling.

A ROBIN BY
ANY OTHER NAME

DAY 16 (10.5 MILES)
QUAD: ARCTIC

Sunny with popcorn clouds (not an official type). Auguring what? Divine cinema? Some kind of vérité? A robin near my tent (one of yesterday's?) keeps pleading *Get the keys, Bernadette*, as if he were too drunk to drive and his spouse nonresponsive. Drunk he probably is, from this morning's balsamic air. Perhaps I'm hallucinating, deprived of human company for too long, but I can see how Alaska Natives believe that in the beginning of time, humans and other animals shared a common tongue. Is the phrase I hear really any less subjective than how guidebooks render birdspeak? All of mine give the robin's lilt as *cheerily cheer-up cheerio*. Did their authors copy from each other or confer about this? Consider the rooster's *cock-a-doodle-doo*. In German, it's *kikeriki*. Their Turkish kin crows *kukuriku* and Chinese ones go *wo-wo-wo*. Do they speak their country's native language? Irving at Anaktuvuk Pass recorded *koyapigaktoruk* as the robin's Nunamiut name, stating, however, that it refers to its "noise" rather than to its song.

So—*Get the keys, Bernadette.*

In my notes and mind, I've been calling the robins "blackbirds." I must have been thinking of their counterpart, the Eurasian blackbird, the German *Schwartzamsel* of my youth. I'm not the only addled observer. Early British colonists swayed by the bird's breast, and homesick perhaps, named it "robin" after the smaller flycatcher they'd known in their parks and gardens. But the two are related only distantly, and the American robin, a thrush, is much larger.

"A rose by any other name would smell as sweet" Shakespeare propounds in *Romeo and Juliet*, a line interpreted to mean that the names of things do not affect their true essence. Knowing the names gives inordinate comfort, especially in a daunting place. We create order by verbalizing. But a species' name is just the first word of its story, a label filed away for future reference. Most people fail to learn an organism's role and habits within its biome, the bigger picture, because taxonomic shorthand suggests that they know enough. There's so much worth knowing that it boggles the mind, and our days are numbered. We often settle for labels, for knowledge without understanding, yet as Barry Lopez pointed out, "Anybody can develop the vocabulary. It's the relationships that are important."

The names we bestow sometimes are downright ugly or inane, commemorating dead White male scientists: Dall (a porpoise and sheep), Wilson (a snipe), McKay (a bunting), Sabine (a gull), Baird (a beaked whale), and that's just a smattering from Alaska. Perhaps there should not be a possessive for other-than-humans; intending to honor, it instead claims. And since we're on the subject, if we absolutely must use people names and possessives, it should be "Dall's sheep," not "Dall sheep," dammit, for consistency's sake and because the Latin name, *Ovis dalli*, says so.

To confound expectations of being spoon-fed information and to spark creativity, I sometimes challenge students or clients I guide. When they ask for a name, usually of a bird or flower, I say: "I can tell you, but what would you call it?" It makes them pay closer attention and use their imagination and can be fun. Edward Abbey's "rosy-bottomed skinny dipper" comes to mind. But seriously, some people consider this naming business—the basic function of language—essential in our relationship with the natural world.

"The itch for naming things is almost as bad as the itch for possessing things," Abbey griped in *Desert Solitaire*, proposing to "leave them alone—they'll survive for a few more thousand years, more or less, without any glorification from us." While I've belabored the beauty and riches of biological and topographic names elsewhere also, and without even delving into their practical necessity, I concede Abbey's point. Does learning a species' name (and place) obscure an intangible essence, though? Does knowledge extinguish magic? Identifying resident beings can be a gateway drug to ecology, spawning a wish to understand the drift of nature's relationships. It might even entice you to spend more time outside.

It's a question of respect, ultimately, implicit too in the use of objectifying versus gendered pronouns. Only the second grant autonomy, agency, to an organism. Don't call an animal "it," which spays or neuters a living being. Use "she" or "he," at the risk of getting it wrong. And dump "common" while at it. There's nothing common about ravens, which in this state we outnumber nearly two to one. The elitist *hoi polloi*, for "the masses" or "common people," to the Greeks simply meant "the many." Need I say words matter to creatures above literati?

Sticks and stones will break my bones, but words will never hurt me, the saying goes. Varmint? Pest? Knowing names saves lives, not just in *Rumpelstiltskin*. It is harder to trample "purple saxifrage" than a "weed," harder to squash an "arctic woolly bear" than a "bug." Look up this fur-coated caterpillar, which survives for up to fourteen years before pupating. All species, not just "charismatic megafauna" and birds, are amazing.

Biologists often refuse to name their subjects for fear of anthropomorphizing, rightfully so, and instead use numerical codes. This ascribes uniqueness to each animal but smacks of bureaucracy. Field ornithologists remark how banding allows them to distinguish birds, which segues into personal names and over several seasons the recognition of personalities with attached biographies, as in the case of Wisdom, a seventy-year-old Laysan albatross, the world's oldest known wild bird who still lays clutches of eggs.

I've ground my axe. I shall speak no more of these matters. Need to get out more. Fresh air should blow such cobwebs from my head's dusty garret. Except that often it doesn't. "Must scribble less," I end this lengthy musing on my map. But I don't always heed my own admonishments.

A golden eagle patrols the mountainside so close to the rocks that he almost links up with his shadow. What is he hunting? Lemmings? Ground squirrels? Marmots? His dark doppelgänger?

I've cut the thumbs off my first-aid kit's surgical gloves and wear them to keep my cracks from getting deeper. This could be a new outdoor rating system: "Michael Engelhard gives this hike two blue thumbs up." Perhaps more expensive poles with cork grips would have been better. Oh well, I have what I have. Here. Now. (Wanderers only had crude, unwieldy alpenstocks once.)

MICHAEL ENGELHARD

Bearflower, harebell. A strong west wind slows me down. There will be a surfeit of that on the Noatak.

Like humans and other creatures in subzero climes, some arctic flowers bank on insulation. Silky-haired leaves trap warmth, retain moisture, and protect yellow glacier avens from ultraviolet rays. Dark-brown hair coats sepals cradling the crowns of snow buttercup, another sun rotator. Fuzz silvers immature woolly louseworts. As soon as spring prances in, ranks of their tender mouths parting gossamer fleck the tundra with flamingo accents. These adaptive traits tie plants cut from the same cloth as glaciers and rivers into a larger landscape. Winter's interregnum is the overarching theme of everything here.

I sometimes look at the actual ground of the route I so brazenly penciled on maps in the warmth of our carpeted living room and think, *Holy cow. I have to go up this?*

Two lambs with their spiky-horned moms watch from an opposite ridge while I descend, but then, upwardly mobile, I go "where sheep fear to tread." A client once said that, meaning to compliment me. It is not true, much as I'd like it to be. My skills and tolerance for exposure near edges pale in comparison to the wild sheep's and in south-central coastal Alaska, the mountain goats'. Lithe dancers on the vertical, the Alex Honnolds of the ovine world, they skip from skinny ledge to skinny ledge, sometimes chasing each other in play, where I would struggle for footholds and handholds. They seek daybeds on the highest, sharpest ridges, from which they survey terrain for wolverines, bears, wolves, and human hunters. Golden eagles in pairs may corner and kill a stray lamb. And a few adults misstepping or slipping plunge to premature deaths. Rockfalls and avalanches sweep up others, perhaps explaining the broken bodies I find, including the one on which those bears were feeding.

A former fellow Outward Bound instructor in his blog spelled *Dall sheep* "Dull sheep." They're anything but. I love outwitting them, crawling behind ridgelines on all fours or Groucho Marx–walking till I'm close enough to pop up and see how they react. Sometimes they just stand and stare in the sheep stance of head scratching. They may not recognize unmoving shapes or not read them as dangerous. If you sit and avert your stereoscopic stalker gaze, one may tiptoe closer, so close that you discern amber eyes—until she catches your scent. Their pupils are flattened, not round like ours, which makes them alien, snake-ish, penetrating.

It's a shape evolved in grazers that allows them to scan for predators even while feeding. When they lower their head, in a neat gyroscopic trick the eyes rotate up so the pupils stay level with the horizon. That creates a blind zone above, to the advantage of climbing human hunters and eagles. With eyes on both sides of their head, sheep have an almost 360-degree view of the ground. This means they can notice things sneaking up from behind.

Ellen Meloy's mulling of glances across species boundaries illustrates my meetings with Dall sheep and bears: "Each time I look into the eye of an animal, one as 'wild' as I can find in its own element . . . and if I get over the mess of 'Do I eat it or vice versa?' I find myself staring into a mirror of my own imagination. There is in that animal eye something both alien and familiar." Indeed, stories we tell about animals say as much about our reality as about theirs.

Desiring this intimacy, trying to lull wary sheep, I've sung to them, which seems to intrigue them and prove that I'm not a malicious, armed creep. Unlike caribou antlers, the horns of wild sheep are never shed and grow over a lifetime, which can result in "full curls," 360-degree head-butting spirals crowning mature rams. Strong horns the color of golden heartwood announce status to ewes and competitors. Plentiful forage and good summers add tree ring ridges or "annuli" faster than meager winter does. Ironically, Dall are "thinhorn" sheep, their weapons longer and narrower compared to those of their bighorn cousins, whose rams weigh a third more. Still, their blunt bumpers pack the punch of two sledgehammers backed by 250 pounds of muscle accelerating.

What I would give to hear clacks of skulls meeting in fall jousts echoing off these crags!

Two connector valleys running east to west from Cane Creek to the Marsh Creek headwaters look feasible on my map. Dropping into Cane Creek, I cast a glance into one of the two, and it makes me shudder: steep, narrow, tortuous, lined with tons of snow. "If you gaze for long into an abyss, the abyss gazes also into you," Nietzsche wrote. This one certainly does, and I hurry onward, banking on the other, which branches off about a mile downstream.

Its mouth, when I reach it, evokes the Mines of Moria in Tolkien's Middle-earth. I enter with as many forebodings as the fellowship had. Past the first curve, damn, a waterfall set in bedrock blocks my way. I cut to the ridge on the north in a slippery traverse on a 40-degree slope. And slip I do, almost dislocating my shoulder again. Having my hands grip the hiking poles is the perfect setup for overextending an arm in case of a fall. It's like feet in stirrups. Before the trip, I cut off the loops, so at least I can drop the sticks without entanglement. Still, I hear that sickening socket crunch, the sound of molars on gristle, but my humerus stays where it belongs. I'm two days from my resupply at the Marsh Fork of the Canning, the refuge's western boundary, so the pack is not very heavy, which may have saved the day. Coming down on that joint with a bigger load could have popped it. It did happen in the Grand Canyon, but here, even more remote, it would be worse.

Rather than face more treacherous footing back into the canyon beyond the falls, I follow the ridgeline almost to the summit. It looks easier from there to sidehill to a small saddle at the head of the gorge. But it isn't. Despite stepping carefully, I dislodge rocks the size of suitcases when I put my weight on them, and, *Khazad-dûm, Khazad-dûm*, they rumble into the deep.

At the saddle, finally, it is too windy to camp, though I'm tuckered. Its swayback marks the Continental Divide, and I cross to the north side again. I start down the connecting creek, which—no way—constricts into a bedrock gullet with cascades that ring ominously between old-snow bridges that have remodeled the creek bed into a bobsled luge. More traversing on tippy boulders on the north side, then. Each time when I think it is safe to cut back and follow the tunneling watercourse, another breakneck stair step of tumbling snowmelt deters me.

I finally bottom out, figuratively and literally. My knees ache, my thighs are filled with jelly. The canyon yawns where another one breaches it, and I make camp on a dry springy meadow. I am too wasted to really enjoy shooting stars dazzling pink on the ground. Today has been not only difficult but also scary. The ten miles I've hiked feel like thirty. And the fifty from Windy River to Atigun Pass are supposedly worse. Yikes. I barely manage to finish dinner before a rainsquall drives me into the tent.

THE LONGEST DAY

DAY 17 (13 MILES)
QUAD: ARCTIC

Summer solstice, I think. It always tastes bittersweet, as from here on daylight dwindles again. Hope this won't turn into my longest hiking day yet. Cloudless, then a slow buildup from white sheep to gray mammoths. Some excellent walking on dryas benches—just what the doctor ordered. Before my first break, I make six miles in a little more than two hours. I do not obsess over times or distances normally, but on this adventure I finely calibrate efforts and reserves, such as the fuel stoking this fickle engine. The numbers also bolster me with a sense of security, proving steadfast progression in the right direction, that movement is assuming the shape of this longtime ambition.

Dwarf fireweed or "river beauty" tints gravel bars, the only bars I'll be seeing for another two months. Fireweed is a choice material for Rika Mouw, an environmental jeweler living in Homer, on Alaska's Kenai Peninsula. Trained as a landscape architect as well as a goldsmith, she has long pondered how to harmonize artifacts with their natural contexts. She no longer uses metals, because the mining causes collateral damage.

Rika was a client on that momentous river trip with Robert Thompson on the Hulahula on which I shared my yen for this traverse. In her piece *Arctic Caribou*, a spray of dozens of polished antler cross-sections translates the Porcupine herd's milling around the calm eye of a storm. *Mark of Time* honors fireweed's role as a seasonal carpe diem with a time-lapse collage of deep rose seedpod wreaths in different stages, some already splitting, feathering out for the wind to release their progeny. The terminal, downy ringlet in this series would make a fine crown for a king of the autumn enthroned for a single day.

Gift of the Arctic Refuge is my favorite work by this artist of gentle, refined bearing who has wept at the power this place exerts. Text from the decree that established the Arctic Wildlife Range, as it was named, lines her wooden treasure chest. From it, snow geese wing upward, better angels of our nature—a chain of hand-torn-paper messengers bearing the words of those who fought for this sanctuary. "Through bird migrations alone," Mouw says about this potent conceptual piece, "the Refuge connects peoples and places all over the world."

Beauty, sanity, wisdom, and wholeness, not just mineral resources, can be extracted from this land.

At this point, I figure the trip will take longer than it does in the end, when I will understand that I underestimated my eagerness on the river run and the rain-swollen Noatak's on its rendezvous with the sea. I've barely started, relatively speaking, and yet it feels like forever since I climbed out of Kirk's Cessna on Joe Creek. The subjectivity of time is a well-known phenomenon. Though a week here holds the same number of minutes and hours as one in town, it stretches under the weight of a gazillion impressions, rich and packed densely with life. Strangely, once you reach middle age, years already lived seem compressed. They've run like grains through the waist of an hourglass, blurred as a picket fence seen from a speeding car.

At the junction with the Canning River, I get a chance to inspect the other Cane Creek connector, the road not chosen. It is truly spectacular. The south side of one flanking peak rises near vertically in ranks of flat, smooth, symmetrical slabs and pinnacles, stegosaurus scales, but tiered, with the larger ones near the base. They are Lisburne limestone, most likely, but Brooks Range geology is complex, contorted with folding and intrusions that bewilder laypeople like myself. The living world has always been my priority, even though the tectonic foundation determines the biosphere everywhere. More of these dragon backs serrate the upper valley, all tilted at the same angle. Below green rolling foothills, the creek's ribbon winds between willows. I'll have to come back to this glen someday to explore. I'm still glad I did not choose the route through there.

Refreshingly after the grim high country, summer here rules with a floral vengeance, scattering saxifrage, oxytrope, and some yellow vetch sweetening the air on mossy flats where aufeis has receded just recently. Petite pinkish bells of low bearberry plants are easily overlooked in this riot. Come fall, their leaves will glint like splatters of freshly spilled blood.

"The world reveals itself to those who travel on foot," the German filmmaker Werner Herzog said, a dictum Bruce Chatwin adopted. The kindred spirit and travel writer is best known for his book *Songlines*. Songlines are paths of mythical other-than-human Dreamtime creator-ancestors who left signs of their passage on the land. Aboriginal Australian tradition bearers on walkabouts sometimes with young initiates still retrace those tracks as a form of spiritual surveying. The joint singing of different clans and regional bands weaves a forager's basket of stories, taboos, and tribal memories, a receptacle for their culture. An elder following his group's particular course recites the appropriate, required chant, which serves as a mnemonic but also brings the continent into existence once more. I think it was Chatwin who once gave a ride to an elder in the Outback who kept up with landmarks as they flew by the car window by speeding up his song.

The world still is best, because most deeply, imbibed at a pedestrian pace, one step at a time, not from behind a windshield, not disembodied in a jet, not even from a bicycle seat, but at three miles per hour (on a good surface). My ball cap and sweat rag are off to Paul Salopek, who endeavored a twenty-four-thousand-mile Out of Eden Walk, a decade-long exercise in "slow journalism" on which he retraced our trek out of Africa, all the way to North America, our last destination. A vector graph showing the place-names, flowers, mammals, topographic features, and physical sensations from blebs to bad gas along my arctic route would form a songline less venerable if equally telling. Various dictionaries define the related *walkabout*, which has entered the common vocabulary, as "a periodic nomadic excursion," "a rite of passage," "a short period of wandering far from towns and cities," or "an adventure of highs and lows, trials and tribulations." Much of this captures my undertaking.

Can anything besides bare facts be learned from a journey through such a landscape? Yes: Trust your instincts. Be prepared and steadfast but stay limber. Expect the unexpected. Forget about arriving; be as present as you can. Modest doses of hardship build stamina if not character. Make a home wherever you find yourself to be. Leave as small a footprint as possible, aware that all beings share life's adventure with you. To a teen Aborigine, these insights might be fresh. But to a middle-aged guy, they're truths already learned, truths too often ignored or forgotten.

Backcountry lessons in the crush of clock-driven cities have the shelf life of yogurt. My clan, enviro-elders who walked the earth—Olaus and Mardy Murie, Aldo Leopold, E. O. Wilson, Robert Marshall, Edward Abbey, Ellen Meloy, and Diane Fossey—is long gone. Many of them were outdoor enthusiasts first, before they became activists. What they knew and held dear they saw being threatened, which prompted them into action. I consider this ground my inheritance—and that of all Americans; nay, of the world—thanks to people like them. Drawing strength from it, I acknowledge responsibilities. Where are today's conservationist icons who dwell for a time in the wilds?

I hear the first Lapland longspur's plaintive call. *Tee-lee-oo. Tee-lee-oo.* Then a plane overhead, droning toward the Canning's Marsh Fork. Perhaps it's my cache number two taking a scenic flight. Whoever it is, I don't think he sees me. The pilot responsible for that load, Dirk Nickisch of Coyote Air, would dip his wings in recognition.

A field of dwarf lupines smells like a ballroom of debutantes. Bumblebees stick their heads into the plants' violet slippers, having a ball of their own. Furry, plump, boldly patterned, tricky to tell apart, bumblebees are "panda bears of the insect world," and the Himalayas, fittingly, are the Amazon of *Bombus* ("buzzer") diversity. If the whole clan is pandas, then its nine North Slope representatives should be polar bears. They lie torpid nine months, chambered bullets on south-facing slopes where the snow melts earlier. Glycerol, the bees' antifreeze, keeps water in their cells from crystalizing. By mid-May, as soon as arctic willows blossom, pregnant queens brave subzero weather, even blizzards.

"To bees, time is honey," punned the author of *Bumblebee Economics*, Bernd Heinrich. With daylight returned and summers beyond the Brooks Range brief, these most northerly of social insects—among the few that thermoregulate—forage 24/7. Invertebrate workaholics weaving livelihoods from floral candescence, they commute for miles on half-hour trips, faster than charging honeybees and galloping horses, before flies and mosquitos can travel. They siphon nectar and collect up to 80 percent of their weight in pollen from early-blooming pink louseworts, yolk-eyed dryas, and later, violet monkshood and lemony poppies. The gold-dusted bruisers are the primary fertilizers of eighty threatened arctic plants, and thus their buzzy sipping at willow catkins and berry bushes resounds through moose and grizzly populations.

Circumpolar *Bombus polaris* thrives farther north than all but one parasitic species, the cuckoo bumblebee. The larger body of *Bombus polaris*, velvety, stocky as a bulldog's, retains heat well. Internal flight muscles twitch more than a hundred times per second, raising its temperature to 95 degrees, similar to a human body's. The black-and-orange-banded dynamos weigh a tenth of a jellybean, which makes their output even more impressive. On sunny days, queens and their female cohorts bask in the open, engines idling. Resting in reflective poppies, "shivering" rapidly—pumping hidden beefcake lats and pecs—they generate extra warmth. "Cold-blooded insect" is a misnomer, really, for *Bombus polaris*. UAF Museum of the North entomologist Derek Sikes compares their caloric requirements to our culture's octane consumption: "As long as we have lots of energy, we're going to burn it like hell until it's all gone. That's what they do." *Their* fuel, of course, is renewable, high-sugar nectar and pollen stoking amped-up metabolisms. I salute their blazing lifestyle, crazily burning glycogen myself.

Offhand bee-watching suggests whimsical frenzy, like Rimsky-Korsakov's concert piece, not beelines but all-hands-on-deck tacking or manic meandering drunks. In truth, members of *Bombus* are rather efficient if hyper navigators. They and their apian kin don't see red but do ultraviolet, bees' purple. Zooming about, they identify flowers five times more quickly than we would from moving cars.

Another good camp amid dryas on a Marsh Fork tributary near aufeis. The mountain chains to the north, which that fork breaches, are a fortress that titans created to dwell in this country. The slanted evening sun bronzes motes of mayflies and willow fluff, the seeds drifting steadily on the breeze, the flies dancing erratically with a will of their own. Midges whirligig in lit columns as if caffeinated. Fitful yet stationary, they're particle physics materialized.

For dessert, I treat myself to a solstice peak. I cross paths with a rock ptarmigan and share the summit with a Zorro-masked northern wheatear, a summer guest from West Africa, before he moves on. It's warm enough at the top in a T-shirt, and the view fills me up.

Glory bee—today was much better than yesterday.

BARREL IN A HAYSTACK

DAY 18 (8 MILES)
QUAD: ARCTIC
CACHE #2

Cloudless. This resupply day will be more challenging than my first. I worry a bit. These are critical times, the only occasions short of death or injury that can undermine my project, the only parts for which I depend on outside help. I am two days early because I got to the Sheenjek faster than expected. Still, except for today's lunch, I've run out of food. That's just as it should be. I hope the pilot dropped off my goods before the due date, the day of my scheduled arrival. Also, my GPS—a Magellan, a name that tickles me—is about to croak: its digital display has become faint, barely legible. And yes, I did check its battery. I've gotten too lazy relying upon it anyway. That's consumer culture for you. They'll gladly upsell you on a new one because the cheap model you bought is crap.

It's hot, buggy, and swampy as I crash through alders. What a dismal little ditch, the antithesis of yesterday's promenade. This cut through the mountains seemed so inviting from the solstice-day summit. I look forward to talking to Melissa tonight if the satellite phone is not going wonky on me.

When I get to where I've marked the airstrip on my map: nothing. In fact, the location for which Kirk gave me coordinates and that I reach just before Magellan's life flame flickers out would not be fit to land on, not even for an Evel Knievel of bush pilots. It's a gnome's bumpy bowling lane. The floodplain of the Canning, on the other hand, a broad sweep with a thin skin of lichen and soil atop river gravel, looks perfect. But I detect no sign that it ever served human purposes. There should at least be scars from plane tires if it were visited regularly. I did not find any either hiking down from the heights. With my heart aflutter, I call Dirk in Coldfoot, little more than a Haul Road truck stop. He was supposed to place this cache. The first outfit I used, Kirk's, is based south of the eastern part of the refuge, in Fort Yukon; and the second, Coyote Air, south as well but more centrally located. I had split the supplies between them according to the proximity of the two outfits' home bases to the intended drops.

At both numbers Dirk gave me, a recorded voice greets me. The season is short but the days long, so the flyboys stay busy, hauling hikers and hunters, floaters and scientists, workers and government staff, and freight throughout the summer. It could have been him buzzing by earlier.

Thirsty from my search, I grab the water bottle and bear repellent from my pack and head for willows seaming the river. A few hundred yards later, I cross a trail, a rut in the dry tundra, with tire tracks. And promptly, another, bald twin of the first. It's the runway. Hurray. At its end sits a low black metal barrel, which in profile could pass for a boulder. It contains my fuel and grub, plus a note from a Swiss couple Dirk flew out for a few days of hiking. They wish me a safe trip and ask if I have a website where they can see my adventure. I did not even buy or borrow a camera—do not want to be glued to one, letting one rule me.

Thinking back now as I write these recollections a decade later, those were simpler, more unencumbered days. I had not planned to create a website until a publisher suggested it. Marketing the fruits of my labor never was my strength, and the thought of taking photos, of "painting in a hurry" to promote my experience afterward was anathema. As much as I love artful photography, I won't kowtow to the dictatorship of the image. We used to have readers; now we have gawkers. And what would it say about a writer if he could not evoke mountains and rivers, tundra flowers and caribou, the depth of solitude, the quicksilver weather and light, and the timelessness of this land through his words?

Eschewing complex technology, I've not driven a car since the age of eighteen, when the army made me. For decades, before computers, the most complex gadget I owned was a white gas stove. I detest watches, the Man's stylish shackles, though my guide work requires that I carry one so I won't miss my clients' arrival at the outfitter's shop in Fairbanks or our pickup rendezvous in the field at trip's end. (A happy-go-lucky guide friend once missed his plane, and his were not happy campers.)

I proudly overcame my inner *Schweinehund* ("swine-hound"), that beast of routine and procrastination, and bought and learned the ways of a GPS partly for my peace of mind and partly for Melissa's. Who says codgers can't learn new tricks? The computer too came with my professional territory; I know of no publisher that accepts typewritten manuscripts anymore. I hacked out the pages for my first minor opus at a computer in the Moab public library. But the reserved time slots were short and I was slow and the librarians refused to lock me in overnight.

In short, I caved in and slaved and became dependent on and incompetent in the use of advanced technologies. I should just shove Magellan's corpse deep into a pile of bear shit—I suddenly realize he has become my Wilson, Tom Hanks's volleyball buddy in *Cast Away*, only less accommodating.

The idea of wilderness, Bob Marshall stipulated, among other criteria "requires anybody who exists in it to depend exclusively on his own effort for survival." Strictly speaking, this disqualifies me from being a wilderness traveler, since I depend on these food drops and the orbital web of satellites. But are maps not external support too, the fruit of someone else's efforts? Weren't the Wiseman locals whom Marshall enlisted as travel companions and whose expertise he welcomed? Call it the purist's dilemma. Indigenous wayfarers helped each other with provisions and canine logistics, as they often did White explorers. They acknowledged that no man can be an island, that a man alone is as good as dead, and that the Brooks Range hasn't been wilderness in thirteen thousand–plus years.

I once more phone Dirk and cancel the express food request I made earlier. Even before lunch, I've already run the gamut from anticipation to worry to disappointment to teeth gnashing and last, relief. Perhaps it's the hormonal changes in men of my age that I've read about.

At dinner, there shall be elation. I decide to put in another couple of miles. Rewarded almost instantly, I flush a red-necked phalarope from almost underfoot, which seeks refuge in a pond. In this species, the only swimming sandpiper, cocks are the nest sitters while brighter plumaged and larger hens go off gallivanting. Its Eskimo name translates as "blood-like" and its German one as

"Odin's chick"—in the ornithological sense. Bobbing and spinning up to nine months each year on the water off South America's coast, these phalaropes with their needle bills swirl up invertebrate prey, which they deftly spear.

I then spot an empty nest five feet up in a willow. Robin?

A bird, to the environmental activist Mark Cocker, is "life quickened and intensified beyond our range," our range being a cumbersome earthbound biped's. Who has not envied raptors regally shedding gravity's shackles? Ever since Icarus botched his attempt, we've tinkered to make it happen. Early Christians saw hell as a place without birds, drawing on an even older Greek idea about an underworld lake whose toxic vapors killed birds in midflight. Consequently, any place hosting emissaries of the upper realm, these puffs of fresh air from faraway lands, cannot be hell. Even house sparrows, grackles, and starlings put balm on harried city souls. Not pigeons, though.

Camp tops a low bluff next to the river. The Marsh Fork gathers beryl in the deeper channels on the outside of its crooks and in holes where grayling hang as if suspended in paperweight glass. The Canning's lacy waterfall and a watery slot canyon farther downstream are gems that could have been cut from the Grand Canyon's scenery.

Back to frustrated: I lose the signal seven or eight times while speaking with Melissa and have to call back; the connection crackles when I have one. *Vox clamantis in deserto*. I can empathize with Isaiah (though this is clearly a Jeremiad), a voice crying out in the wilderness that nobody hears, not even God. Or if he does, if she exists, he/she/they do(es) not respond.

As wags say, when God created Man—and through him, all of Earth's gadgets—she was only practicing. I'd just like to put this day behind me.

POST-SOLSTICE BLUES

DAY 19 (11 MILES)
QUAD: ARCTIC

Cloudless. On the way up and out of a westerly Canning headwaters branch, I surprise an arctic fox napping. He stands up and yawns and then lies down again. As he isn't going to dance on his hind legs or play the flute for me, I keep going. The fox gazes at me from his hollow, and only his muzzle and ears poke out from the tundra. Here by the river, I reflect on good water again, a luxury for most of the world. I fill my bottle anywhere without thinking twice or filtering it. On arctic float trips, I sometimes just dip a cup in it, drinking straight from the source. It is water so cold it induces ice-cream headaches, so clear it magnifies bottom cobbles as it slides over graveled beds. Ricocheting off bluffs, it braids and unbraids. Once in a while, it feathers into riffles or crests into rapids. Often, I have to acknowledge, it falls on me from the sky.

Perhaps I should feel a bit blue as astronomical summer has peaked and we're racing toward winter again at the speed of an extra minute or more each day. But there's a strange disconnect between the length of daylight or "photoperiod" and terrestrial changes. Because the ground takes longer to warm than the sea, summer arrives later on land, still ramping up weeks after the solstice, as evidenced in flowers and other three-inch vegetation, the waning of aufeis, and rising air temperatures. While the minutes flee imperceptibly, I feel that each day spent out here, strengthening body and mind, adds a day to my lifespan, and in my ledger, one summer day easily beats two good winter ones.

What I hate: panting uphill, breathing deeply, and then inhaling a mosquito. It's disgusting and you cough and get thrown off your hiking rhythm.

Fair enough, though. They eat me; I eat them. And pop them like ripe cherry tomatoes. I haven't seen any caribou in days and miss their sometimes shy, sometimes curious company. Their skittishness can betray a close bear, since their noses are so much more attuned than mine is. Still, I do not walk unattended—a swarmtrooper cloud shadows me.

I come upon another airstrip, one with four empty gas cans rusting away. This would be a better staging area for hikers than the previous runway, less willowy and with more scenic possibilities.

Off and on, scraps from movie soundtracks play in my head. I'm embarrassed to find a *Lord of the Rings* theme among them. But the book and the films are long walks into the unknown, after all, with Strider a central figure. And director Peter Jackson's take on the Middle-earth kingdom of Rohan—filmed in the Rangitata River valley in New Zealand's Southern Alps—matches the peaks and outwash plains here that enchant me. The orchestral grandeur of strings, brass, and woodwinds fits this landscape as well. I chuff these melodies, which textures my breathing like a voiceless mantra or army cadence call, especially during steep, strenuous sections.

First Dirk and then a golden eagle zip by while I lunch. I can tell it's him from the plane's color. I leave the Marsh Fork to cut over to the upper Ivishak, which Ron Yarnell said could be difficult. Ron is the former owner of the Fairbanks guiding outfit for which I work. He sold the business to three of his guides and now enjoys retirement, staying active physically and politically on behalf of this refuge. It's an endless battle, since each Republican administration rekindles efforts to develop the 1002 Area, a cradle of life and the refuge's biological centerpiece. The corporations that have probed the contested ground do not disclose how much or how little oil lies hidden there. However, environmental organizations estimate that even just inflating car tires properly would save more fuel in the US per year than the suspected reservoir could yield. Never mind the added carbon dioxide emissions from burning that fossil hoard.

Ron, who has traveled all over this country by boot and by boat, sometimes scouts put-ins, routes, camps, and scenic places from the air. His assessments are mostly spot-on, as in this case. The connecting canyon is a tight and steep ankle twister with slick cobbles, ice plugs, and waterfalls that require detours on loose scree on par with that of the Cane Creek defile. It is very time consuming too.

Another long day, if not in miles. I'm camped on the far side of a saddle near the snowfields that birth the Ivishak under a leaden, all-encompassing sky. Gray above and gray all around absorbs me.

The fixed-length carbon ski pole that props up my tent's gable teems with skull-and-crossbones designs, which under the circumstances, or even for alpine skiing, I find rather macabre. I loathe adjustable trekking poles. At worst, their joints are breaking or bending points; at best, they shorten, telescoping under my full weight, a problem with the locking mechanisms. I therefore brought this one and its twin, and removed their baskets for better purchase in snowy couloirs and so that the tip, dulled with a magic marker cap, would fit into the gable's sleeve pocket. Now, though, the poles embed deeply in mud or turf with each step hundreds of times every day, and yanking them out burns energy and strains my bum shoulder. It's the law of small decisions that will haunt you, their consequences lingering, adding up incrementally and compounding those of other misjudgments.

MEMORIES OF
THE CORPUSCLES

DAY 20 (4 MILES)
QUAD: ARCTIC

Sunny. When I went to get a midnight snack from my bearproof barrel in the kitchen, a dozen sheep had bedded down on the slope above camp. In the quiet, I later heard *baa*ing, lambs calling to their mothers. This was a first for me in wild sheep and created a strangely bucolic mood. Half expecting clanging bells, I did not need to count the vocalists behind closed eyelids to fall asleep again.

I tumbled on the ice again while descending the creek this morning. But the terrain is not nearly as rough on this side of the saddle. I am famished all the time now.

Bundled caribou trails lead to the Ivishak, grooves the Porcupine herd's annual ambulation has left on turf greened and sprinkled with wildflowers. "The animals dominate the landscape wherever they are, a river of life, always moving," George Schaller wrote about these trailbreakers in his 1956 journal. I think of their trails as capillaries with caribou as flowing corpuscles, the lifeblood of the body that is this land.

On her one and only Brooks Range trip, Kate, along with her fellow hikers, was blessed with a spectacle I've witnessed but thrice in my life. Having crossed Guilbeau Pass, we were camped one easy day from Grasser's airstrip, the finish of our weeklong backpacking trip. Because the morning was drizzly, my hikers still hid inside their sleeping bags. Over a contemplative cup of joe in the kitchen area, a stone's throw away from our tents, I noticed shifts in what in the flat light looked like a boulder field.

"You might want to come outside. The whole hillside is crawling with caribou," I roused the sleepyheads, unaware yet that I was seeing ten thousand, a prong of the southbound transborder migration. After days with few animals, we had suddenly struck it rich.

We sat and breakfasted quietly for about three hours, afraid that a loud word or brash gesture would turn the approaching herd. The tide of furred bodies divided and flowed around us. Their gamey, dense musk saturated the air. To Mardy Murie, the herd's collective sound was "a permeating, uncanny rumble, almost a roar" she could not liken to anything else. We distinguished geezer sounds and with each step clicks from tendons that snapped back splaying, "snow-shoe" hooves—like the bow-flex camber in cross-country skis—that help caribou preserve energy. The animals were fat from the sedges, willow leaves, mosses, flowers, mushrooms, and cottongrass on the Arctic Coastal Plain. Cows had shed their antlers after dropping gangly calves there in early June, but the bulls were still geared up for the fall rut near the tree line.

We broke camp without causing so much as a ripple and then hiked against the current, down-valley, through the herd. The drifters eyed us inquiringly: *Don't you know winter is coming? You are headed the wrong way!* They were ready to cross Guilbeau Pass, which we just had, in the opposite direction.

After the rush had subsided, we traveled freshly tramped filaments, past wisps of fleece caught in bushes and dung pellets soft in the tracks. We ran into strag-glers: stilt-legged offspring heeling five females, "The Moms"; a bull with a dozen cows, "The Harem"; and, heartbreakingly, "The Casualty," a calf limping behind his mother. The doe kept glancing back as if to encourage the little fellow, but we were sure he would end up feeding a bear or wolves or perhaps a golden eagle.

I have not encountered any wildlife above the size of a robin today, not even ground squirrels. That is the Arctic—famine and feast.

I spontaneously camp where I'm taking a snack break. It's too precious to rush through, this junction of four upper-Ivishak valleys issuing from the Philip Smith Mountains to the north, and I don't have many miles to cover on this leg to the Wind River cache, number three. Going for a hike up a ridge, I turn around without summiting when the footing deteriorates into serious rubble.

I've just been through a day and a half of that. And the view could not become that much better: waterfalls lacing a side valley headed by a mountain whose face is draped with hanging glaciers. I also want to return to camp and jot down some thoughts concerning migrations. Yes, the mind does wander independently when the body does, but more of that later.

After dinner I hill-walk a stair-stepped chain of knolls behind camp. A question pops into my head: Why, unless you're one of Joseph Campbell's heroic types, is a loop, or even going only from A to B, more rewarding than going from A to B and then back to A? It must be the novelty, though landscapes always appear different, Janus-faced, depending on whether you're coming or going. Come to think of it, even Odysseus returned the roundabout way to Ithaca, his point A. It's more gratifying for readers too.

ONE BUNTING A
SUMMER MAKES

DAY 21 (4 MILES)
QUAD: ARCTIC

Sunny with breakfast sprinkles. It's the buggiest morning yet. I especially hate dropping my pants when they're raving like this. Time is not fun when you're having flies.

I decide on a layover to explore the valley I saw yesterday from the ridge. There is plenty of time—I actually should have put the next cache on the Middle Fork of the Chandalar to even out the two legs of this journey east of the Dalton Highway. Perhaps next time.

The valley, cradling a clear creek at its bottom, pinches into a neat little gorge so twisted you don't know what awaits you upstream. The bends that scuba divers fear affect hikers differently: you want to know what lies around the next one and the next, and before you have walked even half of a canyon, dusk surprises you. Luckily, that isn't a problem here in the summer.

Up close, the dead-end headwall looms even more impressively, slightly curved, an amphitheater. It is a cirque, clearly, and my map shows the glacier that carved it, now receded, higher up. Cirques rise in clean-cut monolithic profiles like the Arrigetch (Nunamiut for "fingers of the hand extended") Peaks on the Alatna—three-thousand-foot spires, sharks' teeth, and cliffs of intrusive-magma granite that erosion exposed. Bedrock bays at the bases of cirques often cup meltwater in a lake or "tarn."

The day has turned gray and drizzly, the light flat. I cannot complain, though; the weather has been good so far, except for the snow squalls when I crossed into the Sheenjek valley. How many months ago was that?

Sunny in the p.m. In western Ireland they say, "If you don't like the weather, wait fifteen minutes." The Brooks Range is massive enough to brew up its own systems, and it often divides the Interior's high-pressure dry spells from fronts enshrouding the coast.

A lone sheep—and *snow buntings*!

Forgive my excitement. Only someone who lives for six months in a meat locker understands the import of these harbingers of warmth, light, and plenitude. One swallow may not make a summer, but one bunting does. "I never tire of the snow buntings," Olaus Murie wrote. He painted a pair at the nest, adding, "Each time, the bird bursts upon my view in fresh purity of white set off by the black pattern." The "snowbirds" sometimes delight my Inupiaq friend Robert Thompson before he sees them. One heard upon awakening, singing atop a wall tent or through a home's air duct, "adds much cheer to your day."

This circumpolar pip, the planet's northernmost passerine and perhaps toughest bird, nests farther north even than ravens. It inhabits nunataks, stone islands like the ones Greenlandic glaciers engulf; and US Navy submariners have spotted it at the pole. For Arthur Cleveland Bent, the author of a twenty-one-volume work on North America's avifauna, it was the "very epitome of an arctic bird." It snow bathes and burrows into drifts during minus-35-degree spells, overnighting in digs thus established. One chased by a hawk might plunge into deep powder. Audubon watched several, hoar frosted, too numb to fly. Snow buntings that arctic storms delay in Fairbanks refuel for their journey's finale by gleaning dead bugs or shriveled chokecherries. Grounded, they roost in huddled, hungry masses yearning to stay warm. Downy ankles reduce heat loss through the migrants' naked feet. Still, the icy gusts of such an existence snuff out four in ten adults every year.

Even airborne, glimpsed easily from the corner of an eye, the plump black-and-white finch-size "snowflakes" can't be mistaken for other birds. Billowing flurries—Audubon's "compressed squadrons"—will "relax the closeness of their phalanx" and sweep low across foreshores and tundra, where, jumping or wing-brushing beach grass to drop seeds, they hustle before pairing up. Traveling day and night in chirping currents of hundreds or thousands, this blizzard of urgency picks up geomagnetic clues. Males, among the first birds to return to North Slope breeding grounds, after wintering in the northern United States touch down in early April and right away chime, rattle, and buzz, gaudy wind-up toys claiming territories and honing individual tunes. They flit about, snatching materials for sturdy cups of moss and dead grass that they line with fur and shed ptarmigan feathers. Females join them three to six weeks later. Both sexes linger until the earth freezes rock hard again in September, and some lag into November.

Nesters on treeless tundra become easy prey. Cautious snow buntings rear their broods in rock crevices, vacant lemming burrows, hollow driftwood logs, or sod-*iglu* ruins. Humans provide fox-and-snowy-owl-proof egg-laying nooks under snowmachine hoods, in pipelines, rusty barrels, empty tin cans, junked cars, and in one case, a "well bleached" Inupiaq skull. It's no surprise buntings thrive throughout Prudhoe Bay's oilfields, Cold War Distant Early Warning sites, and Inupiaq settlements. A hen, camouflaged like a sparrow, often won't leave her half dozen bluish, brown-speckled eggs because of a nest's chillier setting, and depends on her mate feeding her.

Predecessors of hobby and academic ornithologists long studied the comings and goings of *amautligauraq*, "the one with a pouch," an allusion to the bunting's piebald back. Inuit, who told a myth about one that forecast good weather for departing geese, built stone piles whose cavities appealed to the songsters, which to the people were auspicious. Families caught some as pets. Their cairn-dwelling free kin revealed caribou happenings. The fledglings' feathers turn rusty brown when calf hair takes on a similar tinge, announcing prime skins for certain light garments. In August, after chicks have mastered flight, buntings gather for their southward migration, just as caribou do for theirs into hunters' ambushes. In a wayfinding feat that must be the envy of every outdoorsman, fogged-in Native Greenlandic kayakers steered not only by judging echoes reverberating from dangerous cliffs but also, even more astoundingly, by the slightly differing songs of cock buntings rising from each headland. By memorizing the exact melody of one bunting nesting at the cape that marked the entrance to their home fjord, they knew to veer there without hesitation.

In a justified tit-for-tat, we cater to the snow buntings' housing needs unknowingly, but human actions (and inaction) also threaten them. Though today's climate disruption expands their ranges, earlier springs outrun migrants, dooming chicks missing the peak of fly, beetle, mosquito, and caterpillar bonanzas. More bad news yet, higher temperatures bring competitors and red foxes to the bird so charming in its voice and appearance, its looks and longed-for arrivals.

Thundershowers pound the earth—the hardest it's rained yet.

Note-taking in such weather is a royal pain. Ink smears, limp maps tear along their creases when I unfold them. There's poor light and barely enough room to sit inside my tent in the camp chair. Counting on all-night sun, I did not bring a headlamp. Was Gilbert White in Selborne or Thoreau at Walden productive under conditions like these? But then, the upper Nile explorer Amelia Edwards, getting "a foretaste of cremation" with sand silting up her paint box and slapping flies with "a morbid appetite for water-colours," or Henry "Birdie" Bowers, on "the Worst Journey in the World" to collect a penguin egg at Cape Crozier, struggled with worse. Bowers's fellow birder, the superb draftsman Edward "Uncle Bill" Wilson, who sketched outdoors in the Antarctic summer, nearly snow blind after a day of heavy sledging, reported fingers "all thumbs" that were "soon so cold that you don't know what or where they are."

THINKING ON YOUR FEET

DAY 22 (6 MILES)
QUAD: PHILIP SMITH MOUNTAINS

I've been sitting around too much during the past two days and am eager to be moving but get a late start because it is raining again, and I've been procrastinating in the tent. When the rain breaks, cloud tatters linger in the mountains, veiling and then unveiling wells of blue. It actually isn't that bad for hiking, better than buggy or sweltering air. A ram fords the creek while I breakfast, a rare sight, and he's clearly wary, uncomfortable at this low elevation.

Drizzly and gray all day—the tatters win. Crossing valleys at right angles repeatedly is so much harder than traveling with the land's flow. I've lost considerable weight—the waist of my hiking pants tells me so—and on some days feel weak. I'm always hungry now, eating more than a day's share, but my mind works in overdrive.

I do some of my best thinking while walking and again find myself in good company. "I can only meditate when I am walking," Rousseau confessed. Kierkegaard insisted that he composed all his literary works on foot. An entire school of sages, the Greek Cynic philosophers, lived vagabond lives, berating the settled that stooped in the market places. Diogenes, who might have slept in a wine barrel or not, thought Aristotle's legs were too skinny. A walk down memory lane is not just metaphorical either—Charles Darwin acknowledged the mnemonic edge sauntering gives. A long trek is like stream-of-consciousness writing: the senses regard an incident or shiny object from various angles before taking leave, moving on to the next. Similarly, both the essayist and the river runner meander to advance in the main direction, toward some kind of closure.

Topography structures cerebral cadences. Deep breaths perfuse thoughts. Footfalls yield a rhythm for language and song. The semi-automatic, repetitive act leaves the creative part of the brain free to scamper. In walking, the mind unkinks for its dialogue with nature, and the longer the walk, the deeper the dialogue. There is scientific truth to all this. Regular walkabouts stifle angst, depression, and the phantom dementia while juicing up memory. They keep you mentally spry. Another fringe benefit of thinking afoot is the distraction it offers from blisters and stiffened joints.

It's a sad thing when the wandering body and mind forever decouple. Approaching ninety, my father, who introduced my brother and me to alpine splendor—we climbed Europe's highest peak, Mont Blanc, together—no longer could do even yard work, which he loved. He misplaced tools. His body stayed strong, but his short-term recall flickered. It was little consolation that some earlier memories remained intact. Walking about, he could not generate new ones, which for me was a main motivation for undertaking this traverse: experiences that, barring brain injury or insanity I naively thought then, would cast their warm glow into my rheumatic twilight years. Perhaps writing is my attempt to save such recollections from the teeth of erosion. Time like a glacier already has planed too many details off undocumented adventures I had before I became a writer at the ripe age of forty.

Dwarf hawksbeard, a circular yellow starburst from which pea-green tracers radiate. It's a pincushion of miniature dandelions.

I have made a navigation error again, going up the wrong upper-Ivishak drainage. I rushed since it was raining and did not bother putting the two map sheets together for the bigger picture. I was right on the edge of one and now am just on edge. My maps are not laminated, and I can ill afford to have them fall apart (not to mention that soaking them would wipe out my journal entries). Neither do I want to get Magellan wet—only a landlubber imbecile would. He hardly displays anymore and might short-circuit if moisture gets inside. I didn't buy the waterproof model, so what. Walled in by this dead end and weepy sky, I call it a day.

TWO TRAGEDIES

DAY 23 (12 MILES)
QUAD: PHILIP SMITH MOUNTAINS

The cloud ceiling—what an appropriate word—has dropped all the way to the valley bottom, brushing against my tent. It looks featureless, almost like fog, but it isn't fog. Nimbostratus, *The Cloud Collector's Handbook* says, is a form that arrives "surreptitiously and without fanfare" with steady precipitation that can last for hours and "gives all the other ones a bad name." The world is duotone, shades of gray plus white, a waiting room for lost souls. When the clouds immured me last night, they brought rain as predicted.

They are lifting this morning, and so is my mood. The sun struggles to elbow through as I backtrack to the valley's mouth where I think I went wrong. The zone of brighter gray in the sky promises light at the end of the tunnel, the soul's delivery to a glorious future. For now, it's a female griz and her cub in the willows, just where I most fear to surprise any bear. Naturally, Murphy's Law, they meander into the direction in which I am headed. When I round a blind corner, carefully, I see both on talus scree, cutting upward diagonally. This time, they've seen (or smelled) me first.

Mama takes her time, stopping repeatedly to look back at me. *Don't you worry—chasing you is the last thing on my mind.* Her struggling cub gets separated in a crumbling cliff band. His shorter legs and smaller muscles and lack of experience prevent him from keeping up. I hear her calling half a mile below. I don't know if ursine distress calls exist, but her bellowing raises hairs on my neck. A note of agony rings in it and another of loss, and the harmony is touchingly human.

I'm booking it as they're both still cruising toward the pass to the Ivishak for which I am aiming, one of the Continental Divide's highest in this region. Short of an about-face, all three of us have nowhere else to go. I would really like to overtake the bears, hoping she's busy for a while reconnecting with her cub and hoping she won't hold a grudge. I fear, irrationally, that she might try to hunt me down and teach me manners.

Like people, bears, while engrained opportunists, are creatures of habit. Over decades and sometimes centuries, generations of them commute to and from work—their work being fishing and grubbing, napping, mating, putting on pounds for winter, fighting rivals, dodging hunters, and caring for cubs. Their entrenched lanes are rarer and longer lasting than individual pigeon-toed tracks.

Bears pad on byways through muskeg or northern rainforest tangles. Soft shod, they mosey down deer trails and dirt roads. They skirt wetland meadows, truckin' between trees where soil is firmer and forage better. They ford rivers, balance on logs above streams. Hunger and memories entice them to trundle across scree into valleys. Do they contemplate shortcuts? Plan rest stops? Switch to cruise control? Follow mental maps, favor faster lanes, or feel traffic has gotten worse? Their local positioning systems process whiffs, sounds, visual clues. During salmon runs, they stitch waterways into arcane rounds, surprising bipedal berry pickers and anglers. It pays to be mindful traipsing through brush, more so at dusk, grizzly rush hour.

Postholing in marshes or ankle-deep moss, bears ration their strength by walking in each other's imprints. In difficult terrain, they step in "direct register," placing a rear foot in the track left by a front foot, which further defines links in home ranges as a rule undefended. Over time, offset parallel lines of ankle-deep pits form. These are awkward for hikers, since grizzlies have broader shoulders and hips. "In order to travel in these," our expert tracker Olaus Murie wrote, "I found it necessary to make a half hop from one [footprint] to the other." Be careful when practicing this technique; you might meet head-on traffic.

I'm back on the proper route. The Continental Divide at the head of the Ivishak could compete with Tibet's scenery: craggy; humongous; unscalable, like the roof of the world—you expect yaks or a yeti. It lies snow-free for just about ten weeks each year. I don't know if I'll make it to Seefar Glacier today, a name that speaks volumes. Perhaps I should try to, in case it socks in again. This would be lethal country to be moving through in a whiteout. It's sunny right now, with clouds snagged on the peaks, a place in Earth's past.

Bear diggings here where nothing much grows suggest mortar bombardment. There is nowhere they won't traipse in this country. Canada lynxes are creatures of the boreal forest, with their northernmost range in Alaska around Coldfoot, that Dalton Highway truck stop on the Brooks Range south side. And yet, one was shot at the Barrow dump on the Beaufort Sea coast; another, satellite data showed, explored the Noatak headwaters; eight-hundred-mile, ten-week two-way and loop lynx rambles have been logged. Superweasels, wolverines too have been fitted with radio collars and tracked to alpine summits, clawing their way up not for food or sex or to escape a rival but for the sheer hell of it. We'll never fully fathom the minds of these others and don't even those of our own kind.

A northern wheatear, a bird of the high country, peeps and bobs and flicks his tail in avian curtsies while making lip-smacking sounds. He is ashy gray with a buff throat and brown back, and a black eye stripe gives him something rakish. The rump of the wheatear, who owes his common name to a sixteenth-century corruption of "white arse," flashes only when he flies off.

Ron Yarnell was right: the walking is pretty good, at least to the scree field below the pass. There, on the unstable slope, incongruously, lie twisted metal scraps of a plane that disappeared in 1958 for twenty-one years. Debbie Miller, the Arctic Village schoolteacher who hosted Jimmy Carter and his wife, Rosalynn, discovered the wreck on a backpacking trip. She found vintage unopened 7UP and Coke cans among the debris. The plane had burned badly, but her party could read its identification number and retrieved a metal case containing the largely undamaged flight logs.

Miller and friends later learned that the US Fish and Wildlife Service regional director had piloted a twin-engine Grumman Goose that also carried his twenty-two-year-old son and another USFWS officer, and that nobody on board had survived the crash. The most extensive search mission in the territory's history involving hundreds of aircraft and surveying 280,000 square miles came up empty. As winter shut down all operations, the families hoped that somehow the missing men would make it out alive. (All Alaska bush planes carry survival kits, and the director, a former game warden, was an experienced outdoorsman.) Some people thought the Russians might have shot down the plane or forced it to land in Siberia—not a far-fetched idea, since that same September, four Soviet MIGs had intercepted a C-130 Air Force transporter over Armenia, killing all seventeen of its crew.

Investigators Miller led to the crash site found "five-gallon gas tanks that had been flattened like pancakes upon impact" in the nose of the plane. The throttles were set on forward mode. Death in the explosion would have been instantaneous, they concluded. Iced-up wings, poor visibility, or winds buffeting the plane inside this tight valley each or in combination could have doomed the trio on that August day decades ago.

I pause and contemplate the remains for a few minutes, reminded again how easily one becomes a fatality here and how easily one disappears. As recently as 2022, the FAA added two passes known foremost to local pilots to its Brooks Range charts. I pity the Goose's pilot and passengers. Judging by the position of the wreckage five hundred vertical yards below the notch, they almost made it.

This arctic range crushes the careless or unprepared even more easily than it does the circumspect and experienced. It claimed its own kind of Chris McCandless, the Denali hiker made famous by Jon Krakauer's *Into the Wild*.

In 1981, the Anchorage wilderness photographer Carl McCunn, age thirty-four, took his own life while stranded near the confluence of the Porcupine and Coleen on the south side not far from the Yukon border. He had been freezing and starving in a tent after a misunderstanding with the pilot whom he believed would get him in August, before winter's onset. Friends believed McCunn had already returned. He wasted his last chance, inadvertently hand signaling "All Okay—Do Not Wait!" to a state trooper who flew repeatedly over his campsite. Planning to stay roughly five months for wildlife stills, he had left only a vague itinerary. Because he felt like "a war monger," he threw excess shotgun shells into the river. Still, he tried to subsist on ducks and muskrats he shot and on the meat of a caribou he saw die in a lake. By November, suffering dizzy spells, he considered hiking seventy-five miles to Fort Yukon but was too weak.

McCunn wrote his final journal entry on December 18:

Am burning the last of my emergency Coleman light and just fed the fire the last of my split wood.
When the ashes cool, I'll be cooling along with them. . . .
I [chickened] out once already, but I don't wanna go through the chills again. They say it doesn't hurt . . .

He pinned his driver's license to a farewell note and will, suggesting whoever found him should inherit the shotgun and rifle for his troubles. He then shot himself with that rifle.

The view down the upper Wind River that Seefar promised is one of the trip's most magnificent, which is saying much. The backside, where I ascended, isn't bad either: kitty-corner to Windy Glacier, Seefar Glacier plunges from its summit past a black horn into a cirque that the ice gouged from tilted rock layers.

I negotiate some tricky parts coming down, though nothing too bad, and camp in the bottom of the Wind River's valley in the shadow of a 7,740-foot peak. Such elevations may seem puny compared to Denali's 20,310 feet, but Brooks Range summits thrust up from only 3,000 feet above sea level in the upper Wind River.

It feels good to be in cushioned country again, even though snowmelt soaks the mossy green. My knees and ankles rejoice. Still, my left Achilles tendon hurts. This pass would have fried me without hiking poles. It's been a long day, nine hours straight with minimal breaks and few tent-site options along the way. I'm on the south side once again. The cloud vault creaking open spills robin's-egg blue, a hopeful color.

I FEEL LIKE FOOD

DAY 24 (8.5 MILES)
QUAD: PHILIP SMITH MOUNTAINS

Last night crud blew in from the Continental Divide. And it rained. I lay in my sleeping bag glad I'd beaten the weather over the pass. It probably looked up there as it had on the day of the plane crash.

Around midnight an arctic fox trotted past, curious but distrustful of the flapping thing on the tundra where nothing this big had flapped before. I love my open-front room; it's like a bed in the first row of an IMAX theater. Winter foxes are all tail, and snow white or ivory, which makes their skins a coveted luxury. The summer version in its skimpy coat looks slimmer, dull brown and gray, blending in perfectly with that landscape also. A "blue morph" rare in Alaska is charcoal in fact. These solitary rovers venture onto the sea ice where they follow polar bears from whose kills they pilfer and surprise the occasional seal pup. On the mainland, they hear rodents under the snow—footage of foxes jumping several feet into the air as if on a hotplate to then pounce on unsuspecting lemmings is as iconic as it is comical. In the summer, they nab chicks, eggs, and ground squirrels; hoping for scraps, they trail wolves more than ten times their weight and twice their size that might eat them.

Morning bear—not referring to myself here. Within five minutes of my leaving camp, one towers on hind legs near where I meander. When I address him— memory fails as to the exact words—he drops on all fours and ambles off, stopping repeatedly and looking at me over his shoulder. A juvenile, definitely. He then circles around, behind my back, now and then hidden by a rise. It's the creepiest experience imaginable, at least if you're a guy. I do not like it one bit and keep on walking, trying to retreat without showing signs of panic or assuming the body language of prey. He quarters downwind of me finally, and it's goodbye.

Arctic explorers supplementing their shipboard fare with polar bear sometimes became a meal for the camouflaged lurking beasts instead of securing one. The phrase "serving as food" itself hints at subservience, at inferiority and a lack of agency and control over nature. These feelings are hard to accept. We think of wildlife as largely subdued, relegated to and aestheticized in coffee table book pages and on TV, except in rare shockers like *The Revenant* or Werner Herzog's blood-curdling *Grizzly Man* documentary about the deaths of Timothy Treadwell and Amy Huguenard down in Katmai National Park. Belying his surname, Treadwell, a self-declared bear protector, had camped for weeks on end during thirteen summers in Katmai's backcountry among brown bear daybeds and food sources, yards from junctions of tunnels in alder thickets through which they swaggered but that forced him to crawl. In 2003, this intimacy proved fatal. A rogue silvertip mauled him and his girlfriend, whose death sounds their dropped video camera captured.

Robert Thompson, who once shot a polar bear charging him on his doorstep in Kaktovik in self-defense, has an equally harrowing story. He was the first to come upon the scene of a double slaying in the Hulahula foothills. A grizzly had killed and partly eaten an Anchorage couple in their tent. Floating by their camp with two clients on a rafting trip, Robert noticed torn gear strewn about and landed to see if he could help. When he set foot on shore, the bear guarding his food stash attacked, and they quickly retreated. The bear followed them on the benches and eventually dove into the river trying to board the raft. One client, a Colorado river guide, rowed while Robert, gun ready, watched their pursuer from the stern. At some point, they hung up on a gravel bar and the bear came very close, but they made a last-moment getaway. Game wardens Robert alerted in Kaktovik flew to the site and shot the bear from the aircraft because it still was defending the camp.

This happened the summer during which the mom with the two cubs had mock-charged my party in Joe Creek. Freshly returned from that trip, I thought I had a scary story to tell—until I heard Robert's.

In the real living bear in a wilderness, the literary theorist Kenneth Burke writes, we once again face the "staggering disproportion between man and no-man" that for so long has been part of our mental makeup, as beings who "built their cultures by huddling together, nervously loquacious, at the edge of an abyss."

Nervously loquacious I would be, but there's nobody else here, and I'm not yet ready to gibber to myself about the horror that currently chills my frame. I suddenly feel like food, and it's not because my belly is growling again. Death in the refuge is a constant companion, but so is life in all its varied forms and exuberance. As proof, I next bumble into a sandpiper family. Two chicks pop from the vegetation and scurry off in different directions while the hen engages in the lame-wing fake.

How quickly my role has reversed, from hapless prey to monstrous threat.

It rains all afternoon. And after I praised soft country yesterday, I get swamped and tussocked today on truly soft ground. It is brushy too and my nerves are still frayed.

Tussocking should become an Olympic discipline or a punishment the penal system adopts, although human rights organizations would object. Jails would be empty and everybody on their best behavior. It's an all-limbs no-mind form of locomotion, as draining physically as it is emotionally. Sometimes I growl and shout in frustration, but nobody hears. When I close my eyes at night, the vile ranks march past me unceasingly, Mao's drab army, its helmets camouflaged. I'd like to grab a flamethrower and mow it down. "Pain is weakness leaving the body," a staff sergeant with more hair on his chest than on his head told me a lifetime ago. I wish he were here for a dose of mine.

The rain barely stops long enough for me to throw up the tent without its interior and my sleeping bag getting drenched. I should be less than half a mile from the Wind River cache, if it is there. When the rain briefly lets up and the clouds part, I see aufeis blink from the bluff where I've made my home. A thunderstorm unleashing pellet showers that take turns mills above my tent. During another lull I dart out and brew a cup of coffee, which I drink inside. I think dinner will be served cold and indoors as well.

GODZILLA IN THE MIST

DAY 25 (8 MILES)
QUAD: PHILIP SMITH MOUNTAINS
CACHE #3

This is a hard country for a hungry man.
—VILHJALMUR STEFANSSON, ethnographic diaries

I call Melissa in the morning thinking it is her birthday—except it was yesterday. *Where did I lose a day?*

More rain in the offing. Not thinking the cache would be in the floodplain, I slightly overshoot it hiking on the riverbank. But half the airstrip that two arms of the Wind River clasp is submerged, and the container *is* there. Are any of these resupplies going to be easy, a stroll up to the barrel? The river must have risen recently, because I cannot imagine Dirk landing within a strip this cramped or even trying to.

I wade some thigh-deep channels to retrieve cache number three after dumping my pack's contents on the shore. Aiming for Treasure Island, I shuffle sideways with the toes of my boots pointed upstream, trying to present the least amount of body surface to the pushy current. It's so strong that my hiking poles vibrate. I think I can hear them hum above boulders thudding in the streambed like icebergs against a ship's hull. Cobbles roll underfoot. A bow wave pillows on my groin. Having left the hip belt unclipped just in case I'm pulled under, I barely stay balanced and fail to keep the pack's bottom out of the water.

Back on the bank, having depleted my tank and feeling shaken up, I inhale a snack of pilot bread slathered with sunflower seed butter. Song snippets to the tune of *Rosamunde* rise from my Teutonic subconscious:

Then they hear a rumble on the floor, the floor
It's the big surprise they're waiting for . . .
Roll out the barrel, we'll have a barrel of fun . . .

I do not take to this Wind River country. It's brushy, boggy, tussocky, and wet-socky. An aufeis rink issues steam tendrils into the warm air above it.

Dear smart caribou. "Beaten men follow beaten paths," an old saying goes, but I gladly latch on to their trails, which line the fine shale in the drainage above the infernal willows. I ford a creek swollen by the storm and choked by alders. Near the valley's steep head, I slide one step back for each two I take upward, Sisyphus on crutches. On top of the "little pass" my map had led me to expect, clouds blot out the world, swirling gray with darker gray here and there, pieces of a mountain flank. White swaths appearing out of nowhere become snowfields. It's decidedly Hadean, a walk in the afterlife while carrying all my wrongdoings on my back. I'm not one hundred percent sure this is the right valley, but I drop in.

Just as I look forward to finally sailing down an open alpine meadow, I spot another bear. I labor uphill again to cut around her. Him? She does not notice me, although I am upwind. Perhaps she's just as fed up with this as I and wants to get the hell out of here. Or she may have just eaten. The valley bottom lies clear, a stage set for a drama, but from a tributary, clouds pour in as if from a special-effects machine. Wagner couldn't have arranged this any better. I glimpse the bear only now and then when I look over my shoulder, understanding how troll and Sasquatch myths congealed. I'm so glad I did not run into her higher up in those pea soup conditions.

I'll have to camp much lower in this valley, though the bear is feeding into that direction, leisurely, as they all do. She might walk through my camp later, I fear. I'm drained physically and mentally, and there are no decent campsites on hand. I can't do anything about that. Sometimes out here, you simply yield to fatalism, not expecting to wake up in the morning. If you do—all the more reason to celebrate the new day.

How many types of scary bear situations could there be? How many possible moves on a Rubik's Cube?

Abbey never saw a grizzly in his life.

Really? If you want to, you know where to find them. They will find you.

The weather breaks long enough for me to pitch my tent and cook dinner. Then it's back into seclusion, with the fly zipped by necessity, blinding me to what could come down the hill. The lone limping calf we saw on the Hulahula last year is suddenly me.

CARIBOU MINDS

DAY 26 (8 MILES)
QUAD: PHILIP SMITH MOUNTAINS

It's a leap day. At least that's what my notes for today say. Occasionally, I can no longer make sense of some cryptic map remark scribbled during the trip.

I did not get much sleep last night, afraid that the bear would show up. Rain showers move through the valley this morning, and the cloud ceiling obscures summits, but at least it has stopped pouring for now. The worst part of the day is peeling myself from the warmth of my sleeping bag and putting on damp socks and pants and especially clammy shoes, neither of which lately have had a chance to dry overnight, since I cannot drape clothes on the willows.

Surely, caribou fanning out and finding their route in varied terrain exercise some form of intelligence—it requires plenty from me. You learn a lot about them just by following them. They avoid ankle-busting cobbles and brush and tight gorges, preferring stretches that expose slinking predators. So do I, as a rule. They otherwise choose the most straightforward option, at least from their perspective, like water seeking the path of least resistance. Who says time does not figure into their calculations? They do err gravely at times, and hundreds have been found washed up dead in one five-mile section of swollen river on a single occasion.

A smart trail is logical, unavoidable, as much a product of physical as of mental efforts. It is "predetermined by the shape of the topography and the needs of its walkers," writes the environmental journalist Robert Moor. The same holds true for off-trail routes, some of which "are so elegant that they seem to lie sleeping just beneath the surface of the earth."

I'd like to think big game laid out all our original roads. Flying through tussocks, causing speed envy in me, caribou high-step and throw their legs sideways, flappers doing the Charleston. On hooves that splay as wide when pressing down as a man's hand with its fingers extended, they sail through swamps as if on snowshoes while I founder. They survived where camels, horses, mammoths, and scimitar cats did not, in part due to a "knowledge of danger and darkness and fear, built into their tissues by the centuries," as the nature writer Lois Crisler put it. I stick to their trails especially when they traverse steep scree or cut through alder thickets, though the caribou's narrower hips at times force me to walk pigeon-toed in their ruts. The songlines of our genome that the cultural critic Richard Louv references in *The Nature Principle* make us kin to the migrating creatures. We left Africa and we never arrived at our destination.

Psychologists now categorize sensitivity to the natural world as a type of intelligence that augments musical, spatial, emotional, logical, linguistic, and other forms. The complexity of the environment in which we grow up affects our perceptions and wayfinding skills. Worldwide, people raised in rural settings outperform those with roots in urban "training grounds much too undemanding for our spatial systems to develop anywhere near to their full potential," in the words of Erik Jonsson, the author of *Inner Navigation*. And among urbanites, people from cities with grid designs, say, Salt Lake City, score lower than those from Kathmandu, a maze that grew organically, like the layers of an onion. A full third of test subjects in another study were unable to form cognitive maps, models of learned fixed points, distances, and directions we hold in our mind and use to navigate. These folks wander confused around parking garages or when they step off a forest trail, getting lost in an elevator, one might unkindly say. "When we were a bit more nomadic and had to look around for things to eat, it probably mattered more," the lead investigator surmised.

Linguists chipping in add that speakers of about one-third of the world's languages do not employ left and right as their frame of spatial reference, terms relative to a person's position. Instead, there are absolutes, like cardinal directions, or parts of speech rooted in a local landscape, as in Yup'ik Eskimo upstream/downstream/across-river and up-coast/down-coast oppositions. Speakers of such languages are said to be more skilled at keeping track of their relative position even in unfamiliar places.

MICHAEL ENGELHARD

Caribou are as curious as toddlers. On river trips I sometimes stand up in my raft and, waving my paddle overhead, bait them; or I might put my hiking poles to my head like antlers and sway my body side to side. More often than not, the caribou step closer and closer, eyeing me nervously, until they can scent me or have had enough of this silly game and resume their trek.

A "guttural thrumming" at key moments in the migration surprised Karsten Heuer and Leanne Allison while eavesdropping on the Porcupine herd. Low-frequency "infrasonic" exchanges across distances much greater than those bridged by ultrasound have been documented for whales and elephants. I myself have never heard the phenomenon, which, Heuer believes, could be important to understanding communication that orchestrates the herd's moves and even may transcend species boundaries. This idea strongly resonates with the beliefs of Gwich'in Indian hunters who, claiming caribou as distant kin, say that they can converse with them.

Known special powers help caribou to forage more efficiently in the winter, when the landscape is bathed in bluish hues. Since they have ultraviolet vision, the UV-absorbent lichen on the reflective snow stands out black to them, as do urine splotches, a warning sign of wolves nearby. And their tapetum lucidum—a "bright tapestry" lining behind the eyes' retina—changes for the dimmer days so that extra photons bouncing back can hit their receptors. That change turns the resulting eyeshine (the proverbial glowing "deer-in-the headlights" stare) from golden yellow into a rich blue for that season. Caribou never suffer snow blindness, but human light sources at the oilfields may affect them.

When you're airborne, you appreciate differently the lines that their foot-loose generations have scored into turf. At times, they braid like the region's gravelly rivers, since herd members too can be choosy, setting divergent courses. In passes or similar bottlenecks, multiple strands become unified lanes, tokens of a single directional will. Staying on tracks, besides being safer, saves calories. Break a leg in this vastness, and you're in trouble. The routine inherent in trail hiking relieves the mind of route-finding tasks. This encourages daydreaming, and perhaps caribou aim their freed focus there.

When I doubt their sense of the landscape, or hundreds of hooves have churned their paths to mud, or I tire of waddling through swamp or tussocks on my relatively (to theirs) stumpy legs, I trade the slopes' dwarf birches (not nearly dwarfed enough) for a different punishment: river rocks the size of babies' heads.

I've wasted half the day looking for the up-and-over to the Middle Fork of the Chandalar. My waypoint, instead of marking the turn in the valley onto a new course, was a distance up that side drainage, and, trying different approaches, I could never get closer than 1.5 miles to that point in this involute country. Magellan on a good day could sail on a straight course, at least in theory. When I tried to go as directly for it as fancy flies, I got into some really rough country.

Monkshood: also "wolf's-bane" and "devil's helmet." I contemplate poisoning myself with its alkaloid, aconite, with which Aleut hunters killed whales, and Japan's Ainu killed bears, by smearing it on projectile points. I'm second-guessing my planned route at large. Should I have left later in the year and stayed more on the divide's north side to avoid brush? This will not be the last time I ask myself that question. The actual traverse into the Chandalar headwaters, when I find it, is embarrassingly easy. Unfortunately, the Middle Fork in this section is just as brushy as the Wind River.

It has been cloudy but not rained all day. Still, inevitably, I get doused just before I make camp at the only willow-free spot around—hallelujah—on a bluff overlooking the river, which roils latte brown from the recent rains.

At streamside camps like this I stash my bear barrel away from the river's edge after dinner, preferably hidden in a hollow or bush, paranoid that a griz batting it around might roll it into the current, which would turn it into a buoy bound for the Bering Strait. Petroleum deposits also attract bears as much as they do magnates, and I've seen punctured fuel bottles bruins chewed on, but there's nothing I can do about it. If it comes to that, I'll cook on a willow stick fire. Fossil fuel junkies, brown bears in a nature preserve in the Russian Far East have become hooked on discarded aviation and generator fuel barrels. They huff leftover gasoline and kerosene and have been found lying blissed out on their backs in the snow. Armed, twelve-hundred-pound addicts hoping for spillage even accost helicopters.

I pad and level the tent site, which is a bit lumpy and sloped, with reddish sphagnum, a peat builder with which the Nunamiut buffered "moss houses." Then there's a strange color in the sky too: blue. Not just patches either, but enough sun to dry out my gear and let me sit outside and read after dinner. It might be a fluke, but I'm as happy as if I had won the lottery. You have to gamble in order to win. In this light, even the shrub jungle looks like precious filigree.

ROBINSON CRUISING

DAY 27 (11 MILES)
QUAD: PHILIP SMITH MOUNTAINS

Back to gray and rain. It's hard not to let the weather's vagaries color my moods. "Considering its power over people's lives and emotions, it is not surprising that weather is the most fully personified element in the Koyukon physical world," Richard Nelson writes in *Make Prayers to the Raven*, his study of their belief system. I once more realize how sheltered from the elements we live inside our houses, apartments, and cubicles of transportation. They are parts of civilization's veneer that most of us take for granted. Lengthy solo backpacking in bear country reminds you of many of these, restoring them to their rightful position: a good night's sleep, human company and the exchange of ideas, a shower, truly clean socks, a bed you can simply fall into. While I cherish these luxuries upon each return from the wilds, their luster soon fades and other things again beckon. Is it just a memory lapse, forgetting the suffering hitched to beauty, or is this a case of grass always greener on the rougher side?

Crossing the river unnecessarily, I almost get swept off my feet. Cobbles slick with algae pave the bottom, which I gingerly feel with my feet before putting my full weight on them. Eddies downstream of boulders that breach the surface promise momentary relief from the current's insistence but can also mark pits it scooped out. I thought the going might be better on the far side. It isn't, and I recross. Weeks from now, such random lane switching will save me from serious injury.

The day passes with gravel bar walking, frequent willow thickets, and the fording of channels as the Chandalar careens down its bed like a drunk driver a road, ricocheting from bluff to bluff on its appointment with Alaska's matriarch river at Fort Yukon, 130 miles or a packrafting week to the south. I feel I spend more time in the water than out today. After open ground intermissions, approaching willows crowning above my head, I hail those stands with a hearty "Hey bear!" to alert any that might doze or browse inside that not-food is coming their way. When I get hoarse, I blow the signal whistle I tied to a backpack shoulder strap. Something inside me recoils from announcing my presence to a grizzly—I'd rather pass through unnoticed without drawing an ever-curious attention. It would be more foolishness, however, to surprise one and thereby provoke a defensive charge.

Wildlife has been absent since the grizzly in the mist except for the alarm calls of gray jays, a grating scolding. Perhaps animals are not fond, either, of this logy land, or its food sources are pitifully few, though more likely it simply better conceals the wildlings. I suspect the terrain and weather may skew my perception with tunnel vision. Still, I make excellent distance on this riparian route, reaching camp in the early afternoon. Or rather, I decide to call it camp (as I have none that are predesignated) since the sun puts in an appearance and I'd like to dry my stuff. I treat myself to a cuppa caffeine and enjoy the view up three conjoined valleys of a green knife-edge ridge that separates them.

I had my Robinson Crusoe moment today when I saw human footprints. I thought I was alone on my island. The boot print size hinted at a male. And the interloper could have run out of food and be prowling the tundra for man flesh. It's easy on this traverse to forget for large chunks of time that other people exist, and I certainly do not expect or want to cross paths with anybody. Except for the Kongakut packrafters and folks on the Haul Road and in Anaktuvuk, I won't before I reach the middle Noatak River.

My best chance of seeing a wolf is along such riverbanks, habitat seams that they patrol for birds' nests and ground squirrel burrows. I saw numerous tracks today, larger than those of dog paws, but so far, none of the track makers.

A ragged eye opens reluctantly above one of the mountains, framing a contrail, the trip's first, strangely ominous and somehow out of place. The white razorblade slash across blue jolts me from my reveries, from the refuge's timelessness.

I wonder if this journey will change me, and if so, how. Even before I left, I had a low tolerance for our society's take on modernity. You probably know by now what I mean, and I don't want to ruin the moment by diving into all that.

I think I will plan more long treks after this. The Grand Canyon (for next year?) tops my very short list.

Today, it takes fifteen minutes inside the sleeping bag to rewarm alabaster feet wrinkled like lumps of a French specialty cheese. Wringing out socks makes the difference between putting on wet ones or damp ones in the morning. If only I could force myself to tuck them inside the sleeping bag to dry them with body warmth overnight. I leave muddied pants in the vestibule, keeping a clean house.

FAREWELL TO A REFUGE

DAY 28 (11 MILES)
QUAD: PHILIP SMITH MOUNTAINS

Every man, every woman, carries in heart and mind the image of the ideal place, the right place, the one true home, known or unknown, actual or visionary.
—EDWARD ABBEY, *Desert Solitaire*

Overcast but with a high ceiling. Excellent walking up the creek, to another small but momentous divide. I am about to cross into Your Creek, to leave the refuge. Hiking its entire breadth has given me a better sense of its scale than the fact that it is as big as Georgia or Maine or some such state. (I had to look this up—it actually is about the size of South Carolina, more than thirty thousand square miles.) I realize that as in the Grand Canyon, all my journeys here—mere filaments on the map—can ever only scratch the surface. This place is too vast, too varied, and changing daily, to be contained in one person's mind. In one's soul? More likely. And yet, bureaucrats drew another line on their maps here, calling it quits.

For me, this sanctuary continues. It oozes beyond boundaries. Migratory birds and caribou leave for their wintering grounds, carrying this land's bounty as subcutaneous fat. Calves and chicks born here bear the memory of the coastal plain, which compels them to return. Arctic char visit the Beaufort Sea where they feast on krill. The bowheads and belugas never belonged to this soil but on their fall journey may recognize spits, barrier islands, and capes, and the taste of various rivers transporting the mountains' minerals. Creeks and streams fat with snowmelt will ring in my head as some blessed tinnitus wherever I'll go.

I have to kick steps up a snowfield on the last incline before the saddle. Fortunately, it isn't too icy or steep. In soft spots, I posthole up to my thighs.

Snow turns into Chandalar runoff with a melodious chuckle, eager to start its downhill rush to the Bering Sea. It clucks as it percolates through rocks underneath the crust. Don't break a leg here, getting caught between boulders a weak snow bridge may hide, I remind myself.

On the far side, in upper Your Creek, still three hundred feet within the refuge according to my map, I pass through the densest patch of arctic forget-me-nots I have ever seen. Whole fistfuls cluster in minibouquets. If you could fill their scent into bottles, you'd get rich. Has anybody tried? It's a flashy send-off, a prompt to remember this heath.

Except for their white wings, showing only when they rattle off as I flush them, the rock ptarmigans or "snow chickens" now wear summer outfits of brown-and-golden chain mail armor. Their deranged, staccato, guttural *kok-kok-kok* still startles me every time, making my heart jump, an uncontrollable reflex. The flashing white and alarm call serve to distract enemies from a nest. They can also spell the birds' death. When discovered and "put up," Audubon noted, they are "easily shot, on account of the beautiful regularity of their flight." Painters, like hunters, excel with a steady hand.

The refuge shows its best side just to break my heart and make parting difficult. You never know if you'll return to a beloved place. The gods laugh while we're making our plans. It has been rewarding to spend enough time here on this traverse to witness incremental changes as the season unfolds—flowers blooming, green berries forming, then blushing, mushrooms popping from soil, tender sticky buds on the poplars exploding, chicks scuttling about, midges jigging exuberantly, bumblebee queens hustling after overwintering underground, and bears teaching their cubs and filling out, approaching peak plumpness again.

At the lower east fork of Your Creek, I pass a cabin and outhouse, the first human structures besides airstrips since I flew out of Arctic Village a month ago.

I cover much ground today and even manage to set up camp by the creek without getting spit on. This milestone calls for a celebration, and I allocate an extra round of sunflower seed butter on pilot bread. Cache number four waits on a strip beside the Haul Road three moderate days to the west.

Whenever the weather allows it, with my journaling and exploring of the neighborhood finished, dishes done, and my ration of book pages devoured or saved for the morrow, I spend hours lazing outside my tent, simply being, thinking, and taking things in. Away from the built environments, e. e. cummings's "world of made" that makes us mistake ourselves for gods, I realize again that my worth equals that of a pika, a dryas, a bee, or a moss. If physical adaptation is the measure, they even surpass me. They all fit their niches, the "world of born," belonging without knowing it, while I, chafing against few life paths mapped out for me, have never felt that I really did.

LIMINAL

DAY 29 (11 MILES)
QUAD: PHILIP SMITH MOUNTAINS

The instant I put my pack on, it starts to rain. Well, you can't get wetter than down to skin level, and the goal is to stay warm, not dry. Based on an ultralight handbook's recommendations, I bought Special Forces raingear that I wear almost daily. It was cheaper than Gore-Tex, which half the time does not fully protect you either. The Green Beret suit barely slows down seepage, while the fumes from its coating give me headaches.

There are more cabins at the mouth of the east fork of Your Creek. I am on state land now, so these could be homesteads. No airstrip is evident; the building materials were possibly sledded or helicoptered here. Inupiaq allotments inside the refuge were grandfathered in when the Arctic Range was established—Robert Thompson owns one at Lake Schrader between the Hulahula and the Canning and talks about wanting to build a fishing cabin there. The lake trout, he says, are delicious. These "dinosaurs of the deep" really are landbound char that can live more than fifty years and weigh as many pounds.

I circumvent a female bear and her yearling cub on a hillside unnoticed. Up, up, and up I go.

Another day, another pass.

A pass a day keeps the doctor away.

This too shall pass.

That is the price of the headwaters route I chose through the Brooks Range, not that I know of any that could avoid such a slew of divides.

Descending on the opposite side, I step through rotten snow in the gully and almost dislocate my shoulder again trying to break my fall. Camouflaged with a layer of gravel and grit, it promised firm ground. Watching my steps carefully now, I nearly miss a sublime scene. Light angling through a sky portal falls on a mountain's wet stone flanks, which briefly gleam like old silver.

I have difficulties finding a campsite and end up, tired, on another river bar. After raining on me during dinner, the weather turns sunny. It's nice to just sit and not have to move. As my next resupply is close, I wolf down a second dinner. The metaphor has never been more apt, mainly for the sound effects.

BASIC INSTINCTS

DAY 30 (9.5 MILES)
QUAD: PHILIP SMITH MOUNTAINS

Overcast with a high cloud ceiling gray as a prison blanket. Altostratus is generally considered the most boring of all cloud types. Two yellow warblers pursue each other in the bushes in a flurry of hairpin turns, vying for a warblerette or a prime nest site. They are streaks of color, sun flashes brightening this drab day. A lesser yellowlegs squirts out from underfoot. Two turquoise eggs dappled with brown sit between rocks near the creek on a thatch of collected compressed grass reminiscent of my own sparse furnishing taste. The clutch looks incomplete. It is a redpoll's, I think. I see these tiny puffballs in April at our Fairbanks birdfeeder, where they stop to stuff themselves on the way north. Some of these finches overwinter in the Arctic, as do ptarmigans, ravens, and snowy owls—only eleven bird species live here year-round. The male redpoll "courtship-feeds the female by regurgitation," my guidebook says. Similarly, in Eskimo societies a young man desiring a woman would bring game to her father's household to prove his competence as a provider. Thus, the biological once more intersects with the cultural.

Things also look spartan on the far side of my daily pass: a fun jungle-gym scramble down a tight gorge that forces me to rock hop and wade ankle deep in the icy creek.

I next find a ptarmigan foot, with its digging claws. Its white winter feathers insulate the bird's culotte legs and the snowshoe feet that let it float on top to reach buried willows on which it feeds. There's nothing else. Some predator must have dropped it or lost its appetite after consuming the rest. A foot or severed wing implicates a raptor; true gourmets, falcons above all relish ptarmigan breast muscles and brains. Feathers as if from a pillow fight signal the less surgical feasting of a wolf or a fox on a heavenly dish descended to earth. I love the mystery of animal signs for the yarns they make me spin. They're clues for the naturalist's reverse engineering of stories. While tracks dominate in the winter, at this time of year there remains plenty of evidence strewn across the tundra.

I, on the other hand, try to pass through without leaving a trace. I bury my crap (did not bring toilet paper), build no cairns, no fires (not needed in the summer and the wood has been very wet anyway), and take nothing from here, no souvenirs, not even photos. Once in a very rare while I harvest clumps of moss to cushion an ascetic tent site or more often, spongy handfuls as bum wipes. These scars may heal within ten years but are nothing compared to those bears inflict on the landscape. I take pride in blending in rather well, not needing reassurance that I existed through my mark left on the world. It would not be right to needlessly mar the land that so enriches me.

The North Fork of the Chandalar, which I enter only briefly, as far as I can tell is the first stream since before the Wind that is not complete 'shwhack—that's guide lingo for a bushwhack. (Yes, we can do the Aussies one better.)

A ptarmigan I flush flies at me, hissing—very unusual. In the commotion, five, six, or seven brown sparrow-size birds also scatter. They must be her brood. She then sprints ahead of me, low to the ground, her back hunched, her head down. A ruse to lure me away. I hope they all reunited.

Boykinia or "bearflower," which grows only in Alaska and the Yukon, densely spikes a slope with spires of many white blossoms. It's a survivor of the ice age, the last of at least four that gripped this range, and grizzly bears relish it. *There should be a bear here given all these*, I think. Next, I poke some scat that looks pretty fresh. *I better blow my whistle.* I do and keep walking. Less than ten paces later: a bear in the creek, with her head up, scanning the area. Perhaps she heard me. I duck and walk uphill and around her. I believe she never senses me. The sighting happens close to today's destination, but since I don't know if she'll go up-valley or down-valley or stick around, I don't want to camp nearby. I continue to a mountain meadow close to my final pass before the Haul Road. There seems to be no food of interest to a bear there, so I feel better.

MAGELLAN AND ME

DAY 31 (10.5 MILES)
QUAD: PHILIP SMITH MOUNTAINS
CACHE #4

Heavy rains and gusts last night. This morning, cloud remnants boil in the valley and altostratus puts a lid on it above those. I rally for this section's ultimate pass.

From its top, I glimpse the distant gray band of the Haul Road and the silver thread of the Prudhoe Bay pipeline before clouds shutter the view. This is what Magellan must have felt when he beheld the storm-lashed strait at South America's tip that was to be named after him. He'd successfully grabbed the tail of the beast slumbering at the margins of maps, where cartographers noted: "Here be dragons." Actually, my joy rather might equal his upon reaching the home port of Seville again—except that he never did, dying partway through his circumnavigation of the globe. My thousand miles pale in the face of the survivors' sixty thousand, as do my 31 days so far to their 1,082.

I've been hiking for exactly a month now and have never been as happy to see the damn oil drain. It almost chokes me up a little. With this duct in sight, I feel confident that, barring an accident, I can reach the Noatak on foot. Prior to the trip, based on my study of the maps, I thought the leg from the Wind River to this pass would be the hardest. Now that it lies behind me, I hope that it was. It tested me with six major divides compared to the two that await me before Anaktuvuk. The country was brimming with brush because most of the drainages I traversed ran down the south—the forest—side of the Continental

Divide. It rained on me or my tent, from a sprinkle to a downpour, every single day. My feet were only ever dry inside the sleeping bag.

Naturally, the weather and bugs could get so truly atrocious in the weeks ahead that I'll miss my good old days in the refuge.

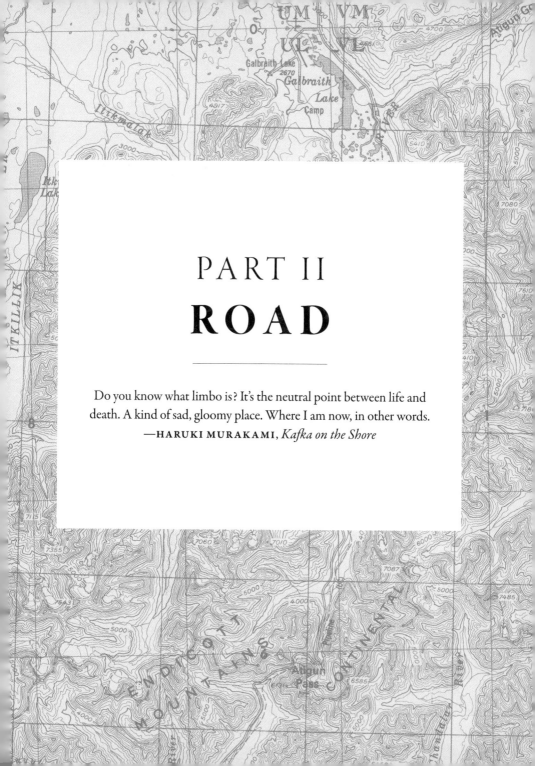

PART II
ROAD

Do you know what limbo is? It's the neutral point between life and death. A kind of sad, gloomy place. Where I am now, in other words.
—HARUKI MURAKAMI, *Kafka on the Shore*

TROUBLE AND COFFEE CAKE AT THE DOT

Many men are happier, and find it less strain, to fight against
wind and wet, cold and fatigue, than against telephones and timetables.
—**CHARLES EVANS**, expedition leader on Kangchenjunga

Three miles south of Atigun Pass, I cross under the pipeline that in some places is elevated, allowing the passage of wildlife, mainly bears, muskoxen, and caribou, but foremost, to keep the hot pulsing oil from melting the permafrost, which would skew the structure. I idiotically wait to hear crude being pushed south in the steel life-support system's four-foot pipe. But it makes no sound. So much concentrated power, so quiet. This may be a feeding tube for an ailing patient, but it spells trouble for the planet. The engineering marvel impresses the techno-logically minded, people who believe with religious fervor that human ingenuity will vault all hurdles, including a global reckoning.

I once toured the crown and guts of Glen Canyon Dam, the concrete arc that stoppers the Colorado and bloats it into Glen Canyon Reservoir, better known as Lake Powell. The tour guide's litany of gigantism quickly numbed my mind. His statistics, and the pipeline's, toot the horn of a species impressing itself. The blare drowns out tallies of other species disappearing; numbers of decimation within species still hanging on; graphs of sea and land temperatures rising beyond anybody's control. And the gap between the two data sets since that visit has only widened.

I follow the gravel track blazed parallel to the pipeline to service it. Ned Rozell, an acquaintance, once walked its eight hundred miles from the Valdez shipping terminal to the Prudhoe Bay source with his dog, Jane, and wrote a book about their experience. He retraced the steps of that 120-day journey twenty years later, again with a dog, which admittedly offers some bear protection. Friends and family joined him for a few sections. While I doff my cap to the feat, I can't quite comprehend the desire behind it.

How strange to walk on a path this wide and smooth. It jars after the soft tundra as if I were wearing wooden clogs. My progress seems slower, though it is not, and quickly gets boring. I already drool at the thought of the cache's contents and tonight's splurge. I wonder if during my absence a nuclear flash or flaring pandemic has ended civilization, a thought other arctic wayfarers relay. The last man alive frets about pasta and Reese's cups.

When I arrive at the Chandalar Shelf strip, a graveled affair much longer and broader than previous runways on this trip: nada. *I cannot believe this*. I scurry up and down it in distress like a commuter who missed his flight or lost his wallet on the tarmac. This was supposed to be easy, a smooth drop-off and pickup—the strip, obvious on the map, is only sixty-seven miles from Coyote Air's home base in Coldfoot.

After searching for about half an hour, I walk to the DOT complex on the other side of the Haul Road to get to the bottom of this. (The depot must be one of the country's most scenic, but I don't currently have an eye for the beauty.)

Before crossing the road, I look right and look left, a compliant first grader. How ironic and unfortunate it would be to get flattened by an eighteen-wheeler after sleeping with bears and scaling icy passes for a month.

The DOT camp looks deserted. Armageddon is still in the cards. I knock on a few doors. Nobody answers. I finally enter unbidden and walk down a hallway, through another door into a garage the size of an airport hangar. A guy in oil-stained coveralls at a workbench is on a phone, a radio playing softly next to him.

"Excuse me," I croak, no longer used to using my voice, which sounds unfamiliar. He looks up with an expression not unlike that of the thru hiker I surprised at Grasser's last year, though I doubt this guy is expecting a bear here, inside. After days of silence, I feel I should have more important things to say than "Can I use your phone?" But right now, nothing *is* more important.

I explain my situation, and he offers me coffee cake while he finishes his call. He talks for half an hour, a hallway clock tells me. I'm back in the busy world of men, I guess. Solid walls feel strange too; my semitransparent tent, whose front I roll up most of the time unless it rains sideways, hardly qualifies as indoors.

When the DOT guy hangs up, I punch in Coyote Air's number. I could have on my satellite phone but thought better of it, expecting a lengthy conversation. Money still matters, and electronic disturbances would make an already arduous task only harder.

The pilot's wife, Danielle, answers. She tells me Dirk did not want to leave my cache at the airstrip "too early" because hunters might mess with it. I tell her I am too early because I am starving and that it is not really hunting season yet. She informs me that they still don't know where to put my Noatak cache, with the boat, as the river's level has been rapidly changing. I do vaguely remember that from the cache I retrieved on the Wind River like Moses parting the seas. She wants me to call from Anaktuvuk again so that she can give me the Noatak coordinates once Dirk has delivered the big steel drum holding my kit. (Bears are notorious for chewing on nonedibles also, snowmachine seats and rubber boats.) But she does not want me to call before the thirteenth—that's ten days away, and it will never take me that long to reach Anaktuvuk. I tell her I don't want to hang around the village for days only to make a call. She hasn't even mentioned how I'm to receive the current cache before dinnertime. Dirk is probably out flying. I am starting to percolate.

She suggests "we" should perhaps cancel "the whole thing" because I seem unhappy. *Seriously? Damn right I'm unhappy after all the planning I've done.* I sense the past month's magic slipping away like shed snakeskin. I was trying to minimize human contact and complications for the duration of my traverse. Something else must be wonky, I suspect, but I have no idea what it might be. Impatient, I offer to hitchhike to Coldfoot to collect my stuff in person.

Perhaps out of guilt and a smidgen of professionalism or else not wanting to lose the delivery fee, she says she'll drive the supplies up to the DOT, which will take a couple of hours. *Never mind that I paid for air freight and will not get a refund.*

I wait outside by the airstrip. Eventually, her office assistant pulls up and hands me my garbage bag full of grub. Danielle either lacked time or the spine to face me. I vow to never do business with Coyote Air again. The outfit I work for uses their services though, so this could become awkward on some future trip I might guide. I realize what a litmus test soloing has been in regard to responsibility. With no one around, and the terrain and the weather irreproachable, you cannot blame people when things go sideways—a burden as much as it is a relief.

Dreading the thought of spending a night near this semi-industrial site, I hike another four miles south on what is officially the Dalton Highway to pick up my route on the west side, very close to the boundary of Gates of the Arctic National Park.

This two-lane 414-mile umbilicus linking Fairbanks and the Arctic Ocean is my favorite road, but that's not saying much, coming from a tree-hugging Luddite. Lovers of disturbed soils, bird vetch and white sweet clover have colonized the highway and river corridors, kept barely in check by volunteers. A crashed tanker truck spilled two thousand gallons of oil, and wildlife has become more accessible to hunters; I met a trucker who shot a six-foot wolf there opportunistically. The road was named after James W. Dalton, a graduate of UAF serving with the Naval Construction Battalions (CBs or "Seabees") in the Pacific theater. He helped engineer the Distant Early Warning Line during the Cold War, remnants of which can be seen in Kaktovik, and worked as a consultant for the North Slope's Naval Petroleum Reserve. James was the second son of Jack Dalton, who in 1896 pioneered a livestock route from Pyramid Harbor on the Lynn Canal in Southeastern Alaska to the Yukon interior's goldfields. His was the Klondike's only trail built largely by a single man. The Skagway paper called him "perhaps the most famous pathfinder in Alaska." Tougher than fossilized mammoth ivory, he put snowshoes on packhorses, thought nothing of snowshoeing fifty miles to a cache in one day, and kept a shotgun loaded with rock salt chunks under the bar of a saloon he owned, to deal with unruly customers.

The sun appears, and with each mile I simmer down. Drivers pass me in their bubble of engine roar, glancing curiously but without a wave, or flashing headlights or a thumbs-up, or stopping to ask if I might need anything. I don't. Nothing they could give anyway.

I stop briefly at one of the Haul Road's tourist attractions: a black spruce. It's the northernmost one along this truckers' route, a sign proclaims, a lone outlier of the tree line. "Please don't cut it down," the sign pleads. I think this means the tree, not the sign. The tree's pitiful state reminds me of a Koyukon myth about a woman who heard a tale so sad that she gouged her skin until she started to cry. She transformed into the very first spruce tree, with skin equally tortured and rough, and wept resin tears.

Unfortunately, this roadside specimen is no credit to a race that, looking as if a drunk trimmed each tree with a chainsaw, does not elicit gawps or applause even in its prime. I am not badmouthing *Picea mariana* here, a true survivor whose shallow root system can take hold in acidic thawed soggy soil only ten inches deep. Hardy evergreens also save energy by not regrowing leaves each year, as deciduous trees must. At their farthest north extension, their tops thicken like clubs above skinnier waists.

In 1956, Olaus Murie found one white spruce ten inches in diameter on the upper Sheenjek that was 298 years old. Now, beetle invasions and drought weaken Alaska's boreal spruce, which increasingly wither, fall to high winds, or go up in smoke. In evolution's arms race, the bugs developed pheromones to communicate with each other, thereby locating mates and susceptible host trees. Black spruce seldom gets infested, and white spruce targets insects with special chemicals of its own.

The farthest north Haul Road spruce is dead—killed perhaps by exhaust or shame from the mockery of too many tourists. Yes, vacationers ride to Prudhoe Bay in camper vans, shuttles, trucks, and rattletrap cars, and on motorcycles or bicycles. Years ago, a Japanese man walked north on this highway harnessed to a rickshaw-style trailer in which he would sleep. People noticed it parked by the roadside at some point, without any trace of him. It turns out he was recovering from his ordeal, with friends in Whitehorse, Canada, I believe. I don't know if he returned to finish his walk to the Arctic Ocean.

I too have utilized the Dalton as a springboard with belly-flopping potential for bargain high latitude ventures. Though traffic tends to be sparse, you are constantly dodging semis, which is especially scary in muddy conditions. On dry days, the monsters fling shrapnel, spider-webbing your windshield. You can tell veteran Fairbanks Haulers by their trucks' scars. Vegetation in the margins gets coated with dust, and at crucial curves like the Atigun Pass switchbacks, sprinkler trucks dampen the surface with recycled lube oil or with water sucked from a tundra pond. With permafrost in decline now, the road is prone to flooding, washouts, and burial by debris flows. "Them State Boys" on the Chandalar Shelf will stay busy for years to come.

I turn off the highway where black spruce trees marching in loose ranks toward the famous fatality up the road crowd into the Dietrich River valley. A witches' cauldron of weather is brewing to the north, so I hurry across the knee-deep river and into the adjacent greenbelt, my only stint of true boreal forest hiking on this trip; my fear of the storm overcomes my aversion to trees. Having located a small clearing on a knoll, I set up the tent in record time and barely manage to flop inside like a beached salmon before lightning, thunder, and rain arrive. I sit enveloped by flapping fabric, hoping it will hold. I've had similar squalls break tent poles before.

Dinner will have to wait. What a day. Happy Fourth!

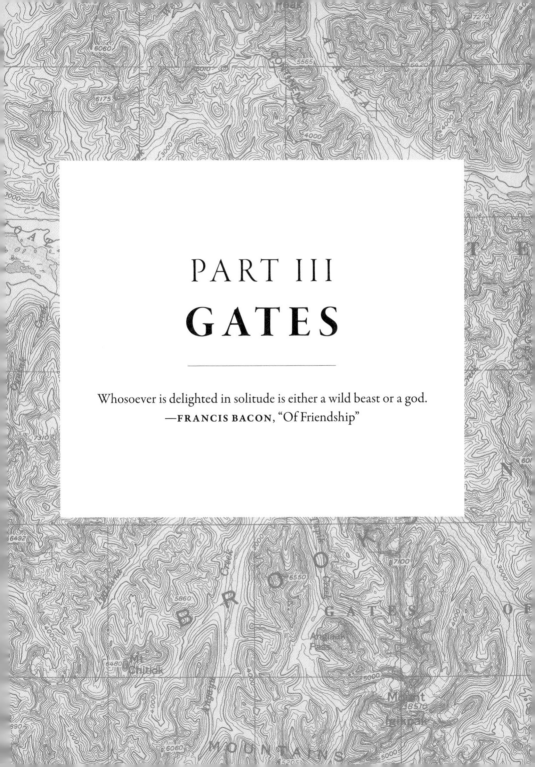

PART III
GATES

Whosoever is delighted in solitude is either a wild beast or a god.
—FRANCIS BACON, "Of Friendship"

INTO THE GLORIOUS UNKNOWN AGAIN

DAY 32 (8 MILES)
QUAD: PHILIP SMITH MOUNTAINS

Around maybe one in the morning, sounds from a creature in pain awaken me. It starts with a barely audible whine, then mounts into a moan, then reaches a fevered pitch, thin, piercing. Again. I pop from my tent, in socks, bear spray in hand, and there it is—slightly downhill, the color of smoke against evergreens, under a single orange-lit storm cloud: my first wolf of the trip. He instantly sees me but keeps on howling, throwing his head back with each new exclamation, nose pointed heavenward. He seems to invite me or to expect a response, so I join in. Not your typical wolf howls, neither his nor mine, but we both understand. Understand what? Certainly not each other. But perhaps a longing for companionship, or simply the urge to let loose, to listen to echoes, to find out if the world might answer. One has to be wary of anthropomorphizing in the presence of such haunting wild music. Still, I'm not the only one doing this. "'Howling' is a poor word to use" for wolf vocalizations, the father of boreal ecology William O. Pruitt Jr. averred, adding, "'Singing' would be better."

After a while, the wolf has had enough and vanishes into the trees as if he had never existed. This encounter less than a quarter mile from the road is extraordinary in the truest sense of that word. As it was happening, a tractor truck's growling mixed with our voices in a strange composition of the motorized and the animated.

I return to my sleeping bag, which has retained some warmth.

I'm still buzzing from this dawn duet, which made it hard to fall asleep again. The old cloud-and-rain show puts in another performance but somehow it bothers me less. If this is the price I must pay for transcendence, so be it.

A Siberian aster is rayed in pale purple—must not overlook the ordinary in search of the extraordinary. This aster, a final bloom, shuts the door softly at the far end of summer.

I enter the park without any admission fee, camping permit, or even a sign that announces it. Its boundary here aligns with the Continental Divide, over which I have just skipped again. On the other side: Kuyuktuvuk Creek. The names alone inspire curiosity, word time capsules that entice dreamers with visionary topographies. Each one is a peephole into the past, a mnemonic juncture of language, history, and geography.

As a graduate anthropology student, I participated in a multiyear land use and subsistence study the Park Service had financed. I collected place-names of Gates of the Arctic and Kobuk Valley National Parks. Preliminary analysis hinted at Athabaskan roots for some of the mostly Inupiaq terms. This was exciting, relevant, as any Alaska Native group able to prove historical use of federally protected lands is entitled to hunt, fish, and trap on them.

Faced with my roll of maps, elders I interviewed spelled out fishing holes, traplines, hunting camps, trading spots, birthplaces, or graves where ancestral bones hallowed the ground like calcified roots. Patterns became obvious. Inupiaq and Athabaskan place-names never elevated individuals. People were simply not important enough to be honored thus in a storyscape composed of larger, longer-lasting things. Anglos, conversely, employed the possessive case and glorifed White explorers, expedition sponsors, surveyors, admirals, traders, homesteaders, or McKinley, a president overseeing the iconic gold rushes who never bothered to visit the new acquisition. There's a James Dalton Mountain thirteen miles to the northeast, a still-glaciered massif, blandly named for the father or son; I don't know which. Eskimo toponyms, by comparison, include gems like "Ridge Where We Cry," "The Old Lady Made It That Far," and another classic, "Where Arrows with Excrement Are Shot Down," an early instance of biological warfare, each hinting at events that changed or ended lives.

The truth behind names can be elusive. Deadhorse, the industrial settlement that sprung up in Prudhoe Bay, commemorates freight haulers whose first contract was for dead Fairbanks livestock; or else, investing in this trucking company was as promising as betting on a nag bound for the knacker. Transplants often projected longings onto Alaska. With its sinuous twists, the Arctic refuge's Hulahula River to whalers suggested dances they'd witnessed in balmy Hawaii. "Landscape," according to the art critic Simon Schama, "is a work of the mind. Its scenery is built up as much from strata of memory as from layers of rock." Place-names accrue into veneers of meaning. They anchor terrain in our imagination, claiming and taming it.

Gates of the Arctic, the northernmost and second-largest US national park—bigger than Belgium—unrolls before my boots under a leaden, squally sky. These are mountains without tollbooths or handrails. It is land free and undeveloped, as some of it should be, land each person should enjoy according to his or her abilities.

We owe much to Robert "Bob" Marshall, a twentieth-century John Muir and advocate of the Central Brooks Range. "Let's keep Alaska largely a wilderness," he urged Congress in 1938. The New York forester with the boyish face and goofy smile arrived in the uncharted territory he'd selected from his atlas months before the Great Depression and began to study tree growth at the northern timberline for a thesis about the effects of climate on political history. He was also searching for a rumored tree with pine needles and the bark of a cottonwood, a Douglas-fir he thought based on the description, which he never found.

He already was larger than life—and brimming with it. He'd summited his first Adirondack peak at fifteen; decades later he still loved running down slopes. Frugal and modest despite being wealthy, shy except during dances and parties, Marshall was a romantic, an admirer of Lewis and Clark who felt he'd been born too late. He sometimes portaged in tennis shoes or subsisted only on raisins and cheese. He planned to take a thirty-mile day hike in every US state. His sense of humor favored the absurd. He once entered a room somersaulting through the doorway, change flying from his pockets, crowing, "I just rolled in." Another time he daubed shoe polish onto his underwear to keep the holes that mice had nibbled into his tux from showing at a formal dinner.

An activist with socialist leanings, he shared royalties from his 1930 memoir *Arctic Village* with the Wiseman folks it so lovingly portrayed. He stayed a bachelor his entire, truncated life. Perhaps his biggest accomplishment was cofounding and funding the Wilderness Society, which focused the movement for protecting what is now Gates of the Arctic National Park.

"There is just one hope," Marshall intoned in a seminal article, "of repulsing the tyrannical ambition of civilization to conquer every niche on the whole earth. That hope is the organization of spirited people who will fight for the freedom of the wilderness." In November 1939, when he was thirty-eight, the dynamo heart that had propelled him up countless mountains gave out on a midnight train ride from Washington, DC, to New York.

While there can be no room for the possessive in wilderness—land "gloriously fresh" with "no musty signs of human occupation"—the rough paradise he helped to preserve will be Bob's Country forever.

The going is the best since before the Wind River. I cross a shale flow where a mountainside is eroding, filling a ravine with a moraine of firm black fine-grained material like compacted mud. The gravel bars along the creek are much smoother too, perhaps because these mountains contain less limestone and more shale. Oolah Pass in the approach looks much lower and mellower than most of the unnamed divides in the Philip Smith Mountains I have put behind me.

I camp early at the pass, unable to resist. It's the most beautiful place yet on this trip of superlatives, beating even my tent site on the West Sheenjek. The map did not, could not, and should not prepare me for this. An emerald lake rimmed with perfect, flat shingle beaches and velvet-green moss banks lights up this mountain bowl. It's truly alpine, this Continental Divide nook, unlike the bug-ridden bogs of lower saddles. The lake by my tent, which naturally faces the water, mirrors snow patches on the talus into Rorschach blots. The tips of distant peaks at my back, where I entered the bowl from Kuyuktuvuk Creek, spur "top of the world" feelings, a euphoria well earned. Gulls and semipalmated plovers wail poised on the tarn's crystal surface, the only sounds besides whispers of a rill spilling from the amphitheater's heights.

I'll be traversing to the north side three times before my next resupply, cache number five, in Anaktuvuk, which also straddles the divide. A curved, naked, sawtooth range blocks the view down the valley I'll be descending tomorrow toward the Itkillik River—perhaps it's the one Marshall named for its resemblance to an Eskimo skin scraper. In his days, North Slope Inupiat traveled this pass in the Endicott Mountains to work or trade in Wiseman, twenty-six miles north of present-day Coldfoot. The latter settlement originated during a minor gold rush to the Middle Fork of the Koyukuk in 1902, when the Klondike and Nome claims had dried up or been consolidated into corporate holdings. The mining camp allegedly earned its moniker from prospectors returning with frost-blackened toes; in its heyday it had two stores, seven saloons, two inns or "roadhouses," and a "gambling house" employing ten "Goodtime Girls."

A little more than a month into my journey, I'm falling apart. Enjoying the luxury of afternoon coffee under a tentative sun, I lose a filling chomping on salmon jerky. My right shoulder throbs from the previous dislocations, and the Achilles tendon on my left foot pinches; my pack is too heavy again for midweight boots that do not give enough ankle support but supposedly keep your legs from tiring as soon. I console myself with the thought that Marshall, famous for forty-mile days, schlepped a seventy-pound pack with a tumpline along nearby Ernie Creek and was forced to rest three times along each mile. This is a hard country.

Marshall learned that early in his Wiseman-based explorations. "Gaily daring the unknown," he had set out with one companion on his first probe of the Arctic Divide in July 1929. The pair almost drowned when the Koyukuk's rain-swollen North Fork flooded their island camp. The experience energized Marshall. Here was a place, finally, where nature had not yet been declawed.

I call Melissa in the evening, venting about Coyote Air. Flickers of distant lightning followed by thunder.

TO THE ITKILLIK

DAY 33 (9.5 MILES)
QUAD: CHANDLER LAKE

Chilly this morning after a hard rain last night. Swaths of gray mix with smidgens of blue. One lonely gull kept me awake for hours, shrieking repetitively, monotonously, echoing in the cirque, beyond the reach of my throbbing throwing arm.

There's a lot of weather talk in these pages, I realize. But it determines so much, setting a tone for the days, creating obstacles and diversions, constantly changing a landscape that can feel lifeless, immutable. Strangely, it provides a grasp on time's slippage when calendar dates and the days of the week have become meaningless.

The mountains appear more dramatic here than in most places I've seen in the refuge, jagged, nose-diving shipwrecks or broken fangs, and more waterfalls vein them. I gape at a truly apocalyptic scene where a slope seems to have melted. The bottom is a dead zone reminiscent of World War I battlefields, a mess of craters and tumuli but studded with cabin-size boulders. I wonder if the devastation came gradually or in a flash, as a landslide. Incongruously, meltwater the color of swimming pools has gathered in ponds, and the creek in a lake where the slide blocked it. Traversing this obstacle course is time consuming. But when God made time, as the Irish say, he made plenty of it. Here, it is visible.

The creek has carved out a breach amid chaos and continues unhindered on its run to the Itkillik. The bugs are marauding in force, spawned perhaps by the stagnant water, perfect breeding grounds for the beasts. Sun wins this afternoon, though clouds like baroque wigs threaten all around. I hike past bleached caribou skulls and antlers, signs of Nunamiut hunters pursuing the Central Arctic herd. These, unlike their whaling kin, truly are "People of the Land," inland Eskimos.

An angelic white wing with its shoulder joint and the bird's blood jeweling lichen unsubtly declares that I too am meat—nothing new there, but the carnage spawns some unease. Landscapes littered with body parts unbalance us. Still, life enfolds me, and death is integral to it. Shrieking jaegers defending their nest strafe me. Smaller skuas, they are acrobatic fliers with hook bills and nine-inch stiletto tails. They swoop in for frontal attacks, target your eyes with their feet, bill, or wings, and then wheel about for a pass from behind. At sea, they're "piratical," hounding other birds until they upchuck fishes they've caught. The German name *Falkenraubmöwe*, "falcon robber gull," perfectly sums up the jaeger's mind and elegance.

Next, I rouse a ptarmigan hen and her brood; seeking cover, the unfledged chicks carom apart like struck billiard balls. The one closest to me, a downy mottle of chestnut, gold, and black, presses itself into a hollow, perfectly camouflaged, as the hen stands by, clucking.

If the land lets me, I'll sleep on the banks of the Itkillik tonight.

WHERE MOUNTAINS AREN'T NAMELESS

DAY 34 (8.5 MILES)
QUAD: CHANDLER LAKE

Sun on the tent wakes me up, but already clouds roil all around. Three lakes and a cabin in the marshy flats—probably an Inupiaq or Anglo inholding—occupy the Continental Divide. The biggest lake supplies the North Fork of the Koyukuk, which hurries south to join the Yukon near the Nulato Hills. The Itkillik on the divide's north side gathers speed and runoff from Snowheel Mountain to contribute to the Colville, whose North Slope meanders unload their cargo in the Beaufort Sea.

According to Orth, my go-to toponymic compendium—it lists tongue-twisting doozies like Dakeekathlrimjingia Point and Nunathloogagamiutbingoi Dunes whose gist remains obscure—an Inupiaq map drawn in 1900 identifies the It-kil-lik or Indian River. An Inupiaq elder in Anaktuvuk Pass remembered it as "the place where Eskimos had a big battle with Indians," most likely Chandalar Gwich'in. I wonder if Koyukon hunters from Hughes or Allakaket traveled along this corridor, in the ways I earlier mentioned, into the Brooks Range.

Sluicing through North Slope foothills, the Itkillik scalloped and polished a hundred-foot bluff of permafrost soil ten to fifty thousand years old like obsidian knapped for a spearhead. Its melting face released early horse, steppe bison, and mammoth bones together with gases from rotting fossilized peat and carcasses, and thus was dubbed Stinking Hills. Mammoths, inveterate walkers like humans, evolved in Africa and, cutting swaths across Europe and Asia, branched into different species, two of which tramped into North America by way of Beringia. About 13,500 BCE, hunters of East Asian descent with their dogs and families crossed Bering Strait seafloor exposed when late-Pleistocene icecaps storing more snow lowered ocean levels 160 feet. They scouted Alaska's interior and the Yukon, opportunistically spearing or scavenging reddish-orange, strawberry-blond, or chestnut-brown woolly jumbos. Those made up one-third of Alaska's paleo-mammal biomass. Tusks or bones eroding from cutbanks and river bluffs remain not uncommon.

In 1815, Otto von Kotzebue probing the Pacific for the Russian tsar found "a very fine tooth" near the settlement that today bears his name. Nineteenth-century rumors of surviving mammoths were owed to a zoologist aboard the US revenue cutter *Corwin* to whom Inupiat on Cape Prince of Wales offered bones and tusks in trade. Bering Strait Eskimos long familiar with half-buried pachyderm parts they carved into tools took them as proof of mythical creatures tunneling underground that died when they surfaced, inhaling. The beast the collector sketched for them on the ship's deck embodied the enigma whose continued existence they might then have affirmed.

From the valley bottom, Peregrine Pass, slotted between two massive knife edges, downright intimidates, especially under the gloom of sky only slightly less dark than the embracing mountains. From up close, I realize that the up-and-over is not where I suspected and is more benign than I thought. I camp early again, at a lake one mile from the crest, saving the climb for tomorrow because rain threatens and my foot could use rest. And because I am just three days from Anaktuvuk and simply because, like Colin Fletcher, I do not need "such fragile props as 'reasons.'"

An arctic tern fishes the lake's outlet. The Cape Cod writer John Hay honored this bird of light with a book. Before each bout of hovering to scan the water for fingerlings with her fork tail spread, the pearly, black-capped angel soars upward on scythe wings and then, building up a harpoon's momentum, plunges with her red bill aimed at the target. She hangs suspended from wings that shine with each beat like sails luffing against a stormy gray background. Basking in unceasing summer, these birds overwinter in Antarctica and on voyages up to forty thousand miles long chase the sun—that's three round-trips to the moon in a lifetime. Feisty colonial nesters, they've attacked clients and me while we rafted through their domain. They also harass gulls and jaegers, birds three times their size.

Living into their thirties, arctic terns touch down on nearly all of Earth's shorelines during their peregrinations. Mark Cocker sees them as "little more than a

MICHAEL ENGELHARD

heart enclosed in wing muscle." Nicknamed "sea swallow," this bird and its gull kin has also been "sun-shard," "sea-gauntlet," "proud fishfeeder," and "sea-lily" in Welsh medieval poetry. Tern radiance on bright days can outshine the snow. The silvery glint comes from unpigmented microscopic structures in the flight feathers refracting sunlight. Given the importance of courtship flights in this species, it would not surprise me to learn that the attractive shimmer is a trait evolution selected for.

After dinner, the tern is back diving in the shallows with a different hunting technique, plowing a furrow into the lake with her bill. She now is a pendulum. Her flight's flat parabola creates the illusion of her glancing off a solid surface at the contact point. Once in a while, she pivots on a wingtip at an arc's end, changing course. I hope to someday observe the pairing ritual in which the male woos the female by gifting a fish.

In the late 1800s, stuffed terns adorning women's hats as fashion statements sparked the birth of Audubon Society chapters and eventually the Migratory Bird Treaty Act, which protects this tern I am watching before turning in.

BOB'S COUNTRY

DAY 35 (8 MILES)
QUAD: CHANDLER LAKE

Clouds creeping up the valley obscure the pass and I'm glad I have my Magellan, even though he is on his last leg. I crest a swell, not the pass proper, and therefore descend to it. From this notch among whalebacks, I see an inkwell of a lake at the bottom of Grizzly Creek, twin to the one I camped at last night. The view, clear below an overcast canopy, is one of the best so far. Bob Marshall in time-honored tradition peppered alleged terra incognita with his own coinages, as if he'd built the ice-clad peaks scrumming around me: Cockedhat, Snowheel, Inclined, Alapah (Inupiaq for "cold"), Doonerak—his "Matterhorn of the Koyukuk"—and square-jawed Limestack Mountain, each summit clipped by the bruised sky's blade. Many indeed had never been climbed. Foragers had no reason to. Peaks, promising neither game nor raw materials, did not figure into subsistence rounds.

An obsessive list maker and timekeeper and the first to map this region, the East Coast visitor bestowed 164 place-names on the central Brooks Range, including Boreal Mountain and Frigid Crags, a gateway for the Koyukuk's North Fork that became this park's tagline. The US Geological Survey, denying that the "so-called exploring expeditions" of adventurers, mountain climbers, and newspapermen contributed usable map information, stuffily credits Marshall's headwaters sketch as the "exception to the unimportance of individual exploration in Alaska."

Nowadays, few new names in official wildernesses are approved and only after thorough review by the respective land-managing agency. The Board on Geographic Names, the USGS branch responsible, wants to minimize the human touch in these areas, be it ever so slight, in accordance with the spirit of the Wilderness Act. "Although wilderness designations are a modern invention," the board insists, "a fundamental characteristic of elemental wilderness is that the cultural overlay of civilization is absent. Place-names in a wilderness area might diminish the sense of discovery that those who visit ought to be able to experience." Of course, too many visitors also diminish that sense—and the physical integrity of a place—but zoning and permits, let alone carrying capacities, for Brooks Range wildernesses, parks, and preserves have never been established, for better or worse. Embracing both solitude and discovery, Marshall could not have foreseen crowding or serious human impact in his beloved mountains. Even his naming mania might have relented had he lived long enough for his zeal to mellow.

Marshall and a Fairbanks prospector friend also christened Grizzly Creek, which flares below me. On my heels I glissade down a black shale ramp splotched with arctic poppies, all the way to the valley bottom.

A self-diagnosed "ursa-phobe" who once escaped a grizzly by climbing a tree, Marshall admitted panicking when faced with another, "11 miles from the closest gun, 106 from the first potential stretcher bearers, and 300 air-line from the nearest hospital." At his camp near the mouth of Grizzly Creek, "an immense, whitish-brown humped mass" spooked and stampeded the pack stock. Dragged behind one crazed nag, he shot at the bear from the hip and, after letting go of the halter, managed to wound it. He then chased the runaway horses on foot. The next day a cold rain soaked him, and he saw little, as fog mantled the "ragged giants" bracing this glen. A soggy slope crashing into the creek two miles below camp caused more excitement, with horses once more spooked.

I do it again: I outrace ominous clouds, chugging up the Valley of Precipices, Marshall's "great gorge of the north" with its pillars Boreal Mountain and Frigid Crags, forming the "Gates," and last up a slope stubbly with tussocks to a small Ernie Pass tundra lake—Ernie Johnson having been one of Marshall's Wiseman companions. As Marshall often did, I go unarmed and on this marbled day at the very head of the Koyukuk's North Fork don't meet any wildlife. Bathed in theatrical light, I take five hasty minutes to floor the marginal site with fistfuls of moss and pitch my tent by the lake before the sky's floodgates sunder with booming claps.

Now, against the advice of bear experts, coffee is brewing in the vestibule while I sit snug in the pitter-patter and thunder. You can't beat that. It reminds me of rainy Sundays on the couch, and my notes show it indeed is that day of the week.

Open and unimpressive Ernie Pass is yet another iteration of the Continental Divide, and I shall walk on the north side tomorrow again.

I saw bladder campion today, a less showy relative of moss campion. Its white, purple-ribbed "bladder," a calyx like a Japanese paper lantern, is a greenhouse for the reproductive organs. This campion has been called "a strikingly unflowerlike flower," since its tiny petals are tucked inside the bladder. It also is said to be "nodding when young." Isn't that how we'd prefer youth to be, always agreeable? Now, taking to the streets, they're accusing us, justly, of having ruined the planet.

A CLOSE ENCOUNTER OF
THE STRANGE KIND

DAY 36 (9 MILES)
QUAD: CHANDLER LAKE

Clouds jellyfish low on the hills on this cold, sunny morning—an ambiance spelling the brink of fall yet typical of summer here. It's too chilly for bugs, but I'm sure they will swing by later. Watching a red-throated loon afloat in "my" front yard, I wonder how a lake with a single bird can appear more lonesome than one with none at all.

Last night a jaeger's heckling betrayed an arctic fox inspecting my tent. It snuck off when I poked my head out. As I wash breakfast dishes, two golden plovers distract me. A mew gull is trying to snatch their leggy chick. The parents dive at the Goliath intruder in loop after loop, running it off. Virgil envisioned hell as a place without birds. I think our world without birds would be hell.

While the rest of America goes to work, I reach Graylime Creek and the broad Anaktuvuk River valley carved by Pleistocene glaciers. Only twenty more miles to the village post office where I'll collect cache number five, mailed to myself. I salivate at the prospect of cookies Melissa baked and some new books; I've burned pages from the one Dave traded me after reading them to lighten my load but have long since run out of unread material.

Past noon I hit the alder-lined ATV track on the riverbank east of the settlement, one of the webs with Anaktuvuk Pass as their node that connects villagers and their hunting and fishing grounds. Stream gravel under the sod drains the tire scars along much of this stretch except for occasional mud pits causing multilane bypasses. Civilization's debris welcomes me back: fire rings, tin cans, broken sled runners, a rusting snowmachine with its Plexiglas windshield, a *Star Wars* plastic laser sword . . . I imagine village kids mounted on four-wheelers, round-faced Nunamiut Jedi fighting galactic battles.

These miles before the next cache hold many memories. Friends from Germany joined me here for one of my earliest arctic excursions. And with a client I tried to exit from the aufeis here that the Sheenjek gully reminded me of. Most poignantly, I did not climb any peaks girding this valley while guiding a Swiss couple from Shainin Lake in the northern foothills to Anaktuvuk. What was the point with wildfire smoke voiding the views and us breathing harder than we would have under normal circumstances? Even nearby heights loomed barely visible, bleached shadows, while the sun's ember glowed like a red giant in an eerie fast-forward of five billion years. Only after that 2007 trip did I hear about a fire that lightning had started, a blaze unrivaled in modern times that over almost three months burned four hundred treeless square miles on the Anaktuvuk River, well north of the range. It left "a forest of knee-high black pillars," the remains of charred tussocks. It was my flamethrower fantasy realized. Beware what you wish for.

In a chapter on freaks—including diamond dust, fallstreak holes, horseshoe vortexes, and Kelvin-Helmholtz waves, serried breakers—Gavin Pretor-Pinney's *The Cloud Collector's Handbook* covers pyrocumuli. Tumultuous air columns sprouting from wildfires, these grow large enough to produce their own weather, lightning, land- or waterspouts, even fire tornados looking like computer-generated special effects. The "fire-breathing dragon of clouds" can suck up burning branches and drop them miles ahead of the flaming front, where they start spot fires. Some pyrocumuli now reach above the troposphere, the atmosphere's bottom layer, and bloom into the stratosphere, disgorging soot particles that cause asthma. Flying north in small planes, I've watched them rear monstrous gray heads among cotton crowns of neighboring towers. Bush pilots detour to avoid them. With contrails, not counting amorphous smog, these are the only clouds we imprint, visible proof of our reach beyond the planet's biotic skin.

Making good time on the ATV track, I camp off-trail eight miles short of town at a kidney-shaped lake pocketed between a mountainside and ridge of hills. Having stayed here before with the Swiss couple, I enjoy claiming it for myself.

I am procrastinating, delaying my arrival at the village, dreading even the briefest reentry, the punch to quiet solitude that four-wheelers, generators, an airstrip, or the corporation store will deliver. In this, I am kin to Marshall. Finishing one splendid summer string of forty-nine nights camping out, he halted just outside of Wiseman upon his return. He supposedly tried to rack up a nice even fifty, but I doubt that motive.

It has been the first bluebird day in more than two weeks. Taking advantage, I rinse my skivvies and socks, which on this trek passes for laundry day.

"Gates," as Alaskans fond of abbreviations know the park, has another surprise treat for me. As I recline bare-chested on fragrant tundra, absorbing warmth and mulling the lack of fat in my diet and the resulting shrinkage, a canine, coal black like a hellhound, trots along the far lakeshore without noticing me. *Whose dog is this?* Not an outlandish question given the proximity of huskies and town. But something feels off, a feral spring in this animal's gait, a hint of flexed steel in its bearing. Could it be a rare blue-morph arctic fox? Then it hits me: another wolf, though a skinny one.

Afraid that he will leave, I softly call out to him. "Hey. Where are you going?"

Not at all startled, he stops and gazes at me. "The eyes of an animal when they consider a man are attentive and wary," the art critic John Berger writes in *About Looking*. The animal, Berger avers, "does not reserve a special look for man. But by no other species except man will the animal's look be recognized as familiar. . . . Man becomes aware of himself returning the look."

While I agree with Berger that seeing and being seen by animals and telling stories about them shed light on the human condition, I reject his claim that the wolf looks at us the same way it would at a ground squirrel. The wolf, fathoming deep into you, weighing intentions if not your soul, was always predestined to become a guardian spirit and powerful helper of Eskimo shamans. Differing from the Nunamiut's dogs, wolves were believed to possess souls and, as Barry Lopez relays in *Of Wolves and Men*, share other traits with humans, hence that personal pronoun again: "*Amaġuq* is like Nunamiut. He doesn't hunt when the weather is bad. He likes to play. He works hard to get food for his family. His hair starts to get white when he is old." He regards us as one predator does another.

This wolf approaches gingerly, as if the ground were not solid. Perhaps, I am tickled to think, he detects the faint echo of an ageless bond between his kind and mine.

I keep talking calmly, staying in my mattress-chair, and he comes closer still. He freezes again, his curiosity piqued. The lean body signals no tension, only openness to the moment's possibilities. I can sense the allure that has linked two species since North Siberians first gentled wolves twenty-three thousand years ago. His ancestors carried packs, cornered game, and guarded the camps of Nunamiut forebears on their push out of Beringia.

Deciding that this is too weird, the wolf then circles downwind of me to catch my scent. A shallow ravine conceals the maneuver. Losing sight of him but wanting to prolong the connection, I stand up for a better view. *Amaġuq* jolts at this rude, slightly aggressive move, loping off into the blue yonder.

Sometimes you sit, and good things come to you. Most of my wolf encounters happen that way. Once, on the Aichilik, another north-draining refuge river, I was chatting with a client after dinner while scanning our surroundings over his shoulder as I always do. "There's a wolf, by the way," I slipped into our conversation, casual, as if such a thing were an everyday occurrence.

With my hiking pole I now measure this untamed one's comfort zone. Thirty yards. Our society's small footprint in this expanse seemed to bother neither him nor his pal near the Haul Road.

FINDINGS

DAY 37 (7 MILES)
QUAD: CHANDLER LAKE

I get a late start, waiting for the rain to let up. It does not, so I breakfast in the tent and then pack up inside, everything but its fly. A short day of bleak, soggy hiking on the track. I want to overnight somewhere on the outskirts and set myself up for a resupply that will allow me to indulge in Anaktuvuk's conveniences tomorrow while still leaving enough time to find a good camp west of it afterward. Also, my foot has gotten worse to the point where I doubt that I can finish the trip. The remaining twelve days will be tough hiking for that reason alone. I could fly out from Anaktuvuk on the daily plane to Fairbanks to recuperate but would hate to have the city's jackhammer of demands and temptations interrupt my apprenticeship in solitude. Plus, there would be two additional airfares.

I camp on Dismal Hill—my name, not one of Marshall's. The barely there tent site where two ATV trails join offers views of Anaktuvuk River aufeis, a blinding jumble of channels and broken shelves, at least in between the squalls. Signs of butchery abound: caribou spines and shoulder blades, antler piles, spent rifle brass, fire rings, cigarette butts and burned boards, and a cushioned four-wheeler seat I should repurpose into a La-Z-Boy. There are enough artifacts here for future archaeologists to reconstruct twenty-first-century subsistence habits.

The scene might disturb folks who see national parks as sacrosanct groves, pockets exclusive of residents or materialistic pursuits. But these are Nunamiut Corporation lands, travel corridors the villagers selected in 1971, settling property rights in advance of the pipeline's construction. And is the Grand Canyon's South Rim Village—that concrete implant of hotels, parking lots, interpretive centers, bus and train stops, a clinic, school, faux ancestral-Puebloan watchtower, and mini-mall—any better? (Obviously, a rhetorical question.) The exclusion and forced removal of Native Americans from areas designated as parks are fraught history. The Havasupai had been farming at Indian Garden, a watered sacred oasis halfway down the Bright Angel Trail, for a thousand years before being resettled in 1919, restricted to Supai Camp, their current home in the gorge of the blue-green waters. A move is afoot to rename Indian Garden as Havasupai Garden, an attempt, like the recent excising of "squaw" from Alaska place-names, to mend US government–Native American relations while whitewashing history.

John Muir, heretofore a deity of the conservation movement, supported the uprooting of Miwoks from Yosemite because they threatened its "pristineness." One could argue that these lands were worthy of inclusion among the nation's most beautiful places to be protected *because* peoples through the millennia had taken such good care of them, a skill that western society and federal agencies have yet to demonstrate. Muir moderated somewhat later in life. On a final grand trip in 1881 aboard the US revenue cutter *Corwin* into the Chukchi Sea, he assessed Bering Strait Eskimos in his journal: "They are better behaved than white men, not half so greedy, shameless or dishonest. . . . These people interest me greatly, and it is worth coming far to know them." They did not interfere with his parks there and then.

So, I say, don't begrudge the Nunamiut Dismal Hill. I always put this kind of trash into its anthropological context for clients who complain. Over centuries, Inupiat based in coastal settlements roamed to lightly occupied seasonal camps. In the northern climate, refuse that piled up (and, as "middens," clues in anthropologists), reverted to the earth, or vegetation absorbed it. Organic materials do not preserve well in these conditions; except for the rare lucky mummified frozen find, the deep archaeological record contains mostly stone tools and weapons and fragments of both. Dateable charcoal from a campfire is a jackpot. Compare this to the endurance of the Devil's polymers. Headlamp batteries: one century. Plastic water bottles: four and a half. Monofilament fishing line: six. Crude oil: decades. Uranium tailings: millennia.

Still, one assemblage I discover on Dismal Hill confounds me in its ambiguity. Melissa thinks I make too much of it when I bring it up on occasion. It may seem mundane: somebody placed three crushed soda cans under a rock. I just don't get it. That person apparently cared enough to hide trash. But not enough to carry it out. Did he intend to retrieve it on the way back? Did she weigh it down so it would not blow away? Can I rule out a backpacking culprit? Perhaps I have spent too much time alone lately and therefore dwell on such matters. But to me, they speak of something twisted in human nature, some push-and-pull between doing the right thing and sheer laziness or, worse, disregard. They encapsulate the out-of-sight-out-of-mind attitude that allows us to foul our own nest by polluting the globe.

Again, putting this into perspective, it pales in comparison to what White people do, river runners no less. I did not witness the act, just the profoundly disturbing result. Waiting for our bush plane at a takeout for the refuge's Canning River after a rafting trip, I picked up a muskox skull sitting by the runway to inspect it. To truly value this anecdote, you must understand what a rare thing of beauty such a skull is. The head plate proper, minus the horns, could be that of any old range cow; but the horns are sculptural art, a rich walnut brown, like driftwood boles textured with growth ridges. They sweep downward and out from a forehead bossed four inches thick—a helmet for sexual combat—to curve up into dagger-point tips. A fur patch on the forehead of cows separates her less massive yet equally lethal pokers. While the gap between the two bosses and the horns' flare, their gestalt, recalls the center part and curls of the flipped bob of the sixties (think Brigitte Bardot or Jacqueline Kennedy), they're rugged reminders of the last ice age. Male muskoxen butting heads during the rut can reach bicyclists' top speeds, thirty miles per hour. They often act dazed after bouts and may suffer chronic brain damage as boxers and footballers do, research says.

But I digress in my swooning. Underneath the muskox skull sat a turd flagged with toilet paper. Besides the ignorant sacrilege, the disrespect for this creature and the curious naturalist, the Canning conundrum like the Dismal deposit vexed me: Had the shitter been ashamed?

Desultory phone calls to Melissa crown this day of the blahs. I lose the connection repeatedly, as usual, and she cannot say if my package arrived in Anaktuvuk. I hope this resupply will go smoothly tomorrow, that the PO on whose shelf it should sit for General Delivery has not burned down.

There is always succor from wildlife. I watch a ground squirrel reap grass for his burrow. The sheaf hangs out from both sides of his mouth like a handlebar moustache. Their Inupiaq name, *siksik*, mimics the alarm a sentinel sounds, a kobold standing outside a communal burrow stripped bare of vegetation, whenever bear, wolverine, wolf, fox, weasel, gyrfalcon, owl, eagle, or human approaches. Hearing this quick squeak, or a piercing whistle, other colony members pop their heads out of various entrances to assess the danger.

These tawny spotted marmot relatives are the swamis of metabolic reduction, true cryogenics experts. They're the only known warm-blooded animal that supercools its body fluids to survive a lethal environment, keeping their brains, chest, and abdominal cavities slightly above freezing while letting the rest drop to slightly below freezing without cell damage from ice crystallizing. Their heart and metabolic rates in this state are roughly 1 percent of the summer rates. They lie dimly awake in a state of torpor (unlike bears, which become merely dormant), in essence brain dead, but rally every two or three weeks for periods of sleeping and dreaming, their body temperature near normal. Steadfast hibernators for seven to eight months, arctic ground squirrels thus stunned sometimes drown when spring melt floods their hollows. Where proper snow insulating their time capsules is lacking, others never resurrect. Medical researchers try to unlock the *siksik*'s secrets to help prevent brain damage in humans after cardiac arrests and resuscitations. Insights into the squirrels' winter metabolism also could help treat obesity, type two diabetes, and cardiovascular diseases and prevent atrophy in unused or aging muscles.

With my aged muscles aching and depleted of nutrients, I envy the shrill little buggers. If you pity them, consider that they, like arctic terns, spend almost their whole conscious existence in daylight and summer, the only mammal to do so.

THE PLACE OF
CARIBOU DROPPINGS

DAY 38 (10 MILES)
QUAD: CHANDLER LAKE
CACHE #5

Sunny. A good day, as the resupply goes smoothly.

In a letter to Melissa composed last night outside my tent that I plan to mail from here, I initially claim to write from the Caribou Café, enjoying an Americano stiff enough to float a horseshoe, and an oven-warm blueberry scone, Ben Harper falsettoing on the stereo. It is a fantasy I indulge in, cravings that surface mostly close to a settlement. I know better from previous visits.

Entering Anaktuvuk where the ATV track splices into dirt roads to the cemetery and dump, I make a beeline to a boarded-up house near the airstrip where Dirk has stashed a can of white gas for my stove that I could not send through the mail. I refill my fuel bottles right there. The post office, a clapboard cabin with a satellite dish, comes next. Operating on "village time," it has just opened, casually late. The Nunamiut share a sense of urgency regarding clocks with the rural Irish. It's an adaptation to the vagaries of weather and wildlife honed through the generations, not yet corroded by factories. You can die if you rush things out here, and there's always time to get important work done.

Besides my regular vittles, I pick up a TLC parcel from Melissa. It is heavy with homemade oatmeal cookies, Nutella, hot chocolate, smoked salmon, smoked oysters, salt-and-vinegar potato chips, and three (!) books, enough reading matter, I hope, to last until Kotzebue. I feel like a boy locked in a candy store overnight and devour the chips and oysters—greasy, greasy, and salty; she intuited my deepest cravings—on the wheelchair-friendly post office access ramp. I fish the oysters from the can and, having become wise to the Aussie's trick, finish by drinking the oil and licking my fingers. A lanky guy in his thirties with a Mongol-style moustache asks me if I've seen any wolves. Funny he should ask that. "Yes," I lie, "way back at the Haul Road." Having ratted out a ptarmigan once and still feeling guilty, I don't want to risk having Blackie turned into parka ruffs.

From the PO, I walk to the corporation store seeking a public phone from which to thank Melissa for the goodies. No dice. Apparently, all Nunamiut now have cell phones. My consolation prize is a dinged pint of Ben & Jerry's Banana Split, a bargain at eight bucks. I would have paid twice as much for this second lunch.

A community project, the school's I assume, has beautified rusty dumpsters here and there. The spray-painted messages promote Inupiaq values: *Avoid Conflict. Hunting Traditions. Respect Elders.* And, importantly: *Humor.* These are my kind of people and not just for loving ice cream.

The locals are friendly, with *aanas* (grandmas) and *taatas* (grandpas) and kids asking "Where to?" and "Where from?" and wishing me luck. I'm happy tourism hasn't ruined this Brooks Range village of about four hundred yet.

Anaktuvuk's grid squeezes in among peaks at the watery crossroads where Contact Creek and the Inukpasugruk River merge with the Anaktuvuk and the John. Thirteen nomadic families gravitated there from the Killik River and Chandler Lake in 1949. They founded the insular village three decades before the park around it was established, hoping that air service, trade goods, a school, and a post office would follow. The new PO in 1951 was a domed caribou-skin tent with a stovepipe sticking out, Homer Mekiana's Contact Creek residence. The settlement, a scatter of sod houses and wall tents first known as Summit, brackets the Continental Divide. Grandfathered and -mothered in, Anaktuvuk's Nunamiut are still entitled to hunt, fish, trap, and gather plants within the park boundaries, an exception made for Alaska Native communities.

Every fall, not only animals from the Central Arctic but also the Western Arctic and Teshekpuk Lake herds graced the Place of Caribou Droppings with their presence. Tens of thousands surged through these valleys. Major Charlie Hugo remembers in his youth joining his father to camp for a month and returning with dog teams and up to sixty caribou, enough meat for a year.

Even better than firewood, which warms you twice (once in the cutting and again in the burning), caribou energized Nunamiut hunters thrice: in the pursuit; with their backstrap fat and meat; and through skins lightweight, water resistant, and strong. Dense underfur trapping air under long guard hairs conserves heat just like layering garments. And the honeycombed guard hairs contain tiny air bubbles, much like synthetic Hollofil fiber. In clinical trials, skin-clad subjects stayed warmer, including their cheeks, than those in expedition or army winter getups. Mushers and other outdoors people still consider caribou footwear and beaver mittens top of the line, superior to synthetics.

Nowadays, there are fewer caribou near Anaktuvuk. Biologists explain the herds' declines with erratic weather and cyclical population dynamics. The Nunamiut blame sports hunters north of the park for disrupting the fall migration and thereby harming a unique way of life. Aircraft noise could be a contributing factor. A healthy caribou running in panic, overheating, is earmarked for death after only two or three miles. A pregnant cow stampeded close to her due date dies even faster.

Heirlooms from the semi-nomadic past are curated in the Simon Paneak Memorial Museum, a multiroom modern log house that honors the Nunamiut man who befriended and worked with several scientists and grew into a respected historian of the region. Among hide clothing, hunting gear, tools, maps, photos, and other artifacts, the museum showcases copies of watercolors by an early Outside visitor to the community: Jeffries Wyman.

Wyman was a Renaissance man—a Harvard philosophy graduate with a knack for numbers. In World War II he worked on sonar and smoke screens for the Navy and wrote a seminal paper about hemoglobin based on an insight striking him in a Kyoto Zen garden. After his second marriage failed, the Boston Brahmin spent a month as self-declared "good man Friday" and resident artist with the Nunamiut at Anaktuvuk. His journal and watercolors from the summer of 1951 are snapshots of lives hard yet blessed, of fates inextricably bound to the land.

Wyman first alighted at a camp on the Anaktuvuk River ten miles north of today's village in a floatplane piloted by the second president of the University of Alaska, Terris Moore. During takeoff from a lake in Fairbanks, it almost capsized, and Wyman, fully dressed, jumped into the lake. As it happened, the plane had been overloaded, the cargo unbalanced.

At Anaktuvuk, signs of successful adaptation to a harsh climate and capricious resources greeted the New Englander. His hosts' grandparents had hunted with spears and arrows, hazing caribou into lakes. Their offspring set gillnets for grayling, whitefish, and lake trout; snared ptarmigan and ground squirrels at their burrows, or shot squirrels, even from a drifting boat; and chased Dall sheep and caribou, aided in later years by "Ski-Doos" (snowmachines), four-wheel "Hondas," and tubby eight-wheelers. Elijah Kakinya, who took Wyman in, glassed the valley with a collapsible Yankee-whaler brass telescope braced on a walking staff. He referred to the season's first caribou as "big meat." "Our stomachs are like mountains," his white-haired, patrician houseguest wrote after one feast—and marveled at a five-year-old boy wielding a sharp knife, cutting meat, Inupiat-style, close to his lips.

The families kept meat in "icehouses," caches dug into permafrost near movable summer habitations, white canvas wall tents and skin "igloos" with bearskins as doors. Dead streamside scrub willows were the only firewood. Dogs, the sole means of land transport, packed sixty-pound loads.

Wyman settled in quickly and comfortably, eating, napping, sketching, helping to check nets and haul meat, and visiting much of the time. "Everyone keeps open house, and it makes for a most gracious manner of life," he wrote, impressed by the families' quiet dignity and ethic of sharing. Simon Paneak, a "commanding personality," would have been a shaman in the old days or, among us, "a man of learning." Wyman enjoyed Paneak's stories of Raven and the "little people," Nunamiut elves whose children were small enough to wear hats sewn from a caribou ear.

At Summit, after a foot trip with pack dogs, river crossings, and a toddler stowed in a parka hood, Wyman wished to see traditional singing and dancing. His hosts gladly complied. Two skins were located, soaked, scraped to the right thickness, mended with sinew, and stretched over washtubs—improvised three-person drums. One sod igloo's stove was cleared out for space, and the party began. It ended in the dawn hours, when a couple in fur parkas, with hoods concealing their faces, mimicked caribou mating.

Creating art could be challenging with high winds and cold that numbed fingers until unscrewing caps from paint tubes became difficult. Still, early snow made the mountains look "distinguished," and the weather and light changed "in the flash of an eye." Kids followed Wyman while he was working. Evenings were the most exciting times for painting outdoors, and he often persisted till darkness erased all colors. He wished for the skills of a Turner or Hokusai to do justice to "great clouds, sometimes blue-black, sometimes coal-black, sometimes tawny yellow, sometimes of the light fluffy gray of the gray wolf." The contrast between skin igloos and canvas tents and red, yellow, and orange August hills thrilled him: "The color of the tundra is a most elusive thing and the combined feelings of warmth and coolness which it evokes are incomparable." Translucent tent walls were perfect backgrounds for his indoor portraits and still lifes. Steadfastly supportive, Wyman's new friends provided raven quills for his ink sketching and eagle feathers for journaling, besides keeping him fed and clothed.

"I shall be sorry to leave this life with these people," Wyman wrote the day before his floatplane was scheduled to arrive.

He never returned to Anaktuvuk, but in a fitting coda, facsimiles of his art did. Sixty years after the biochemist's stay, his daughter and son donated seventeen framed reproductions to the museum. (The UAF's Museum of the North holds the originals, too delicate for environments not climate controlled.) In the Elders' Room in Anaktuvuk, the settlers' descendants and future generations can visit them: the folk Wyman so lovingly painted, the ones who charmed and welcomed him, a stranger.

Unfortunately, I can't take in these treasures presently. Must mosey. But the villagers wishing this latest stranger in their midst well for his journey raise a ghost from his own past. At the end of my first season's ethnographic fieldwork on the Kobuk River, I had planned to hike upstream from Ambler to Anaktuvuk, a trek of at least ten days that many elders of the Kuvangmiut ("People of the Kobuk River") had made in their youth. I was naive, a greenhorn in bush Alaska, and when I told one such old-timer about my intention, he just nodded sagely. It's not the Inupiat's way to decide for others what can or cannot be done.

A few hours from Ambler, thrashing through swampy spruce tangles, I surprised a grizzly, the first I'd encountered since I dragged a Steiff teddy everywhere with me as a kid. This one was huge and quite mad or else hungry, digging for something; I couldn't say which. In that instant, I understood coastal Inupiaq tales that warned of the boreal forest, the closed-in country of strange people and beasts, which they shunned. With sod and tree chunks airborne, I retreated, slinking into Ambler to take the next twin-prop plane out.

Today, I am taking shank's mare on the ATV track out of Anaktuvuk. My pack weighs a ton. (Really only half of a moose's hindquarter.) In addition to a small library and Melissa's sweets, I carry twelve days of food and fuel, thereby avoiding another expensive charter drop between here and the Noatak River. I'll haul every ounce of this load, even if it kills me.

Though the ATV track damages tundra and has worsened over the years, I am grateful for it on this slog down a broad valley, wondering facetiously if the divide that runs right through Anaktuvuk splits kin groups or political factions. A convoy of four Cessnas—an arctic Jeep safari—skims the John River valley headed downstream, to put in for a float trip perhaps. That's where I launched canoes with my honeymooning brother and the sister-in-law whom the trail-less country aggrieved.

I may have to budget a layover day or two because of that trail-less country, and my flimsy footwear and recent parcel pickup. It's ironic. Just when the going has gotten easier, I'm going lame. My jokes always have been, but this sort of physical failure is new to me. Ninety-three miles separate me from the Noatak cache, number six: my last. If bears haven't figured out acetylene torches, it will hold my blow-up canoe and three weeks of food. On the river, I'll be doing a lot of sitting, resting my feet. Time to buff up the upper torso and arms, not just the legs!

Dinner tonight is polenta with dried mushrooms, sun-dried tomatoes, and Parmesan. Yum. You'd think I would tire of the same six meals and my snacks. Not so. Each is a feast looked forward to during the day, especially a dreary one. I read Melissa's letter after dinner, glad to have her in my life. And not just for her Cowboy Cookies, which rock. I sit on a knoll above the John River. It's as far as my dogs would carry me today. My water source is a hollow that pools tundra seepage brown as tea from the tannins. Home sweet interim home.

After dinner, a rainbow clasp crisp enough to touch, one of the most awesome ever, points out the gold on the southwestern horizon. It of course comes with rain.

WEAKEST MEMBER
OF THE HERD

DAY 39 (0 MILES)
QUAD: CHANDLER LAKE

Another lovely day, and I'm fated to sit tight. I can't even explore, if I want to give this foot a chance to get better. And I absolutely need it to be.

Feet and footwear are iconic in the literature of serious journeying. Hobnailed, Vibram-soled, reindeer hide with the hairy side out, or, in extremis, wrapped strips of rags—boots rather than dogs have been the adventurer's most valued resource and ultimate friends. I once came upon a wilderness grave in the Canadian Rockies where a cross inscribed *Farewell dear boots* commemorated the lifespan of trusty ones the owner had buried there. (Did he bring a second pair or rob a hiker or hike out in socks?)

Sir John Franklin, reduced to boiling boots for food, achieved immortality not as a loafer but as a man hellbent for leather. "We drank tea and ate some of our shoes for supper," he reported from the Coppermine River, with a stiff English upper lip. Then, there was the Danish friend of the explorer-ethnographer Knud Rasmussen, Peter Freuchen, who amputated his own frozen digits with a hammer and chisel. "Perhaps one could get used to cutting off toes," he quipped, "but there were not enough of them to get sufficient practice. An Inuit treatment for gangrene saved his life: fresh lemming skins, with the warm, bloody side on his rotting flesh. Each new wound dressing peeled off decayed tissue until, sleepless at night, he stared, grimly fascinated, at the bare bones of his toes. A trained surgeon later removed the rest of that foot.

What do I have to bellyache about?

Packing up and moving daily has become more than a routine. It's an urge unlike the caribou's, a wanderlust that the desire to reach my destination doesn't explain sufficiently. I can see how some contemporaries through personal trauma, bad luck, financial hardship, or pure volition may abandon sedentary lives to never settle again. Mobility itself may be enough. It's been a characteristic of the nation's economy too, not just for wilderness guides or during westward expansion or the Depression. In the post-World War II industrial boom, Americans on average pulled up stakes every five years, a number considered high compared to most other countries but low compared to my own history. Now, digital nomads live almost anywhere in the world, working while ambulant and being chic.

The Highlands looks of my surroundings, paired with thoughts of ailments and restlessness, set the needle in the groove of "The Ramblin' Rover," a favorite song, by Andy M. Stewart of the Scottish band Silly Wizard:

> If you're bent wi' arthritis,
> Your bowels have got colitis,
> You've gallopin' bollockitis
> And you're thinkin' it's time you died,
> You've been a man of action,
> Though you're lying there in traction,
> You will get some satisfaction
> Thinkin', "Jesus, at least I tried."

HALFWAY POINT

DAY 40 (9.5 MILES)
QUAD: CHANDLER LAKE

Overcast, drizzly. Thirty-six hours of rest on this knoll seem to have worked a miracle on my left foot. Raring to go, I rejoin the ATV scar. Phlox, fireweed, and Indian paintbrush ("Eskimo paintbrush"?), a flower familiar to me from Canyon Country. A hunting blind or windbreak built from rock encrusted with lichen crowns a hill. Blueberries have ripened in sunny spots but mostly remain Granny-Smith green.

The only things worse than tussocks are tussocks under dwarf birch, which disguises the pits in between humps. The vehicle trail ends at a hunting camp near the mouth of Masu Creek, where Nunamiut women gathered "Eskimo potatoes," starchy roots of *Hedysarum alpinum*, alpine sweetvetch, a fragrant legume with purple flowers listed in US Army survival manuals. There are frames of lean-tos cut from saplings, a blue tarp and plastic bags, bones, rotting caribou skins, metal water basins, fire rings encircling blackened cans . . . and a kid's basketball, deflated like my spirit was yesterday.

And this is where tussock torment truly begins. *Hell, hell, hell,* my annotations read for this stretch on the map. It's some of the boggiest, lumpiest, nastiest terrain of the entire trip. And I was overly enthusiastic about the foot. Within half a day of this, the pain has rekindled already, which really blows, as I wanted to enjoy this final hiking section. Instead, I'm counting the miles and hours to the Noatak.

In the afternoon I pick up the ATV trail again, which helps a bit. Ironically, my tent site is on some of the driest, most level ground I have had so far, though a bog pond below is my water source.

Consulting the map, I realize I passed the halfway point of my traverse some-where near the Masu Creek hunting camp. I am nine miles closer to Kotzebue than to the Yukon border near Joe Creek, Magellan tells me: 282 miles versus 293 miles, and 76.5 miles from the Noatak launch point—that's the *direttissima*, mind you, impossible on the ground—and I have nine days of food to get there. These figures may not be that impressive; they don't mean anything anyway.

HELL IS A PLACE
WITH TUSSOCKS

DAY 41 (9.5 MILES)
QUAD: CHANDLER LAKE

Overcast, gloomy. I am adrift in a sea of vegetation, except that "adrift" implies effortlessness. It's not just bad tussocks either. Last night's rain pearled chest-high willows that now drench me as I wallow through. I wear little leaves, spangles of desperation. The Special Forces raingear clings to me, a wet, heavy frog skin restricting movement. I detect overgrown ravines by tumbling into them, with my heavy pack pressing me into the moss. Bashing through alders is like breaching a dull triple-concertina-wire fence with your body. Branches claw at me, holding me back. Marshland wobbles or swallows me up to my knees. Willows ensnare my feet, tripping me up and really hurting the game foot by overextending it.

Isn't it Bastille Day? Weren't the tortured supposed to be freed from their prison? If one applies Bob Marshall's yardstick for wilderness as possessing "no possibility of conveyance by any mechanical means," then this valley qualifies. The valleys that Anaktuvuk's ATVs churn do not. Here, even my natural, all-round means of conveyance almost lets me down.

The creek, when I try to walk there, is freezing and has to be crossed every two minutes, and my feet on the cobbles soon feel like woodblocks—but hey, no trouble from the Achilles heel. In addition to mosquitos, today we have horseflies, Magellan and me.

This is my Via Dolorosa: Ekokpuk Creek.

Ekokpuk Creek.

Ekokpuk Creek.

EKOKPUK CREEK.

A name worth remembering. It is seared into my brain.

I don't know what it means.

"Don't go there," probably. (Back home, Orth's tome of place names informs me it may mean "Split in Two," which I find side-splitting.)

It's twenty-two miles long. I will flounder through eighteen of them.

There's no sign of wildlife other than two dark-brown ears of an animal that has spotted me from a low bluff. A moose is my guess, my hope. This would be bad country for rousting Old Ephraim, as the mountain man fraternity to which the mauled Hugh Glass belonged called the griz.

A duck and five ducklings flee from me down a rapid, with the youngsters' stub wings whirring like pocket ventilators. Two songbirds pester a large raptor. Some fish in the creek do fishy things. I've no energy left for species identifications.

I camp early—surprise, surprise—wasted and hurting and barely having made the miles I needed to. It's another marginal site, above the creek, that requires padding. I hope the country will ease off as I gain elevation before Agiak Lake. This has been some of the worst stuff I've hiked in in forty years and one of the most taxing days of this traverse. Sixty-nine miles to the Noatak. One more week.

I may have to stew rock tripe, the *Umbilicaria* lichen that saved a Franklin land expedition and Washington's troops at Valley Forge from starving. "The *tripe de roche*," Franklin wrote in his account, "even where we got enough, only served to allay the pangs of hunger for a short time. . . . This unpalatable weed was now quite nauseous to the whole party, and in several it produced bowel complaints." Did he think it sounded better in French? Their mistake perhaps was eating it raw, as this trifle produces an enzyme that allows it to digest rock. Before the end, men on Franklin's last expedition resorted to eating "long pig"; fittingly, for the Inuit's Innu neighbors in eastern Canada, rock tripe was *windigo wakaw*, "cannibal's cabbage." The seaweed-like crust may contain more calories than honey, cornflakes, potatoes, or hominy, but one tester who soaked and repeatedly boiled it to leach out the bitterness found it to be spongy and bland. Others praise the flavor as earthy, "not entirely unappetizing." I think I'll give my insoles a try first.

Spells of sun in the p.m., but I remain cold to the core on Dismal Hill Two.

CUTTING CORNERS

DAY 42 (9 MILES)
QUAD: KILLIK RIVER (WHICH I DON'T HAVE)

A man can't just sit down and cry—he's got to do something.
—**ALEXANDER VON HUMBOLDT**, *Voyage of Humboldt and Bonpland*

Sunny and clouds. After some of the worst hiking comes some of the best: firm, dry alpine ridges confettied with flowers, including thick patches of forget-me-not and enough monkshood to poison a whale, lead up to Agiak Pass, which itself is marshy. I wonder what this new country holds.

Well, here is what it holds. I've walked right up to a grizzly scrounging sixty yards away. My bear radar must have slackened, as I haven't seen one in ten days. This is the first I've encountered west of the Haul Road, and I wonder about their absence in Gates. It's too late to retreat, so I try to sneak past. I've almost succeeded when he looks up, locks eyes, and starts to follow, and, worst of all, accelerates. I keep walking steadily, trying to appear calm and confident, but he's still trailing, closer now, looking pretty excited. I don't know if grizzlies, like wolves, test the responses of caribou to target the herd's weakest or a sick animal based upon its appearance; in that silent predator-prey dialogue, any visible impairment will spur them to persist in their pursuit. From an ecological perspective, culling keeps the herd healthy, weeding out the unfit, keeping the gene pool strong, the senses honed. This knowledge is no solace to me currently.

Soon enough (but not soon enough) the bear hits my scent trail, and it's *adios*. Two rough-legged hawks circle me, keening. It is now overcast, and the heel hurts despite easier terrain. I camp at the head of Agiak Creek next to a game trail, against better knowledge, on ground that lichens emblazon with splashes of mint green, safety-cone orange, and lemony yellow.

You could call lichens the poorer cousins of plants, though they pilfer other kingdoms, combining algae and hardy fungi, thus forming miniature ecosystems underfoot, a whole world easily overlooked. Long lived and slow growing, lichens thrive where no plants can survive: in extreme climates at extreme elevations or latitudes. As rootless pioneer species, they cling to bare rock, dead wood, bone, humus or moss mounds, to buildings or rusty metal, lying dormant for long periods when conditions turn too inhospitable for them. Unlike vascular plants, these brittle survivors remain metabolically active under snow even in a frozen state.

They contribute to rock weathering, which frees inorganic nutrients, and they prepare the field for plant succession by catching soil particles mosses germinate on. More than five hundred biochemical compounds they produce lessen UV-light damage and deter microbes, browsers, and their plant competition. In arctic Alaska or on high mountain peaks, they are often the only life visible. Their biomass and diversity surpass that of the vegetation in places—three hundred species were recorded around Anaktuvuk Pass.

Their looks match the labels of naturalists: crustose, leprose, umbilicate, filamentous, gelatinous, fan-shaped . . . More specifically, they are described in common names as red-capped, ramrod-straight "toy soldiers"; seafoam-green "fairy barf" bubbling with fleshy, mushroom-y bits; pixie cups, sunbursts, Devil's matchsticks, or dead man's fingers palely poking from the ground; and rock tripe, which indeed looks like a cow's stomach lining. More names allude to internal organs, to lung, kidney, belly, gut, or heart. Like all organisms, lichens have specific requirements, ecological niches. Crinkled snow lichen prefers melting snowbanks. Goldtwist or limestone sunshine lichen brightens calcium-rich soils. Wind-driven, branchy arctic tumbleweed balls into thickets of tiny caribou antlers that pile into tundra depressions as its namesake does against barbed wire fences.

Lichen applications are as diverse as their shapes, preferences, and colors. Arctic species yield brilliant purple or ruddy dyes and, in a pinch, have been alchemized into beer, vodka, or molasses; Melissa steeps muskox-wool yarn in a rock tripe solution for a pretty lilac. Witch's hair caught campfire sparks on the soggy North Slope, and lacey snow lichen bulked up duck and fish soup. The stunning rosettes of jewel lichen pointed Eskimo hunters toward prey: its scab on outcrops feeds on nitrogen from perching raptors' and ground squirrels' urine. Partly digested, fermented "caribou moss"—a grayish lichen—still finds its way from caribou stomachs into those of people in Eskimo ice cream, mixed with raw, mashed fish eggs.

Hundreds of thousands of equally dedicated connoisseurs subsist exclusively on carbohydrate-rich carpets. A few closely related species of reindeer lichen account for up to 90 percent of caribou's winter intake, about ten pounds per head per day, and for half of their summer diet as well. Special enzymes in the ruminants' guts break down the fibrous fare. Considering herd sizes and lichen growth rates, swaths scoured down to the land's bones are unsurprising. Lichen recovery takes decades.

Caribou avoid ranges of lichen younger than fifty years, favoring greener pastures, which goes a long way toward explaining changes in migration patterns or why they linger where they do. "They have a knowledge of some kind—of when it's time to shift to a new territory," Olaus Murie wrote. Moose, muskoxen, and mountain goats substitute lichens at ground level for scrub they favor. Tree varieties stock the winter larder of northern flying squirrels. Golden plovers nest in white worm lichen that further camouflages the speckled eggs. Regrettably, climbing temperatures and precipitation seeding the Arctic with shrubs will replace much lichen cover.

Because lichens lack an outer, epidermal, layer, they cannot tell nutrients from pollutants and absorb both. Chernobyl's fallout poisoned Norwegian landscapes on which Sami herders let their reindeer graze. Thousands of animals had to be killed and their meat destroyed. As recently as 2014, hundreds marked for consumption were released from corrals, riddled with cancer from radioactive residue. As litmus of environmental health—the test strips' active ingredient indeed comes from lichen—lichens monitor dust-borne heavy metals near the Red Dog Mine in the western Brooks Range. Their diversity has decreased along the busy Haul Road.

Equally handy in research, mosaics of black and asparagus green known as map lichen help date rockslides and glacial debris. The first life gaining a foothold on moraines as ice recedes, they expand 0.02 inches per year. Samples endured ten days in outer space without damage. Colonies of this splendid stone rash exceed eight thousand years in age, which makes them living fossils of the North Slope far older than Sierra Nevada bristlecone pines. Lichen circle diameters at Atigun Pass fix the most recent cirque glaciers' disappearance there at four to five millennia BCE.

Outpacing glaciers, even quickly shrinking ones, we humans miss much. This landscape's scale and the need to look out for bears cloud the magic of the minuscule. I vow to bring a loupe on my next arctic adventure and to explore this wild microcosm on my belly but leery of the undead reaching up from the earth.

"Is it entirely imaginary that the ground underfoot somehow transmits its character and energy to the person who walks upon it?" the homesteader-poet John Haines wondered in *The Stars, the Snow, the Fire*. I assume that he alluded to a sense of place or a sense *for* a place, as he was not a mystic but someone who tried to find beauty and deeper truths in building a woodpile or setting a fishnet. This ground does not pamper. It is not garrulous. It hums with silence and space, the expectant air of a concert hall before the first note. This ground waits long for a brief flourishing. It rewards patience and attention to details. Its flashiness is a rarity always aimed at survival: the perpetuation of cycles.

When my focus shifts from lichens to cartography and what it purports to show, I realize that I'm not on Agiak Creek. I am off the map.

To save money, stupidly, I did not buy one of the 1:250,000 quadrangles, one the route intersects only minimally in the bottom right corner. I thought I could wing this stretch, flow with the landscape's flow, trusting my orienteering instincts. I cannot. The Continental Divide wanders drunkenly in this area. I am two miles southwest of Agiak Lake and need to get to Lonely Lake and Easter Creek, on my next map sheet.

"You're not lost when you can backtrack to the last place in which you still knew where you were," we used to tell Outward Bound students, "you are momentarily misplaced."

At a junction with a broad valley, I cannot decide which way to turn. I stand bedraggled, up Snowmelt Creek without a paddle, Hänsel trying to trace breadcrumbs with the help of a malfunctioning satellite phone. That piece of junk sputters like water in a hot greasy frying pan, dropping the call every other minute or so. When I tell Melissa my current coordinates a revived Magellan has given me and ask her for those for Lonely Lake to enter into the gadget, she, consulting Google Earth, tells me there is one lake with that name *thirty-four miles* from my position.

She also mentions more Coyote Air bullshit about the Noatak cache, which I fail to appreciate at the moment. She says they've been rude to her on the phone.

Aaaarrrrgh! This beats the tussocks and my ailing foot. I set off scouting while Melissa researches further. It is late, and unlike in Fairbanks, no place in Nome sells maps and the library there doesn't have any either. And I doubt that the relevant quad, the one with the missing corner, is online.

Leaving my pack at the junction, I jog half a mile upstream and downstream, twice, anxious for a clue. Nothing looks like it should. Even the sights first of a marsh hawk and then a ghostly white owl skimming the tundra for lemmings cannot console me. And it's only my second snowy ever. "Practice is finding yourself where you already are," the thirteenth-century Zen master Dōgen wrote. He meant it as advice for reaching equanimity in meditation by casting off striving. As a navigation tip, it makes your head spin.

One time in Nome, Melissa and I had just gotten into our truck to drive to town when we spotted a ptarmigan in the neighbor's yard caught in a similar mental loop. A freestanding thirty-foot fence section barred her path, and the fool hen, frantic in her search for a gap, dashed back and forth, back and forth but never as far as either end. Finally stepping outside, I shooed her away.

It was funny then. Now I feel what that bird must have felt.

In mounting desperation, I call Melissa again. She, bless her heart, finally has a fix on my whereabouts, having located online maps and matched my landscape description with contour lines on her screen.

The want of a nail almost cost me my kingdom, my one-time shot, and my sanity. I never anticipated this problem. Some shortcuts will bite you, adding distance and stress. Practice being where you already find yourself!

It is after midnight when I crawl into my down bag ready to forget this day.

THE MOTHER OF WOLVES

DAY 43 (13 MILES)
QUAD: SURVEY PASS

Another drizzly, fun day of tussock wrestling, but at least I am back on the map.

I *was* camped on Agiak Creek after all, I realize as the landscape coheres again, but underestimated the distance I would be traveling off the map and therefore the distance to Lonely Lake. Half of my scouting was in the right direction—upstream. I simply did not go far enough for the lake, like the fool hen not venturing to the fence ends. Without that landmark, I was second-guessing my position and went down the slippery slope of soliloquy. Perhaps my brain is not being perfused enough or I'm lacking nutrients or some such thing.

It turns out that a good seven miles separate last night's campsite from the lake. I should at least have measured that distance when I looked at maps before the trip at the university library. But maps can be rabbit holes. Each quad in that drawer stuck to another, the names sang their promises, and I got sidetracked. For the cartographer Denis Wood, that's "the very point of a map, to present us not with the world we can *see*, but to point toward a world we might *know*."

To travelers on the ground, as opposed to riding an armchair or navigating map drawers, true wilderness can feel downright nasty, as if it were trying to maim, to hinder each step, denying transit. It's a far cry from the aesthete's relaxed contemplation of a book, photo, or documentary. If all supporters of nature were to experience it at its teeth-gnashing, slobbering best, would all still deem it worthy of protection? Of funding? It's easier to love a person or thing idealized in the abstract, at a distance, vicariously. We do need wilderness, among other reasons to humble us, as a reminder that the other-than-human world too can break us.

I have passed no suitable camps, except at upper Easter Creek, five miles back, around noon.

Only afterward do I learn that on that day, I missed out on a special attraction, remnants of a plywood hutch that played a role in the conception of a little-known classic of wilderness writing. I doubt I would have had the additional food or vigor for a side pilgrimage even if I had known about that site. A northwesterly course down Easter Creek that morning would have brought me to a hill two miles south of the junction of Easter Creek and the Killik River, near Lake Tulilik. Little would have been left on that height: some beams and planks, rock foundations, but most important, the skeleton of a chicken wire pen that held wolves beside the famous "Crackerbox"—well, famous among my bookish kind. In 1953 and 1954, Lois and Herb Crisler spent two summers raising wolves there for a film project. The wolves for Lois became a lifelong passion.

Born in 1897 in Spokane, Washington, the daughter of a Protestant minister, Lois Brown married Herb "Cris" Crisler, a mountain man she had met on a climbing trip. The willowy University of Washington English teacher, author of a thesis on Santayana's definition of beauty, a woman, in Rachel Carson's opinion, prettier than photos suggested, was an unlikely match. Walt Disney hired the bearded autodidact Herb, who'd documented Olympic Peninsula elk, to shoot scenes for the Oscar-winning if melodramatic *White Wilderness* (1958), which perpetuated the myth of lemming mass suicides. Handlers dropped them from a bluff for that six-minute, rodent-stampede sequence.

After filming Denali's bears, the lovebirds roosted eighteen months in the Crackerbox, with a stint in a Barrow "wanigan," a "narrow shack on runners." Disney asked them to shelter there lest they die in backcountry blizzards.

The couple, unarmed, never staging scenes, which was unusual for that time, gathered breathless footage of wolves loping after caribou. In their luckiest break, they bought two three-week-old littermates from Nunamiut hunters the first summer. Trigger grew into a "lordly yet shy," "handsome" gray bruiser. Lady, "gay and fearless, and utterly straightforward," was a black "Cleopatra of changing moods." Initially penning both nightly and later letting them roam as they pleased, the Crislers never trained the wolves that escorted their humans and sometimes returned with bloody muzzles. Lois, watching how they treated each other and their adoptive family, considered them more graceful, sensitive, and intelligent than dogs. "Much of their faces' expression," she found, "resides in their quick-changing eyes," and unlike dogs, a wolf "runs with his tail, thinks with it, marks mood with it, even controls with it." In a game Trigger invented, he sneaked up and snagged a mitt though he "gauged his bite to a nicety," never puncturing Lois's skin. Lady loved untying the earflaps on Herb's hat.

In an age that still demonized wolves as bloodlust incarnate in what Lois called "the Grimms' fairytale effect," her words undermined that reputation. Giving one of the earliest realistic accounts of wolf interactions, she would replace Jack London's savage *White Fang*, in one historian's eyes, with "an image tamed for juvenile mass consumption."

"Feral generosity" charmed Lois, who anthropomorphized and wrote emotionally, a lay opposite of Adolph Murie, a biologist observing McKinley's Toklat pack. Lois and Herb joined their pair's howling: the happy, pack-bonding howl; the mourning howl; the deep, hunting howl; and the *Where-are-you?* howl. "Wilderness without wildlife is just scenery," she came to believe. Conversely, "animals without wilderness are a closed book"—wolves remained enigmatic outside their home environment. She saw them test caribou, surprised at how quickly they'd judge a chase to be futile. "In a reasonable world," for a species bent on unlearning war, Lois felt, "these peaceful predators would be the most cherished object of study."

To film puppies, Herb had five snatched from a den, which Trigger and Lady, then yearlings, helped rear. Bereaving the she-wolf of quintuplets haunted Lois.

Her notes grew into *Arctic Wild*, published in nine languages. The son of the conservation icon Aldo Leopold, Starker Leopold, praised her "most meticulous and complete description of wolf mannerisms and behavior." It stressed wolves culling caribou as essential for healthy herds.

Before the Crislers ran out of time on the tundra, a wild female rival killed Lady. Trigger left, founding his own family. Soon after, a bounty hunter poisoned him. The Crislers continued parenting the pups until the fieldwork ended. Fearing they'd starve to death unsupported, the couple brought them to their Colorado cabin. The expats fled their pen, and locals killed all but one: "Miss" Alatna. For the next seven years, Lois dedicated herself to the lone survivor, trying to create a semblance of Alatna's former social life, providing stud dogs that sired new whelps. The hybrids, too fierce, were euthanized.

The Crislers never had children. In Colorado, half-tame 90-to-110-pound carnivores burdened the marriage, and the self-described "mother of wolves" divorced Herb. Back in Seattle, living modestly, struggling to process her meddling with nature, she wrote *Captive Wild* upon Carson's urging. "People suppose wildness is ferocity," Lois had realized in the Arctic, yet "it is something far more serious. . . . It is independence." Wolves had taught her at the price of that independence. "You can't help sharing a wolf's joy," she believed, and "a wolf, it seems, shares your troubles." The words of one who befriended wolves for more than eight years carry weight. Still, sharing their joy, she caused some of her charges' plight, even death.

Lois disliked small talk, her pen pal Carson remarked: "She has forgotten the easy chatting and exchange of not-so-important comment that makes up social intercourse"—as have I, I'm afraid, on this traverse. Her seclusion and beasts red in tooth and claw realigned her as they have me. I also agree with Lois about wolf eyes ever since mine locked onto them near Anaktuvuk: "You can never do justice to them until you are close."

It so happens that I miss a treat at Agiak Lake too this morning. There, hunters six millennia ago erected hundreds of stone *inuksuit*, "likenesses of a man" (singular *inuksuk* or *inukshuk*), a precursor of Gwich'in drivelines that funneled caribou. Repaired and modified for centuries, the Northern Archaic mile-long scarecrow corridor hazed herds toward real men with razor-sharp flint-tipped lances, seated in kayaks, who turned the lake's water red. Adjacent to cache pits and dozens of stone rings that anchored skin tents, these upright slabs still guard the broad valley. Archaeologists snorkeling in Agiak Lake disappointingly surfaced with only a single bone from a butchered caribou. But the communal hunt with kayaks was well documented. In the fall of 1944, nudged by concerns about ammunition supplies during the war, Anaktuvuk Pass families reverted to this old subsistence practice, organizing a three-day caribou drive—a *tuttusiuvaqtuat* or communal kayak hunt—at Little Chandler Lake, ten miles north of Agiak.

The Brooks Range holds more than fifteen hundred documented ancient sites. Given that anthropologists have surveyed only about 1 percent of the total land area, a wealth of secrets remains undiscovered. Some, the herds obliterate on their migrations. I wonder how many I walk past unknowingly on this trek, how many of my camps hosted flint knappers and their families. A park anthropologist told me about evidence of caribou drivelines in every major Brooks Range Valley. It goes to show: what you see is often what you are prepared to see.

I am overdue for stopping, but still the land does not provide a good campsite. Finally, a hillock island in the tussock sea with a dry, level cap big enough for my tent. In an irony of ironies, it's *too dry*, no water nearby, not even one gunky pocket hiding between mop heads. So, I get it from a flooded meadow about ten minutes away, filling my pot, bottle, and a ziplock to last me at least until morning. Balancing everything without spilling the precious wet on this inland chop, I flash back to childhood egg races at summer camp—except that after nine hours of stork-like stilting, this run is not nearly as much of a hoot. Despite the punishing terrain, my foot does not hurt as badly as yesterday and I've covered more miles.

THAT WHICH DOES NOT KILL US

DAY 44 (13 MILES)
QUAD: SURVEY PASS

Overcast and surprisingly cold. It is not a question of *if* it is going to rain but only *when*. The weather illustrates another bon mot I heard on Ireland's west coast: "If you can see the Aran Islands from the mainland, it will rain. If you can't see the islands, it's already raining."

My rain starts an hour after breakfast and with nary a break continues all day. The balance sheet at this point: roughly three weeks sun and three weeks none. Days to come may tip the scales either way. All in all, it's already the wettest Alaska summer I can recall. Or perhaps I'm just spending more time outside.

Raindrops sequin larkspur, another toxic midnight-blue siren like monkshood. Only burly bumblebees can bust through the trapdoors guarding its dunce cap flowers. Throughout the West, larkspur is a livestock killer, but Alaska Natives drank small amounts of a liquid boiled from it to treat tuberculosis. A larkspur wash killed lice and fleas, and some Inupiat poisoned arrowheads with an extract from the roots of a related anemone. "Solely the dose determines that a thing is not a poison," the Swiss Renaissance physician-philosopher Paracelsus famously wrote. Foragers' skills in distinguishing lethal amounts and applications from healing ones stagger the mind, given that they learned through trial and error, word of mouth, and observation.

Wish I had more botanical knowledge. My foot is swollen and the ankle therefore less flexible; I am a senior citizen with edema. Now, where did I park my walker? Perhaps the lightened load, compared to what I schlepped out of

Anaktuvuk, will let me mend. That's delusional thinking, I realize. I know better from wilderness first responder courses required for guides. The cure for bum joints is RICE: Rest. Ice. Compression. Elevation. While I *did* wrap the ankle with an elastic bandage to stabilize it and contain the bloat, there's no ice in sight. I cannot afford rest, and the only elevation that matters is the one I should gain on my way to Kutuk Pass in the Endicott Mountains, another milestone on the Continental Divide.

The ground since I left Easter Creek has improved. I camp in a valley connecting April and Easter Creeks without going on an egg hunt. Humor, especially the childish and gallows kind, helps me cope, so you'll have to excuse me. I cook inside the tent and stay inside afterward. I only want to be dry and out of the wind.

You can borrow a Park Service "bear vault" from the Fairbanks visitor office. Unlike in the refuge, those are mandatory inside Gates of the Arctic, keeping bears from thinking of hikers as easy sources of food and therefore keeping either or both from getting killed. A magic-marker diagram on the underside of each barrel lid shows the ideal camp setup, a triangle of 100 yards on each side with your tent at the pointy bit and your kitchen and storage area downwind, at opposite corners of its base. (Excuse my language—I opted out of math in tenth grade.)

Cooking and eating inside a tent in bear country invites big, hairy trouble. It momentarily skews the safety geometry into a dot. But the daily onslaught of weather sometimes dissolves best practices. Hypothermia is no laughing matter either, and by soloing I'm already ignoring recommendations. Of course, were a grizzly to destroy my tent and were I to live, I'd also face cold nights on bald mountains. As mundane as decisions outdoors may appear, some compound consequences, like the butterfly's wings building the storm. You simply hope the rare breach in routine will go unpunished.

PROFESSOR COLD

DAY 45 (14 MILES)
QUAD: SURVEY PASS

Another nipping, nipple-hardening morning. (It's the goosebump effect, if you must know.) As at Ernie Pass, it feels like the first day of fall. I am hiking in my raingear and mitts just to stay warm and make good time to Kutuk Pass, another familiar place. One early September a few years ago, I guided a family at a basecamp there in similar temperatures. They came self-equipped and wanted to do their own food too, so my duties were simply to lead them on day hikes and ensure their safety. The father, a Seattle banker and bit of a gearhead, had strangely decided to bring neither a tent nor a cooking stove. They slept under a fancy tarp instead and gnawed on imported cheeses and macadamias and Wagyu beef jerky straight from their bear barrels. I felt sorry for the girls, so I brought them hot tea in the mornings.

They still got their money's worth. In the stillness of one night, I crawled from my tent to relieve myself and could not believe my eyes. In a crystal sky sugared with stars, the aurora twitched in all its neon-green glory. Wandering organ pipes, whorls, curtains, and streamers in their eerie silence made me expect some sound effect—the cello wail, perhaps, of a bowed saw playing haunted house music. As if this were not enough, the lake's gloss at my feet doubled the miracle. With the roused family, I stood in silence, the chill night air forgotten. I will treasure those moments for the rest of my life.

Kutuk could not look or sound more different now. Clouds shroud the valley, with raindrops ticking on the lowly vegetation. I am cruising down April Creek, on caribou trails once again, as if on rails, lunching quickly so my pilot bread won't disintegrate. Memories of sunbathing on the tundra seem to be of a former trip. While it is not quite cold enough to snow, I breathe on my Nutella for five minutes to render it spreadable.

I know nothing about the cold tolerance of Laurence Irving, the pioneer of biological cold adaptation research mentioned earlier, but as to mine, during my first Fairbanks winter in 1989 I blistered my Adam's apple biking from my cabin to campus. I quickly realized that a zipper's metal slider is a perfect conductor. (I ditched physics too in tenth grade.) Fairbanksians remember Irving, the first director of UAF's Institute of Arctic Biology—near where frost bit my throat— for his holistic approach. Considering all facets of arctic survival, he was never content with just the nitty-gritty of individual species' survival mechanisms.

Given Laurence's arctic feats and long Fairbanks residence, this student of chill responses certainly knew lunar temperatures. His peers called the Boston-born Harvard and Stanford man "Larry," believing that "Noah's Ark would have been an appropriate location in the space-time continuum" for him because of the menagerie he had handled for his research. His eager mind grappled with beach fleas and ducks; starfish respiration; trout embryo development; seal, porpoise, and manatee blood circulation; and related mammal adaptations, including those of humans.

Considering *Homo sapiens* as merely another animal and therefore fair game, Irving learned that the hands of North Slope Inupiat immersed in ice water stayed warmer and functional longer than those of Caucasian control groups. (He's mum on nipple behavior.) White commercial fishermen too acquire this tolerance, which thus is not genetic. Furthermore, Inupiaq test subjects exposed to moderate cold with scant bedding slept rather comfortably, shivering less than their White counterparts. However, their culture's ancestral technology—sod houses, skin clothing, seal-oil lamps, furs, and such—and savvy regarding snow and ice shielded them better than any physical traits.

Irving soon realized that besides being hardy, the Inupiat were astute naturalists. They volunteered facts gleaned "during a lifetime and in seasons and weather when most scientists remain indoors," he noted in his arctic ornithological study, so "thanks to their careful observations, accurate knowledge of country, and ability to travel" his studies proceeded rapidly. Inupiaq hospitality throughout "greatly eased the burden of working in remote regions." Irving hired Inupiaq consultants in Barrow and at Anaktuvuk Pass, lured by the valley's reputation as a flyway. The moxie of tiny black-capped chickadees wintering in the Brooks Range surprised even him.

"While the aurora flashed in the winter nights outside, the people described many birds with the intimate detail in which I had known them as a boy in the northeastern states," he reported of his first visit to Anaktuvuk. On his next, the locals showed Irving yellowlegs, wandering tattlers, and long-tailed jaegers they'd caught and kept in their tents for him to examine. "The lakes and country are daily searched by the Nunamiut with telescopes in their survey for game," he wrote, "and large loons and even small birds are carefully examined until identified. All birds seen are noted and with other natural phenomena are the subject of careful discussion when people get together."

Irving enlisted Simon Paneak, that able "instructor of scholars," to investigate ptarmigan distribution. His guide discussed the mountain valleys' natural history in "accurate and expressive English." Many elders from the Anaktuvuk Pass region remember winters without ptarmigan when some people starved to death. Unfortunately, like snowshoe hares the fool hens have little fat. Paneak compared eating them boiled without some kind of blubber to dining on moss. Raw eggs made simple snacks out on the land. The stomach content of leafy greens yielded vitamins in short supply at high latitudes. The pungent droppings, which could pass for sawdust Cheetos, seasoned stews of seal meat, oil, and blood. The culinary adventurer and mycologist Lawrence Millman, who tried ptarmigan Parmesan, "would choose it any day of the week over whatever McDonald's puts between its buns." Always traveling light, the Gwich'in cooked ptarmigan by filling the chest cavity with water and dropping a hot rock where a hot heart formerly pulsed. People traded the feathers for arrow fletching or scrubbed hands and dishes after a meal with them.

The bond between Irving and Paneak bloomed into a friendship of more than twenty-five years, with Paneak coauthoring papers and Irving eulogizing the hunter-historian in an obituary. Irving downplayed his own insights from five fruitful decades, commenting, "I do not know what use the results may have, but I have a feeling that, like art, science is as valuable, as it provides pleasurable interest." A devoted mentor, the winter tsar kept a toe in academic waters until his death at age eighty-four in 1979.

The rain never stops until I camp at the mouth of Doc Creek, my cutover to the Alatna. I could be on the Noatak in three days if all goes well.

My clothing and gear are sopping, everything but the sleeping bag and a layer of thermal underwear I sequestered in a drybag. A moose ogles me and trots off. They follow willows up protective drainages from the south side, probing the North Slope, with beavers and snowshoe hares right on their tails. Admittedly, moose do not have much of one, just a stub. Relatively rare north of the divide during the early twentieth century, they became increasingly common in the second half. Winter condemns them to a diet of frozen willow buds, and they need to eat the equivalent of a large trash bag full daily to survive. They still lose up to 50 percent of their body weight, which means some shed 850 pounds. I should not really complain about my dwindling girth, not yet anyway.

Among moose remains hundreds or thousands of years old, scientists on the North Slope found an antler they dated to fourteen millennia BCE. In sync with plant cover and hunting pressure, the small arctic population—Eurasian immigrants, as all North American moose (and beavers) are—shifts like a stilt-legged, rubber-lipped tide. Again and again, the Arctic rejigs our grasshopper perspective, our expectations.

As I sit in the vestibule of my tent after dinner, procrastinating, not quite ready yet to turn in despite the wet nastiness, another clip from *Never Cry Wolf* plays in my head. By the film's end, with the field season over, hunters have decimated the pack. While snowflakes alight on the tundra and melt on his wire rim glasses, the biologist sits on a boulder, playing mournful notes on his bassoon—and a distant wolf answers him.

I hole up early again. Sitting outside staring at gray while wishing for an opening is not my idea of fun.

CACHE NUMBER SIX
OR BUST

DAY 46 (12.5 MILES)
QUAD: SURVEY PASS

Clouds drag their guts across the valley bottom: numbolostrumpus. The mountains, as in Song Dynasty paintings, reveal only a shoulder here, a toe there. It's not raining today; it mists. My long underwear for inside the sleeping bag got damp yesterday, so I stuffed it into the only dry spot, the almost-empty bear barrel on my backpack.

Ron Yarnell promised the hiking in Doc Creek would be good. Initially, I can't see that since tussocks are in the way; but when the creek widens and frays, gravel bars offer decent walking. Grayling hang out here. A momma bear and two cubs on a distant slope do not notice me, and I slink past as if I had picked the bears' pockets.

I hate to pass up upper Doc, very scenic, good campsites, but I need to resupply soon. I'll have to lay over here next time. Yeah, right.

A row of widely spaced stones across the caribou path looks as if someone is rerouting traffic. It is likely the work of a downhill flood. The trail continues unobstructed beyond that apparent barrier. I nevertheless cross to the opposite bank on a whim, although the hiking is no better there.

Not two minutes later, I spot a bear on the side I vacated, a cub. Then another. And another. That curious golden toddler standing up alerts the mother, who muscles in close to investigate. Had I not switched sides, I would have blundered right into this random cluster. I continue upstream, trying to assure Mom that I don't mean to harm her brood. For a moment, for once, it appears to shape up into a stress-free encounter for everybody involved: they move downstream, in the other direction. Then, suddenly, the whole mob gallops over to my side, downwind and behind me, to check out this skinny biped. Tell me there's no calculation at work, no mental abacus clicking that may equal but differs from mine.

I keep a steady course, now and then glancing over my shoulder to ensure she's not creeping up on me from some unforeseen quarter, disguised by a rise. Losing sight of her is much worse than facing her. I expect her to show up on a swell of ground parallel to the trail any second, like a genie from a broken bottle.

But bears don't care about our expectations. Quite high on the mountainside, four rumps jiggle out of sight. Bingo. I guess after forty-five unwashed days I'm too rank even for grizzlies.

As my body odor has sharpened out here, so have my instincts, arrows hitting the bull's eye without aiming. At the barrier, I sensed something amiss, some existential wrinkle reminiscent of the one in the Chandalar bearflower meadow two weeks ago. Counting this morning's trio, that amounts to a seven-bear day, the first since Joe Creek.

Before I pop over to Ram Creek, I skirt two lovely if sterile lakes, sapphire gems set in bedrock on a small saddle. This April-Creek-to-Alatna thoroughfare is bear-y scenic. I can only imagine its beauty on a clear sunny day, as presently all summits have been decapitated.

I camp on a ridge beyond the pass, a broad back with a view down the valley. Dinner is a bit meager, and I'll probably have to split tomorrow's ration in two.

CONDITIONS CANNOT BE IGNORED

DAY 47 (9 MILES)
QUAD: SURVEY PASS

It's as if a wet fleece has been thrown over the valley, socked in, the view obliterated. "Socked in" is pilot lingo: when you can't see the windsock from the control tower. Or from inside the windsock. Cloud vapors invade my bedchamber when I unzip the tent fly. Except for the clamminess on my skin, the morning is a sensory deprivation tank. Hiking feels unsafe. I could sleepwalk into bears or make a wrong turn on the Alatna, getting suckered downstream instead. I'll sit tight for the time being.

The Brooks Range never gets boring. When I start to feel comfortable, mildly competent, mildly confident, it hurls another curveball at me or rather, a missile. Waiting this out would not be a problem were it not for the food shortage. It's twenty-some miles to the Noatak cache, which might as well be the moon. I'm Scott of the Arctic stuck short of the vital depot.

This is not the middle of nowhere, but if the weather cleared up, I could see it from here. We bizarrely define "the middle of nowhere" as "far from any town or other inhabited place," while in fact most of our cities are Anywhereville USA, cookie cutter designs from the same lump of urban dough; John McPhee said as much about Anchorage. In the middle of nowhere, city slickers losing their bearings get lost. To the contrary, subtly varied landmarks stamp this tundra unmistakably. Utopia literally is "nowhere" (unless you're Musk ogling Mars or Bezos the Boastful, Emperor of Amazonia); the best possible world is anchored in real earthly places. The skewed mindset that coined "nowhere" and "no-man's-land" also gave us "remote" and US maps with small Hawaii and Alaska insets. Remote from whose perspective? The axis mundi can be wherever you want it to be. To the Nunamiut, it is Anaktuvuk, and Fairbanks an unreal periphery. The 1002 Area, to paraphrase the poet Naomi Shihab Nye, is famous to the Porcupine herd.

A magic hand parts the curtain, which opens fully an hour later.

Though caribou trails aid my progress in lower Ram Creek, I do my share of ramming through alders—always after blowing my whistle—where they booby-trap transverse ravines that give me the willies. Spruce runts announce the tree line in the Alatna River valley. On a ridge I pause, beholding the stream's fluttering ribbon, old silver lace enfolded in huntsman green.

I am moving much more slowly than hoped, sure now that I'll run out of food before the cache.

Just as I'm about to pack up my lunch stuff, ready to head on down, a faraway bear climbs up my intended route. Great minds think alike where navigation is concerned. I backtrack, ceding open ground I've labored to gain and bushwhack in a boreal beeline for the river. I arrive, topping out on the lip of a cliff band along which I crash upstream through undergrowth hoping for a gap and a ford.

At long last I wade in, and in the current my hiking poles tremble again. I stroll on gravel bar boulevards the Alatna's raveling built, a delight after an ordeal. Tracks of bears, moose, beavers, minks, and wolves on the shoals lift the veil just enough for a peek at alien lives. Pebbles shot through with marine fossils pave the dove-gray sand beaches: jumbled ivory buttons of crinoid cross-sections; white fan streaks or a petri dish's cell cultures of corals; brachiopod raisins in chunks of limestone bread. The patterns look psychedelic, unreal. Serenity washes through me. Fasting combined with exercise reportedly boosts people's sleep, memory, energy levels, and mood, all while reducing inflammation. A cocktail of endorphins and dopamine spikes the bloodstream, feel-good chemicals that laughter and meditation also release and that dampen pain and anxiety. But a little fear is a healthy thing out here. So is a little food. Hemmed by this northern jungle, watched over by frost-riven peaks, I cross and recross repeatedly, setting my weaving against the Alatna's.

Olaus Murie saw a very different scene on a winter collecting expedition with his half brother, Adolph, in 1923. They had left Allakaket with two dog teams on

January 4 after a minus-68-degree cold snap. "Conditions could not be ignored," Olaus wrote, describing these conditions as "almost unbearable, at times." The brothers broke trail on snowshoes and stayed put on days when they could hear their breath crackle as the exhaled moisture froze almost instantly, a sound Finns hear as "the whisper of the stars." Smoke from a stovepipe at such temperatures rises but a few feet and cooling quickly, snakes downward to writhe near the ground before diffusing into a milky lake. When Amundsen sent his victorious wire from Eagle, the cold somewhere had broken the line, and he had to await confirmation that his words had reached the outer world for a week, until after the repair. In denser, frigid, calm air—air that "rings like a knife blade against bone" in the composer John Luther Adams's words—you can eavesdrop on people talking miles away without technology's magic. That's why wolf howls travel farthest at night, up to six miles.

At the Alatna headwaters the brothers shot eight sheep, keeping six as specimens and feasting on the others. Olaus marveled at the boldness of weasels whose tracks they followed in the timbered bottoms as well as on high ridges in the Endicott Mountains. "At one camp, a weasel found our pile of dog feed and made that his headquarters during our stay. Several times as one of us passed the pile of fish he peeped out and chattered, as if disputing our right to the dog feed."

I smile noticing that in his penciled field journal, Olaus personalizes the animal: "his" and "he."

On their return in late March, the brothers ran into flocks numbering several hundred ptarmigans pecking at willows and poplars along the riverbanks. Olaus related how "the natives sometimes snare these birds by constructing a hedge of willows in a straight line across the feeding ground, leaving gaps at frequent intervals in which cord snares are set." Anaktuvuk Pass villagers drove flocks into nets woven from braided sinew and laid out on snow, bagging forty to fifty birds at a time. Indigenous northerners clubbed, stoned, or stunned Alaska's eventual state bird with blunt arrowheads, then roasted, smoked, dried, or stewed it, or ate it raw. (Its East Greenlandic name, *mitigak*, translates as "he at whom rocks are thrown.") Decoys fooled amorous territorial males. An Eskimo hunter would clear a soil patch and sculpt a likeness from snow, dressing it with russet grass around the neck to simulate spring plumage.

Celebrating Thanksgiving with miners, the future director of Berkeley's Museum of Vertebrate Zoology and author of *Birds of the Kotzebue Sound Region, Alaska* Joseph "Chickadee Joe" Grinnell praised ptarmigan, the "turkey of the Kobuk," above all other game. One Sourdough trapper hung his "white pheasants" in a spruce, retrieving the frozen treats as needed from this Christmas tree. In late spring, ptarmigans gobble up Labrador tea and old berries while they wait for willows to bud. This gives the meat an herby aroma, which people prefer over the birds' willowy tang later in the year. They are said to taste best in the fall when gorging solely on berries.

When Olaus and Adolph ran out of the frozen whitefish they carried for their dogs, they killed two to feed the rest before reaching the village completely out of provisions. The year after their trip, surveyors on eight sleds with teams hauled four wooden freight canoes up the Alatna for a summer on the North Slope. Nowadays, traffic flows mostly downstream, recreationists floating from the Arrigetch Peaks—an arctic Yosemite—to the village.

To imagine a starker, wintry Alatna River, I stop the reel of its running. I strip off all deciduous foliage. Darken the conifers' green. Cover river and forest floor with white pile three feet deep. Silence the birds and the current's gurgling. And dim and thicken the light, which dulls blue sky to sackcloth. My breath plumes as I dial down the temperature too. I snap out of my reverie and in an instant, summer enwraps and enraptures me, as it should.

Olaus Murie's Alaska travels closed the era of natural history exploration in North America that Lewis and Clark had launched, the enterprise an outgrowth of the Enlightenment that in the historian William H. Goetzmann's phrasing practiced "science as common-sense descriptive history." Muir, Dall, and Olaus Murie drew on long periods of field observation during which they sketched and collected specimens. This inductive type of research made do without methods like aerial surveys, radio collaring, computer statistical analysis, or experiments. Irving and Schaller represent the newer, deductive, gadget-loving school.

The subject of quantification nudges another memory that rears its grizzled head, smiling. Guiding a Dutch family from the Noatak to the upper Alatna by a route different from mine on the traverse, I performed one of my proudest outdoor feats ever. The father had pointed out fronds of bull caribou antlers sprouted from a bleached skull on the stream bank and keen on numbers, as many of my clients are because figures make the wilds appear safe and contained, asked what the set might weigh. "Twenty-six pounds," I ventured off the cuff, never having been a math wiz and not caring all that much. He promptly pulled a spring scale from his pack, which, being Dutch, he probably used for weighing their loads before the hike; it's a nation that found its feet as merchants, after all. He then hung the rack from it and announced "twenty-six pounds to the ounce." I had earned their full confidence.

After about three miles in the Alatna's glen, I turn and head southwest up a gorge, Gull Creek, which springs from a pass that will be my last before the Noatak. A strange mood suffuses me—anticipation and happiness, cut with early-onset nostalgia. I am reluctant to leave the Alatna, sensing that my adventure overland is nearly finished.

I ascend Gull Creek, literally, as its slopes are too brushy. Where the gorge bottlenecks, the water is wall to wall. I am slow and my foot hurts again, so I fail to reach the pass as I hoped to. Boot prints ribbing the sand precede mine, and while I'd like to think they are those of the solitary hiker I've trailed before, they're too weathered to tell for sure. Camp is rough creek gravel, Lisburne debris. The grist off milled mountains. Just when dinner is steaming and ready and my clothes on a bush have started to dry, rain forces me inside the tent again.

I SHALL GATHER
BY THE RIVER

DAY 48 (16.5 MILES)
QUAD: SURVEY PASS

Dabs of powder blue dispel gray and then vanish, as if the weather were indecisive. I leave the creek bed above the tree line and thread caribou trails that vein the steep slopes skirting the crystalline creek as it worms through narrows. The caribou, as usual, know when to switch sides to avoid sheer drops or brutal talus. The final miles up to golden water-stained cliffs guarding the pass rank among the trip's most picturesque.

On the far side, a valley's sweep ridged crosswise with dikes resisting erosion drops to the Noatak, still out of sight. A haze of young horsetails up to my ankles turns the cut into a Swiss pasture. Living fossils, the whorled feathery ferns through which my boots swish evolved in the Devonian. Species dominating the understory of Paleozoic forests, feeding dinosaurs, could tower a hundred feet tall.

I cross the Continental Divide one last time. From here to the Bering Strait will be downhill, the occasional rise notwithstanding. Lucky Six Creek dug the deepening trench on this side of the pass, and I descend with it for the final four miles to the river. Prospectors after a phony rush on the Kobuk discovered gold here in 1898. The lack of timber made mining the Noatak headwaters difficult. Men and their dogs lined scows loaded with planks whipsawed on the Reed River, a Kobuk tributary near Ambler, thirty miles to the Lucky Six and nearby Midas Creek to build sluice boxes.

Generations of caribou ask me to ignore gravity, to disregard the creek's fall line and instead keep skirting talus on the chalk traces of their trails on Mount

Papiok, shaped like the eponymous Tail of a Fish. Trying to solve the visual riddle, I surprise five Dall sheep, my alpine send-off committee.

It's not over yet. There remain a few gaping ravines to cross, and I scramble into and out of them. I pray the sixth cache will be where I planned it to be, and intact, that it will be my Lucky Six.

Never before has a drink of water tasted this good. I see why baptisms still are performed on such riverbanks. Taking a first sip of the Noatak at the mouth of Lucky Six Creek, I toast the wilds and the river that, knock on wood, will take me home—or rather to Kotzebue, from where I will catch a jet home.

It is still ten miles to my boat cache at Portage Creek, an alternative up-and-down over from the Alatna. I hike the broad gravel bars, repeatedly crossing the Noatak, which here in its upper reaches is less than a stone's throw wide. I daydream about floating already, except that there is no landing strip, hence no put-in this high up. Most Noatak river parties, with bigger boats than mine, launch at Pingo Lake, downstream from my cache.

The light's angle and water's depth change the flow from sapphire to jade. I don't know which looks prettier. Where the stream wheels north I decide to cut off a mile or two by crossing the foot of a mountain that causes the arc. Blueberries have ripened on the tundra, a sign of summer's progress, which has not always been obvious in the high country and with the weather I've had. The velvety spheres, warm from the sun, tartly burst in my mouth.

On a slope with scattered willow and alder clumps I fall into my "Hey bear" routine. Sure enough, there is one, looking for me. I duck behind a rise and circle past him at a respectful distance. He's probably back to hoovering berries, and I see nothing more of him.

A beautiful camp awaits me on an elevated gravel bar lush with fireweed and the bustle of shuttling bees briefly docking. It's riverfront property, with the Noatak ten yards away. I can rest assured that it will still be there when I wake up after tonight, that it is not just a mirage. "He who hears the rippling of rivers in these degenerate days will not utterly despair," wrote Henry David Thoreau. Lately, distance and space have tamped down my despair, making it manageable, with the world's affairs largely forgotten.

I sit *in the sun* after dinner, *outside*, the first time in three weeks, I believe. Stuff is spread all over to dry, as if a pack has exploded. Three handfuls of noodle shards and a pinch of Parmesan from the bear barrel's dregs constitute my celebration dinner. All I have left for breakfast are two pilot bread crackers and coffee. I better find that cache before lunchtime tomorrow.

Droning bees and the river's babbling almost put me to sleep. It's been a long, hard day. I call Melissa to let her know I made it to the Noatak.

A clutch of small cirque glaciers in the Schwatka Mountains births the Noatak, one of Alaska's longest designated wild and scenic rivers. Except for far-flung homesteads and fish camps and a few tundra landing strips, no human construction impacts its 425-mile length. That's a little shorter than the proposed $5.9 billion gas pipeline from Prudhoe to Fairbanks, but the Noatak snakes more and bites not at all—quite the contrary. Its mountain-ringed basin is the nation's largest undammed watershed. Six distinct ecosystems, from the alpine tundra to the delta, form a UN International Biosphere Reserve monitored as a baseline for environmental changes worldwide. About four-fifths of the river unspool within the Noatak National Preserve, beyond Gates of the Arctic National Park. Marked "Inland River" on late-nineteenth-century maps, it has served for thousands of years as a highway between the Bering Sea coast and the western Brooks Range.

Annual trade fairs at Sheshalik, a spit riddled with tundra ponds, near present-day Kotzebue, drew two thousand Siberians and Inupiat from up and down the coast as well as interior regions. Today, only four hundred Inupiat live year-round on this river's banks, in the village of Noatak, fifty miles from Kotzebue Sound. The first Anglo explorer arrived in 1885 on *Corwin*, which had hosted John Muir four years earlier. With a sailor companion, this man, assistant engineer Samuel B. McLenegan, paddled and lined a twenty-seven-foot Aleut skin kayak or *baidarka* upriver and back. "The Noatak is not navigable for other than native canoes," McLenegan wrote, having turned turtle repeatedly. "The constant succession of rapids rendered our work exceedingly hard, but the amphibious qualities of our nature made it a matter of little importance whether we were in or out of the water." I think he meant that everybody knew how to swim when they flipped or fell in. He found it "impossible to struggle against the strong current with the paddles, and the tracking line was constantly in use." Eventually, the hull of their craft began to leak: "The discomfort occasioned by sitting in a pool of water cannot be aptly described, but it is not productive of a cheerful frame of mind."

Compared to McLenegan's journey of nearly one month, mine down the Noatak should be a lark.

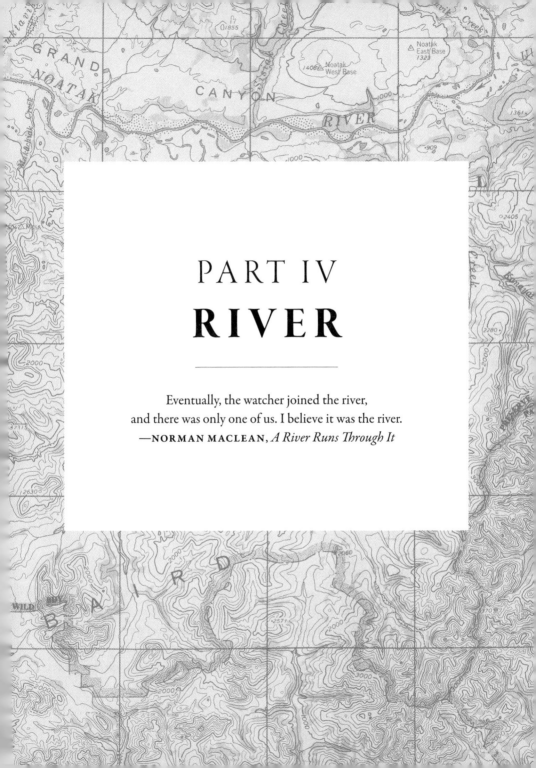

PART IV
RIVER

---

*Eventually, the watcher joined the river,
and there was only one of us. I believe it was the river.*
—**NORMAN MACLEAN**, *A River Runs Through It*

MESSING ABOUT IN A BOAT

DAY 49 / RIVER DAY 1 (13 MILES)
QUAD: SURVEY PASS
CACHE #6

Believe me, my young friend, there is nothing—absolutely nothing—
half so much worth doing as simply messing about in boats.
—Ratty to Mole in Kenneth Grahame's *Wind in the Willows*

Summer is back. Not a cloud this morning, the sky as if rinsed. Last night I could not sleep, stoked with the high of arriving here finally, eager to go boating, and hungry—a late cup of coffee hadn't helped either. So, I broke camp and started to hike around 3 a.m. This late in the summer, you're moving through drawn-out dawn at that hour, and the land is even quieter than during the day.

Watching the first blush on peaks is its own reward, as are some lakes that emit wisps of warmth into cooler air. Hiking this early is a bit creepy, too, as you never know what prowls out there or where, and in the dimness, it will stand out less. Shadows pooling underneath willows and alders and between creek banks or hills may hold threats. I'm reluctant to break the peace with my voice though and don't want to wake up any beasts either, counting on stealth instead.

I walk right up to the cache at Portage Creek on the gravel bar where Dirk landed. Magellan has proven his usefulness, I admit grudgingly. Dozens or more possible routes for reaching this point consolidate into one flow, like caribou trails in a gun-sight pass. From here on, the river will gently dictate my pace and course. This merger, ironically, comes with new freedoms. One is the leisure to enjoy other prospects, other landscape features, or at least to regard them from constantly changing angles. Another is progress even while resting.

Downstream from my Noatak put-in I'm unlikely to see any backpackers, and they certainly wouldn't be moving at my speed. Amphibious, I get to experience both perspectives on this traverse, lucky me.

Just as I arrive at the cache, the rising sun strafes the beach. The fifty-gallon barrel, the standard oil drum sometimes refitted for freight and bearproof storage, here looks incongruous. As the first order of the day, I unsnap its rim, remove the lid, and fish out a breakfast: cream of wheat with blueberries picked on the bank.

Drrrrat! Unpacking my boat, I notice a rip or cut in its packsack. The parcel weighs eighty pounds, and instead of lifting it from the Cessna, Dirk must have just dragged it and it must have encountered something sharp. Fortunately, the bag protected the hull from damage. I do carry a repair kit, but patching the boat before launching would have been inauspicious and an unbearable delay. I'm champing at the bit, raring to row, ready to ride riffles and rapids.

I unroll and inflate the canoe with a small foot pump and quickly rig it. It's a sweet little boat, sixteen feet long, with the capacity to haul a half-ton moose. In fact, Alaska sheep hunters favor this type on bony Brooks Range rivers since its draft is fairly shallow. It has two seat benches and enough room to fit the barrel between the starboard and larboard tubes; listen to the Old Tar already! I cannot leave the drum here as it would mar the place, and I need it to stow my food anyway. This canoe's fiberglass oars give more power than paddles would, an important asset in the Noatak's heinous headwinds. Straps running through D-rings anchor two metal frames that ride on the tubes and have oarlocks affixed, bronze joints of a partial ring on a pin in which the shafts swing.

In preparation for our grand maiden voyage, I assembled Baby Blue in the yard of a friend who for political reasons no longer is one. He took a snapshot of the boat and me, the only photo that exists of us. Technical specs don't do her justice. Length, width, weight, diameter of tubes . . . nothing but silly numbers. She's bouncy, rotund though not curved fore and aft like a classic canoe. Runs bow first as well as stern first. Her color is that of the sky above the highest peaks.

She's a smooth ride, efficient on a river that at times becomes a lake. I won't have to watch my feet, so I'll get to watch more scenery, though I still have to pay attention to channels that could ground me. For a full circle view, I'll lazily spin, pushing one oar while pulling the other, letting mountains parade around me; or I'll wait for the next meander, the river turning back on itself, which will change my outlook the same way. I'll get my choice of beaches for lunching and camping and stretching my legs.

She will still need adjustments after I launch, perhaps more weight in the front so that she'll track better. Moving the oar cuffs that fit into the locks shaped like inverted omegas to their proper position will determine the length and power of my leverage and balance the oars, saving energy.

Assembly completed, I don hip waders and a life jacket, cram the empty back-pack into the barrel, and am primed for my upper-body workout. Time to give that gimp foot a break. I push the canoe off the beach, step aboard, and take my seat at the oars, which I feel have never left my palms. Actually, it is this year's first float because I took the whole summer off. By the end of July, I normally would have guided a couple of nine-day river trips already.

The rocks in the shallow streamed drift past, and my boat's shadow, a huge minnow, glides above them, inducing a sense of weightlessness. I face forward currently, enjoying the pressure on the blades, pushing both as if doing light bench presses, which, facing forward, is second gear. In first, I smoothly alternate left and right strokes, as if I were hand pedaling, with my upper torso rocking side to side as I throw my weight into it. It's a rhythm I can maintain in calm conditions until hunger or sleep overwhelms me.

I started my journey seven weeks ago to the day, and this change in speed and setting makes everything fresh again. The weather helps too; all colors vibrate, and the world has been scrubbed clean.

A ground squirrel dog-paddling struggles to get to shore. It must have fallen off a cutbank near one of the mazes they tunnel into bald bluffs. This, I have never before seen.

Even when I'm not working the oars, I am going somewhere, and in a T-shirt. The valley widens, opening up cinemascope horizons. Mares' tails streak the sky above denser cumuli, adding texture and depth.

I glide past Pingo Lake, the put-in for most Noatak boaters. Too many camping there are denuding the lakeshore now, and the Park Service asks that after unloading the floatplanes, they portage to the nearby river instead. Other three-star Brooks Range attractions, the Arrigetch for example, are beginning to feel the boots and campfires of too many hikers. It's sad, this flocking to places that print, social, and visual media promote. As if on cue, ten canoeists appear, camped on an island and fly-fishing downstream of Pingo, the first people in the backcountry since the bear hunters on the Sheenjek.

How could a day that started serene end up so hectic?

Here's how: at an oxbow, a grizzly and three cubs come barreling down to the water's edge, crashing through willows above the high, steep bank just ahead of me, looking as if they're about to plunge in. Seeking firm ground to make a stand if I must—I certainly don't want to pass them this close—I pull ashore on the opposite, gravelly side. Shouting and blowing the whistle tied to my life jacket have no effect. The foursome appears eager to swim across, the mom pacing, trying to make up her mind. She is agitated yet hesitant and instead works her way upstream. When they're straight across from me, I whisk the bear spray I clipped to an oar mount from its holster. It's only the second quick draw on this trip, the other having been aimed at the overly ardent Joe Creek bear on my first day out.

I rummage through my day drybag for the flare. I was planning to get better organized tonight at camp. By now, the bears are upstream and crossing to my side. If they come closer from that upwind position, she won't be able to detect my scent and I won't be able to use the bear spray unless I want to risk blinding myself.

I cannot make sense of this. It does not feel predatory. She seems slightly desperate, as stressed as I am. She may be fleeing from a male, males being notorious for killing cubs not their own. My presence on the river might have kept her from crossing where we first met. But even in flight mode, if indeed she is, she could still cause me trouble, seeing me as another threat.

I'm not going to stick around to find out. I push off and jump into the boat and water beetle downstream as fast as I can—not very fast. The current is lazy and a headwind harries the surface. I still get away, not knowing or checking if they are following. Perhaps in frustration, the female bellows, which resounds in my marrow.

My heart still races ten minutes later when a red fox stretches and yawns up on a cutbank. He is relaxed while I, terrified, put in a few more miles before camping late. I did not sleep well last night and won't tonight either.

TEEKKONA

DAY 50 / RIVER DAY 2 (13 MILES)
QUAD: AMBLER RIVER

The mares' tails have brought rain in their wake, as they normally do. Against expectations, I slept like a lumberjack. This morning, it's back to the usual: overcast, drizzly. Contemplating the drum in front of me I notice for the first time *Conoco* stenciled on its bottom. I had to buy it from Dirk because I'll have to leave it in Kotzebue at the end of the trip. It must have held supplies Conoco shipped to one of its outposts once, perhaps even to Prudhoe Bay. Oh, the irony. Here I am, traveling the country's last large intact wilderness by muscle power while hauling the Devil's combustible-freight container. My two-grand acquisition of petroleum-based hypalon and neoprene makes me feel decadent, guilty. "The poor still walk at about the same speed as always, but the affluent have accelerated," writes Alan Durning in *How Much Is Enough?* Am I one of the affluent now? In a weirdly appropriate Möbius effect, the refining of oil consumes more energy than any other energy industry in the country. It's Moloch devouring himself.

The human geographer Andreas Malm, a socialist activist with a dissertation on the history of the fossil fuel industry, in *How to Blow Up a Pipeline* (titled misleadingly; I want a refund) questions the efficacy of polite protests and legal efforts aimed at averting the planet's ruination. Call it "uncivil disobedience," "night work," "sabotage," "moonlighting," "monkey wrenching," or "the strategic acceptance of property destruction,"—with each year of heat, flood, and wildfire records broken, and with each delay of global rapport in what another writer termed "climate kabuki," the need for bold methods becomes more obvious. Now, even some climate scientists say direct action is justified and act on their words. Malm warns against "tactics for normal times," that "property will cost us the earth," and that "if states cannot on their own initiative open up the fences, others will have to do it for them." Time is a luxury we no longer have. I kick the barrel, which booms hollowly, a good start.

Where the river curves north again it gathers its branches into a single trunk between bluffs it has carved from a massive moraine laid down twenty-five thousand to fifteen thousand years ago. The sculptor quickens with rare riffles and Class I rapids. In an optical illusion, the downhill rushing steepens into an alley strewn with boulders down which I slide. It can't be the bluffs' horizontally layered sediments. Am I hallucinating, depleted of mental and physical grit?

I'm thinking about parking for a snack when, perhaps lured by my squeaking oarlocks, a wolf appears on the riverbank. Looking at me, he woofs twice, not unfriendly but as if in greeting. He then starts to trot downstream, outlined on the rim, sometimes obscured by bushes. I follow, and we travel together at that relaxed, hypnotizing pace both of us can keep up all day. At one point, unabashedly, the wolf crouches to pee, so he is a she. Each time I lose sight I think she is gone, but we keep up this peekaboo for roughly ten minutes. It's the longest wolf encounter I've ever had. I get a good look at her; she is brownish overall, with hardly a trace of gray, almost cinnamon, her cheeks, stockings, and chest white, and she's still shedding winter fur.

Could she be a spirit assuring me that not every large critter out here sees me as dinner? I'd prefer more encounters like this and fewer of the other kind, but they come as a package.

The wolf finally veers off or finds a morsel that keeps her interest. We never connect again.

The first wolves I saw in Alaska, during my fieldwork as a graduate student two decades ago, were dead ones. An elder in Allakaket, that Koyukon village of one hundred on the Alatna, had much to say about wolves when I questioned him about his subsistence habits.

I had found his mudroom cluttered with the implements of a bush life. There were slumping hip waders, foul weather gear, snowmachine parts, dip nets, a shotgun, beaver skin mittens dangling from a nail, and a chainsaw with a chain that needed tightening. Two wolf pelts flowed from the rafters complete with tails, legs, ears, and muzzles. Before I knocked on the inner door, I had stroked the silver-tipped fur. The eyeholes and the hides' steamrolled appearance had left me slightly unsettled, as did the landscape—muskeg and black spruce—that hid grizzlies and, according to him, mischievous spirits and ill-tempered gnomes.

On maps I spread on his kitchen table he outlined his hunting and trapping excursions, which had taken him into the Brooks Range and as far south as the Yukon River. In the mountains and valleys to the north, bands of semi-nomadic Koyukon and First Americans had hunted Dall sheep and caribou for thousands of years in competition with wolves. With a callused finger, the elder tapped on den sites he knew. His eyes took on a distant expression, as if he were reliving each mile on the trail.

"That *teekkona*, he keeps caribou strong."

An ecological understanding equaling western science showed in that statement. What to the Koyukon and to us now may seem like common knowledge once was a revelation. In 1923, Olaus Murie shared with his supervisor at the US Bureau of Biological Survey the iconoclastic idea that "a certain amount of preying on caribou by wolves is beneficial to the herd," that "the best animals survive and the vigor of the herd is maintained." Murie had scoped the upper Alatna and other regions to determine where in Alaska the largest caribou lived so that wild bulls could be crossbreed with reindeer. Regarding the wolves' culling, the man who would become a leading predator advocate soon realized that "man's killing does not work in this natural way, as the best animals are shot and inferior animals left to breed." Wolves evolved in tandem with caribou. Fangs shaped hooves, eyesight honed sense of smell as pack cunning did herd skittishness.

A life of observing the animals had made the Allakaket elder an expert naturalist and better hunter. In his soft, lilting village English he recalled a rare black wolf he had trapped as a young man. He had traded its pelt together with others in Kotzebue for his first decent gun. I sensed admiration for the sleek, efficient predators under his words.

He spoke at length about the web of taboos spun around this animal, a beast whose numinous power equals that of the bear or wolverine. To appease the spirit of a wolf killed, a choice piece of caribou backstrap should be burned as an offering. Disrespect unfailingly brought bad luck, injury, disease, or even death to the hunter or his family.

The pact binding *teekkona* and the Koyukon is ancient. When such things were still possible, a wolf in the guise of a man lived among them, sharing their homes, participating in their hunts. Before he left to rejoin his own kind, he promised that wolves, grateful for the hospitality he'd received, would sometimes leave food for people. So, to this day, Koyukon men coming upon a fresh wolf kill may take what they need.

I attended a memorial potlatch in the Koyukon community of Huslia on the Koyukuk River also in those years. After a series of songs and speeches to honor Sophie Sam, an elder who had passed away a year earlier, her family handed out beaver skins, wads of cash, rifles, blankets, beaded buckskin gloves, and sundry household goods. I received one of many strips cut from a wolf fleece, which my mother later sewed onto my parka's hood.

Not long after the she-wolf, I glimpse another bear in the bushes. I watch it disappear into the thick greenery, which suits me just fine.

Rivers provide front row seats for watching wildlife. Water draws animals as it does me. Riparian vegetation and its quilt of niches offer food and cover for predators and prey alike. Bars and beaches ease travel, funneling traffic from boggy, lumpy tundra onto natural beltways. Approaching in a boat—if you've silenced your oarlocks with WD-40—rather than announcing your presence with loud footfalls or snapping branches, you get very close, and as soon as you stop rowing, you become part of the landscape. Also, many land mammals may not be programmed to fear threats from the water. Neither do I as a rule, though bears are adequate swimmers.

I don't stop at Matcharak, a Paleo-Eskimo camp on river right, where artifacts and well-preserved animal bone fragments have eroded out of a shoreline bluff. Park Service archaeologists surveying the site have discovered thousands of stone tools, including leaf-shaped "biface" blades of chert, microcrystalline quartz that flakes to knife sharpness. Small hunting bands lived here seasonally, millennia apart. The younger camp has been dated to four thousand years ago and the older to seven thousand.

I spent some time in Lake Matcharak's vicinity during a basecamp with two clients on one of my outfitter's Northwestern Parks Sampler trips. I'd unknowingly chosen a site by the river near a protein glut. We found out that chum salmon were spawning in a tributary about a mile upstream only after a Park Service plane landed on our gravel bar and the ranger opened with, "Did you guys bring a gun?"

Nerves frayed during the next two days. Grizzlies showed up above and below camp exactly at mealtimes, pawing overripe fish from the shallows, their appetites synced with ours. Some came so close we could hear them crunch heads and spines. Banging pots and pans did not impress that lot. Shotgun warning shots I fired when they wandered into our perimeter barely fazed them but did alarm the clients, who looked pale. One monstrous humped male materialized from the brush beside the latrine. After he'd sauntered off, I escorted a woman whom nature was calling there, gun at the ready; I bring one in a waterproof sleeve for my clients' mental comfort and safety on basecamp and rafting trips, where weight is not an issue.

At that camp, I hardly slept for two nights and ran low on ammo before our plane arrived. I was never happier to watch the Noatak's aquamarine sweep shrink behind a cockpit window.

An excellent camp on fine gravel and coarse sand that a slowing river sorted nestles against brush that wove extra shelter, great in case the wind picks up. It's too far to hump the barrel up to it. I leave it with the boat and decide to cook down there. Dinner is two pasta courses in celebration of meeting the wolf and because I don't think I will need twenty days to Kotzebue as I planned.

I can make out the mouth of Douglas Creek as a break in the opposite shore. Tomorrow, I'll leave the Schwatka Mountains to row across the Cutler River's basin into the Baird Mountains. According to information I gleaned before the trip, ten miles of Class II rapids followed by a Class II+ ledge drop and a place known as "The Jaws" await me. At a recirculating whirlpool there—a "keeper hole" that may keep a swimmer or a flipped raft—the river ploughs into a wall on the right and rebounds in a sharp turn to the left. "Lining your boat is a definite option here," the source said.

SMOOTH SAILING

DAY 51 / RIVER DAY 3 (14 MILES)
QUAD: AMBLER RIVER

It took butt welts and two days to figure out that I could rig my sleeping mat chair as a rowing seat as comfy as a recliner. The backrest eases my lower back problems too.

It's a gray day. Five minutes after I launch, a bear on shore stands up to peek over the bushes and hightails it—nice. Brown-and-white bank swallows with notched tails, flying sorties at airborne insects from their bluff warren, dive and wheel like fighter aces. Males chisel tunnels a yard deep with their bills, kicking out loosened dirt with their feet. Females then line the nest chamber with fur, feathers, or grass. Before people learned that swallows migrate, they believed the disappeared birds overwintered burrowed in mud, and one can see how this bit of folklore originated.

Soon after Douglas Creek, channels twisting through hill country twine into a single lane again. The flow, seeded with boulders, gets squirrely; it's the start of the Class II stretch. Some rocks lie barely exposed. Others almost surface, forming watery mushroom caps, so I pay attention to avoid hang-ups.

Perhaps unsurprisingly, given the ease of much river travel, its places imprint the mind to a lesser degree than those encountered more slowly and laboriously, in direct contact with terrain, while backpacking. At the Noatak's leisure, Kavachurak Creek, Atongarak Creek, and the Akiknaak Peaks quickly come and go, transient while I appear fixed in place. On land, I would have struggled up and down their defiles, tasted their waters, and slept on their banks or at their feet. Route choices are fewer afloat, limited to different arms. The river is the only way home, and getting lost is impossible. I therefore tend to pay less attention to my exact position on it.

After lunch, making me eat my words about effortless travel, a headwind rises. Is there any other kind on this river? It cranks up the bench presses to 150 pounds and intermittently pelts me with rain. Gusts rush toward me, raking water, so I can brace myself before each one hits. Memories crop up of my first Noatak trip decades ago, in a borrowed sea kayak. I lost my cooking pot and raingear from the cockpit and damaged the boat when a boulder capsized me. A coat I improvised from a black trash bag was not sufficiently waterproof, and I aborted that trip in Noatak and flew back home to Fairbanks.

When the hills release me, a coastal vibe takes hold. I feel exposed. Space is a circling eagle; topography no longer cradles me. "The eye beholds too much in this land that has no roof and no containing walls," Farley Mowat wrote. Though the Brooks Range has not yet run its full course, for the first time on this trip I sense its end as a reality, not just a cartographic abstraction.

A protected camp for tonight will be crucial.

Two chittering terns skim the river for fish with maneuvers worthy of stunt pilots. Inspecting the boat, compensating for squalls, they fly so low I could reach out and touch them. A finger of land jutting into the river discharges metallic-blue cliff swallows that, unlike their drab neighbors, exit adobe condos glued to the roof of a stone alcove.

I camp early, due to atmospheric interference, on a sweet gravelly point separating the Noatak and a slough, and sip a most welcome hot afternoon drink wearing my down jacket. In Inuit myths, Narssuk was the master of wind, rain, and snow, "a wicked spirit detesting mankind." People envisioned him as a huge baby. Whenever his caribou skin diaper wrapping loosened, he was free to romp about, causing blizzards to sweep the country. Shamans on trance journeys would visit the sky realm where they swaddled Narssuk again to pacify him. Good weather without fail followed.

Damn him and his flapping nappy.

Rain raising goose bumps—tiny impact jets—on the river's skin after dinner drives me into the tent. Then it gusts. And after midnight: eerie dead calm. The weather and late season muddy the wee hours' twilight.

I MEET SOME LOCALS

DAY 52 / RIVER DAY 4 (15 MILES)
QUAD: AMBLER RIVER

Another arctic fox visits this morning. Foxes' scrounging and brazen curiosity make them ground kin to ravens.

Right after launching, I pass two muskoxen on a gravel bar. They are a familiar sight to me. A herd hangs out in Nome, and I mean *in* Nome. Having learned that they're safe there from grizzlies, the headbangers play King of the Castle next to the Alaska Commercial Company store on a hill they have trampled bare. On tranquil days, they mow margins of the bush plane runway, ignoring inflatable grizzlies Fish and Game wardens have positioned strategically and impregnated with "predator pee" bought online, to prevent Super Cub–superbull collisions. Melissa gathers precious shag with which muskies garland the alders, to spin and knit into shawls and neck gaiters seven times warmer than those made from sheep wool. Once in a while a muskox gores a dog chained up in a yard and the owner cries bloody murder, demanding the herd be culled or removed. Why do they live in rural Alaska, I wonder, where coexisting with wildlife is an age-old tradition and where some of us eagerly move for this, among other reasons?

Next, a bear on a rise stands out as a distant profile.

A ferocious afternoon headwind compels me to bust out my secret weapon: the backstroke, my third gear. It requires that I crane over my shoulder as I row backward, looking for obstacles and correcting my course, so I'll likely miss wildlife on shore. Psychologically, it's saying goodbye instead of hello to the landscape, but it certainly eats up the miles. Pulling away from your wake exercises different muscles—calves, thighs, and shoulders more than belly and chest.

At the apogee of a horseshoe, a shriek bounces off a high bluff—a peregrine. He's clearly upset. His partner lifts from the nest and takes a halfhearted swipe at me in a falcon flyby. Loath to interrupt the breeding, I leave them to their fierce parenting and quickly move on.

I've lately spent much time with Fairbanks falconers and gained the utmost respect for these birds, one of which I was honored to take for a walk perched on my fist. While she fed on a dead quail her handler pulled from his coat pocket, I admired the beak serration for snipping a victim's spine and the ergonomic nostrils that let peregrines breathe at racecar speeds. Her chestnut eyes surveyed my soft parts. Never before had I faced such laser-beam scrutiny, hunger so primal, a body so fully inhabited.

The beach cobbles are grapefruit to melon size now, and I have not passed any suitable camps in a while. The wind resumes, threatening general nastiness. I land early in a small cove with a sand crescent and willow windscreen but have still made the most river miles so far in one day.

I value the map's scale bar and even the mileage Magellan displays, undeniable crutches both. Without them and any reference points from the known world, this landscape would set me adrift like the sea. Often, grizzlies my binoculars frame become rocks small as marmots. A peak I can reach by lunch remains distant at dinnertime. Eskimo tales acknowledge this mental unmooring, this funhouse perspective. A ten-legged man-eating polar bear, the *kokogiak*, would lie down supine on the ice, its legs up and bent, imitating stooped men gutting a seal, luring others. There were giants nourishing lemming-size lice and "little people" whose strength far exceeded their Lilliputian frame. They jogged, holding stolen caribou overhead in a *Dirty Dancing* lift, making bush pilots think they were seeing caribou running tipped over. My own scale and personhood amid all that are a shifty baseline.

LIVING THE DREAM

DAY 53 / RIVER DAY 5 (14 MILES)
QUAD: AMBLER RIVER

A second wolf on a cutbank, this one barely past puphood. He sits on his haunches, radar dish ears swiveled, all presence and focus, awaiting a treat perhaps? Three terns hover above him, scolding. Has he just plundered a nest? He keeps inspecting me, and I offer to take him with me to Nome and introduce him to some huskie ladies, but he doesn't budge.

"It takes your stare and turns it back on you," Barry Lopez writes about the wolf. I believe that its entire reputation, its singular standing among all other animals, can be reduced to the eyes. Those of raptors seem cold, clinical, by comparison. Perhaps I misjudge the import of vision for its role in route finding, camping, and writing. A deaf person would do passably well out here.

I sail on by, and only the wolf's gaze follows me.

Gray cloudbanks are racing inland while I crab toward the sea. The light has an underwater quality; the stream crinkles like dull foil. Blue "sucker holes" open and close in the sky. Guides call them that because only a sucker takes off his rain jacket when they beckon. I keep mine on. Daydreams about food: Nachos. Cheesecake. Pancakes with caribou sausages. A Greek salad . . .

Two mew gulls attack, shrilling with entitlement. Do they think the river is theirs alone?

A cabin squats by the Cutler River, a tributary from the south. Beyond its mouth, the Noatak turns into an overstuffed python. Have I missed "The Jaws"? Rapids change with the water levels, and this one could be washed out if the river has risen. For once, a tailwind pushes, but it grabs the barrel in the bow and keeps turning me sideways like a weather vane. I pull ashore in the lee of a willow thicket and brew coffee to wait it out. When I land, the mountains are blue with distance.

It's a strange thing, wind. We feel it but hear and see only its friction, often through parts moving under its impact. Francis Beaufort's twelve-step scale measures its friskiness. The Irish hydrographer was shipwrecked at fifteen because of faulty charts, and as a rear admiral led Robert FitzRoy, under whom Darwin sailed on HMS *Beagle*. The Beaufort Sea, the destination of all the north-flowing streams I crossed on my overland journey, bears his name.

I guess the current conditions are force 5 on his scale: "many white horses are formed; chance of some spray"; I hear echoes of animism in his metaphor. Onshore, "small trees in leaf begin to sway; crested wavelets form on inland waters." It's precise stuff from a soldier, yet poetic. Small trees are the only kind along this inland water. A year ago, the famous Nome blizzicane spewed sea foam onto Front Street and rocked our elevated Icy View Subdivision home, making toilets hiccup. That one easily qualified as a gale, forces 8 and 9.

Since it does not let up, I stay here and camp. Narssuk is tossing, so it takes me half an hour to pitch the tent on a gravel "point bar" curving around the inside of a giant loop. I try to use boat and barrel as windbreaks, and—thank you, erosion—there are large rocks to weight the tent stakes, not always a given with thick tundra upholstery all around. I'm barely set up and preparing for dinner when rain hits, today's first. Great timing. A phrase I've been thinking repeatedly on this trip when things get rough but are also dispensing splendor: *I'm living the dream.* Or am I dreaming this life? If so, I don't want to wake up.

The mileage my ailing Magellan daily coughs up does not mean much. He measures the direct distance to my destination, which the river could double. After lunch at the Cutler today, with the Noatak running north for at least 12 miles, the distance stayed 132 miles even though I rowed for another six hours. Well, I'm just glad I didn't get farther away from Kotzebue since I started this morning. Extreme wind *can* blow you upstream if you stop sculling. With few landmarks in these flats, I'm unsure of my exact location. It could be Okak Bend, where the river swerves west as if foiled by a wall and heads into the Kingasivik Mountains. It's not important.

Unbeknown to me then, on this day one of two hikers en route from the Yukon border to the Bering Sea, whom official sources do not identify, falls to his death at Atigun Gorge near the Haul Road, and the Atigun River sweeps the body a mile downstream. A Coast Guard helicopter rescues the companion.

THE WORD FOR
WORLD IS WIND

DAY 54 / RIVER DAY 6 (22 MILES)
QUAD: BAIRD MOUNTAINS

I could not sleep because the tent fly whapped like someone was beating a carpet. I'm aware that this simile dates me and betrays a pre–vacuum cleaner, working class background. My dad's mom had shoulders that would have made an arm wrestler or stevedore proud.

Insomnia drives me out on the river early. It's another gloomer. I float into a tern blizzard that fishes a riffle with the skim method, not the kamikaze dive, because the water is breakneck shallow. Brush and stands of poplar checker the foothills, and I am glad I don't have to hike through them. With my fisherman raingear, hip waders, and rubberized drybags, I am also not nearly as wet as when I was backpacking.

More concerned peregrines, these guarding three fledglings on the nest. The young face long odds; fewer than a third reach breeding age. Their parents will teach them to hunt and handle airborne prey if they don't know how to already. On a Canning River raft trip, I once saw a peregrine striking a ptarmigan on the fly and handing it off to a juvenile as a relay racer would a baton.

Suddenly, against the drabness that presages winter, the Kingasivik Mountains fill a window of blue that isn't a sucker hole. A long river straightaway, about five miles, leads directly toward them. For once, Magellan's miles will match the ones I row. The window enlarges, includes me. Sunlight lies on the water like a gentle touch. When I land to unbend my legs and water a stone, I step on tundra again. A snowy owl hunts the opposite bank, swinging about, scanning for rodents, as hypnotic a motion as the river's slippage.

Intermission is over. The window has closed. The mountains blur behind rain. But I manage to squeeze a dry coffee break in, lazing fully dressed on black sand on an island beach not quite Hawaiian. Reminder to self: install cup holder in canoe.

On a still, overgrown back channel, fireweed ignites banks otherwise emerald green. The river is a quick change artist, except that it takes its own sweet time, hydrological time, for the trick. Still, it switches attire from threadbare to somber to subtle to flashy, sometimes within a mile.

Mountains enfold me again, in a wind tunnel now. The jagged scrubland shores lack tent sites and could even puncture the boat if I tried to land. New Cottonwood Creek debouches finer material, and I camp near a nice cabin at the brush fringe that reminds me of otherworldly luxuries. The "cottonwoods" here are balsam poplars, the only deciduous trees near the tree line. Their fragrant golden resin, the biblical balm of Gilead, soothes eczema and dried skin. The Gwich'in dabbed it on cuts. Buds, which they boiled for a tea to relieve cold symptoms, exude it in the spring as a sticky insect repellent. I wish I had had some on the Sheenjek to anoint my cracked fingers, and later, when I briefly fell off the edge of the known world, my cracked soul. It now would benefit palms my bench pressing has blistered.

I heard a bush plane take off earlier, the loudest noise since the thunder at Ernie Pass three weeks ago and the loudest artificial noise since the Haul Road's semi growlers. Some people tromp through the poplars nearby. They don't look like boaters, and I've no desire to mingle and have lost what little social grace I possessed anyway.

This time it takes me a full hour to pitch the tent. The wind uproots it when I tend to the canoe, which loaded weighs more than a hundred pounds but is rocking dangerously on high and dry ground, ready for liftoff. I once saw the wind flip a raft even heavier from a trailered stack of four and cartwheel it into the Colorado River, knocking over a guide beside the truck. After unloading my canoe, I place bowling-ball rocks in its bottom, careful not to abrade the inflatable floor.

By the time dinner is cooked, it has turned into a hard twelve-hour day, ten of which I spent rowing. Today's high mileage results from the river's doglegging from north to west after Okak Bend. It also confirms sound river advice: get your digs in while you can. Best do it early, in the morning, while Narssuk still suckles on sleep's teats.

IN THE ZONE

DAY 55 / RIVER DAY 7 (26.5 MILES)
QUAD: BAIRD MOUNTAINS

Another early start, trying to put a few miles behind me before wind rules again. A weird half-light from low clouds curdling in blue sky sheets the land. The mountains, though no longer as dramatic as near Lucky Six Creek, encroach possibly even closer upon the river, which branches so widely and profusely that it is difficult to discern its main channel. Farther downstream, a brush fire has combusted a hill into charcoal slag. Only rusty brush snags stick out from the ashen bleakness. Next year, fireweed will brighten this wasteland. Rebirth will stand stem-to-trunk with death, blazing like the fury that preceded it. Succession's brush will daub pink onto whole hills, visible from the air.

Fireweed or "willowherb," which shoots up six feet tall in our Fairbanks backyard, is another northern signature plant, a pioneer on disturbed ground. It speaks resilience and reconfiguration—the future. In autumn's Chardonnay light, fireweed flowers burn with the transparent brightness of candle flames. "The sourdough's calendar" lets Alaskans compute the brevity of their summers: the fewer blossoms bejewel its spikes, the sooner frost will dye its leaves yellow and red or solidly carmine, then golden ochre, dark sienna, or umber, colors of earth, which the leaves will become. As soon as the seedpods burst open, releasing white silk on the wind, you know that before long a sparkling will fall, what here we call "termination dust." In midwinter, amber fireweed honey sustains you with promise and summer's aromas when color has bled from the land.

Where the Noatak's valley dilates again, its flow has separated two muskoxen. One roots around with his horns as if scratching an itchy head; he's probably rubbing a small gland hidden in the wool in front of his eyes that oozes musk onto the ground or his foreleg. Scent marking signals dominance during aggressive encounters within the same herd, between different herds, and even between muskoxen and other species. If it fails, the impressive horns of both sexes take on rivals, grizzlies, and wolves. Now the bull is snorting heartily, while his partner (a cow?) marooned on a gravel bar midriver longingly gazes across. Mind made up, she starts to wade in but then stops, up to her hump in the water, another boulder to be dodged. The current whisks me out of sight and I wonder if she makes it or loses heart and turns around.

A small party of river runners have beached their paddle raft on an island. I pity non-rowers in such wind. While it blows like a smithy's bellows, sun gilds the day. Now shadowed, now rinsed with light, the Maiyumerak Mountains bulge on the horizon.

A griz lollygags on a gravel bar at the water's edge, a promenade for showing off a fine coat. When I pull even, he notices me, hesitates a few seconds, and then lumbers off a few yards. He stops and now stands there up to his belly in water, reconsidering. In my best bully voice, I tell him to get lost, cocky because I'm afloat and tired of being thought of as dinner much of the time. He decides this might not be a good idea after all and scampers into the brush, after shaking shaggy dog style, spraying droplets in all directions.

I believe the Noatak bears are pushier, bossy in a cavalier way, compared to those I've encountered elsewhere, as if they owned this place, which they do. I wonder if given all the river traffic, they are getting habituated, pegging humans as easy marks. Gwich'in hunters report a similar trend farther east. Bears more easily scared by people and motor sounds in the past now seem less shy. Anecdotally, northwest Alaska's grizzly population is growing, and bad berry years have concentrated it along salmon-spawning rivers and the coast. Marauders gut subsistence cabins by the dozen there, ripping doors off hinges or squeezing their ample behinds through boarded-up windows and popping skylights and upper windows as people do bubble wrap for as little loot as a can of Spam and some Tums. To a Park Service biologist based in Kotzebue, the interior of one cabin looked "like a frat party occurred in there." She has been suggesting "unwelcome mats" (boards spiked with nails) and DNA testing of hair samples to determine if vandalism is a population-wide trend or the work of a few bad seeds.

I'm "in the zone," as if on a sliding rowing seat, stroking calmly, even, and force-fully, leaning into the water's resistance. Push—dip—pull—glide. Push—dip—pull—glide . . . I'm the guy chained to the bench on a Greek galley. "Kick up the beat," an officer tells him, "the boss wants to waterski." It's repetitive, rewarding labor: threshing, wood chopping, nest building, weaving, berry picking, running down prey. I shovel water.

My blades, little miniature maelstroms swirling in their wakes, put yard after yard behind me. On smooth, windless stretches, it's like painting or meditating. But where meditation turns you inward toward the self, rowing like this takes you away from it, stilling the mind's chatter. Exerting equal pressure on both oars, running true as a bullet, I become one giant well-oiled lever. Facing upstream, I anticipate boulders, whirlpools, and shallows by their sounds and gage the river's veer by its banks and currents on either side of me. Stray from the main stream, which helixes between both shores, and I'll lose momentum and likely get swirled into a sluggish eddy. Imagine jockeying for an inside track on a racecourse. It's how you pass slower boats in the Grand Canyon. Momentarily handicapped, you exit the most muscular fiber, the "bubble line" fellow rowers ride, to overtake them in a weaker lane. We call this attention to hydrological details "reading the river," and the more literate you are the more strength you save, even when not racing.

Muscle memory liberating the mind allows an attentiveness that fosters psy-chological "flow." The Hungarian-American Mihaly Csikszentmihalyi coined the term for experiences during which, keenly alive, gladly immersed in actions without external rewards, people fall out of time. Steering thus in the Noatak's currents taps mundane energy strands—as do sailing, surfing, soaring in gliders, and the Zen arts—rather than ignoring or fighting them. The deep focus also achieved in the performance of ceremonies or while meditating, hunting, way-finding, or tracking animals exercises the brain's memory systems as well.

Idea for a bumper sticker: *Eat My Wake.*

While I rest a minute to take notes, a muskox grazes on one shore and a bear on the other. I try to sneak past with small noiseless strokes, but the bear hears me, stands up, and is gone.

Second in size only to eagles, pairs of rough-legged hawks have claimed low cliffs with chalky squirts pointing to their stick nests. The hawks' drawn-out keening—*keeeeeer . . . keeeeeer*—resonates with a note of melancholy in me. I think I've started to say farewell, as if to dear friends. "Swift or smooth," Bob Marshall wrote, "broad as the Hudson or narrow enough to scrape your gunwales, every river is a world of its own, unique in pattern and personality. Each mile on a river will take you further from home than a hundred miles on a road." Except that each mile on this one brings me closer. Starting at Joe Creek, I've found moving toward home to be easier than I have moving away from it, beginning other trips. If only this insight could benefit me in my peripatetic life at large, even on shorter journeys.

Two guys in a forest-green Coleman canoe have pulled over and, seated, are glassing a peregrine nest. I stop to chat. It's time I learned to use my voice again. They are Park Service staff based in Nome filling in for the seasonal Noatak ranger, whose position has remained vacant this year. In addition to grayling, they've caught some nice char that, already faded, lie in their boat.

Another day of almost twelve hours on the river, which by now has completely calmed, shining like plate silver. I snag one of my sweetest camps yet, a sand square on a terrace partway up the bank overlooking a cobble foreshore. A slope thick with poplar cups it. Greenery even frames a mountain view. Normally, unless you sleep on a gravel bar, bushes screen all the sites here. This camp is sheltered but scenic; I should have been here yesterday when Narssuk was throwing his temper tantrum. Previous tenants have left campfire charcoal in the kitchen. I have not built a single fire yet on this trip. It still doesn't get dark, and the days were too sunny early on and too windy later, with wood too wet.

While I'm fixing dinner, the Parkies in their canoe fly past. Must be working overtime, as it's after five. Since I last checked the distance to Kotzebue, it again has not shrunk. Magellan's numerical fits accordion strangely, which takes getting used to. All in all, this has been a first-rate day, a shimmering pearl on a string of fifty-five total so far, one for the memory safe.

A STRONG BROWN GOD

DAY 56 / RIVER DAY 8 (25.5 MILES)
QUAD: NOATAK

I do not know much about gods; but I think that the river
Is a strong brown god—sullen, untamed and intractable . . .
—T. S. ELIOT, "The Dry Salvages"

I never got to enjoy my campsite and its view, as after dinner it started to rain; it has been spitting for twenty-four hours straight now. I still get an early start; the river lapping shore closer and closer to the canoe evicts me from my toasty sleeping bag. "The immense rainfall of the summer frequently causes the river to overflow its banks and inundate the surrounding country," Samuel McLenegan, who also explored the adjacent Kobuk, wrote of the common flooding of these waterways. On their biggest day on the Noatak, trying to save a cache they had placed, he and his shipmate allegedly raced more than a hundred miles on high water. Enduring a one-night drencher on the Kobuk, he feared the unbound river would flush their camp away. When he turned out in the morning, "the members of the party emerged from their wet blankets like half-drowned rats."

Despite the costs and flaws of raingear made from fossil fuels, I truly appreciate it. I commenced my affair with the great outdoors four decades ago in leather boots and gloves, cotton underwear, wool pants and sweater, a felt beret, and a moleskin parka, with a canvas rucksack, under an impregnated cloth shelter-tarp that doubled as rain poncho: decommissioned army tan, army gray, army green. Now it's all thousand-dollar clown suits in bird-of-paradise hues.

The more things change, the more they stay the same. This is timeless country. Animism grows easily here even in campers professing a scientific bent. The river in its many moods *does* appear as a fickle deity, as do wind, bears, mountains, and Magellan. Our minds seek agency even in objects commonly thought of as inanimate. "The whole world is full of spirits," the Mackenzie River story-teller Angusinaq told Knud Rasmussen, with "some small as bees, others as big and frightful as small mountains." Shamans enlisted them as helping spirits, but everyone else trod lightly around them. Animism, the root perhaps of all religion, springs from the wish to confront randomness, to tap into an illusion of ordered security. After all, living beings including humans possess spirits open to supplication, appeasement. People who have lost this belief demote mountains from volatile deities to mineral resources, climbing goals, postcard motifs, habitats, weather stations, or starred attractions.

The rolling bugling of cranes parts the mist. It cannot be time for their fall migration. They wait until August for their colts to grow flight suits and layer on fat. Cranes represent the turning of seasons for Melissa and me at our home on the Fairbanks outskirts. We hear them within days on either side of my late April birthday as they arrow north and west in loose skeins high above our cabin. For a few days in May, peak snowmelt floods front acres of the Creamer's Field waterfowl refuge in town, leaving a lagoon peppered with mallards and northern pintails, white-fronted and Canada geese, tundra and trumpeter swans, and with sandhill cranes strutting their stuff. The polyglot congress reviews flight plans with Klaxon squawks, nasal honks, and creaks from rusty hinges. The cranes curtsy and hop and throw back their snake necks, bills spearing skyward in moves they practiced as juveniles, reaffirming their bonds before their journey's consummation. When they've departed, the field can be a lonely place.

I pack up a tent sopping and, worse, breaded with sand like all my bags and launch into Fog Land, a world packed in cotton. I possibly see another black wolf but cannot be certain since the shadow blends in with the dark earth of a cutbank. It is just a shimmer of motion at the edge of vision, approximately the right size and gait.

When I enter spruce country again, I pass a river party on shore with a packraft and double Klepper, a collapsible kayak that fits inside small aircraft and whose design has remained essentially unchanged since Thule ancestors of the Inupiat stroked across from Siberia. A Klepper's canvas deck and rubberized hull replace the original's bearded-seal skin oiled for waterproofing; the frame, despite being jointed with metal wing nuts and screws instead of rawhide lashings, still is wood, a lightweight and flexible skeleton that can take the sea's punishments. McLenegan paddled and pulled a similar boat, although with three hatches, and the celebrity photographer Edward Sheriff Curtis around 1929 depicted another, with tools strapped to its deck, propelled by a Noatak seal hunter in a hooded skin parka.

Historically, upper-Noatak Inupiat floated wolf and wolverine furs as well as soapstone and jade for carved seal oil lamps to Kotzebue Sound in the summer, hunting seals and beluga whales while attending the fair at Sheshalik; the fair was an occasion for barter, athletic contests, singing, drumming, dancing, and alliance building through trade or marriage. On the upriver return journey, men sailed and lined boats heavy with dried seal meat, oil in sealskin pokes, beluga *muktuk* (blubber and skin), and Russian iron goods, pipes, and tobacco. Their summer fish camps still dot the riverbanks, taking advantage of chum salmon runs. Inland Inupiat also portaged to and from the Kobuk River south of here, where I conducted much of my initial fieldwork in Kiana and Ambler.

In a stunning discovery, archaeologists after a metal-detector sweep troweled four blue glass beads the size of berries from a house pit at an Eskimo hunting camp near the Continental Divide, eighty-five miles north of Ambler. Willow bark twine had strung these together with copper bangles and teardrop-shaped iron pendants into a necklace or bracelet, proving the reach of pre-Columbian trade into arctic Alaska by way of Sheshalik. Traveling on a Siberian spur of the Silk Road (you might call it the "Bead Trail"), traders like Marco Polo and his father and uncle carried beads as lightweight international currency. This azure kind came from Murano, the island on which Venice cloistered her glassmakers, guarding their alchemic craft jealously. At Etivlik Lake, these bits of Adriatic bright sky must have cheered up their new owner on gray Brooks Range days. I try to imagine how many hands cupped them during their ten-thousand-mile journey and how, though connected, neither Venetians nor Thule knew each other's counterparts at the end of the line, nor the continent where those others lived.

The river splits mountains one final time at Sekuiak Bluff, exposing bedrock in Noatak Canyon. Beyond, it hurries south, a greyhound coursing a hare through boreal flats, home to raven gangs and to white-hooded eagles hunched against the wet, stoics perched on bleached snags. Where the current has undermined banks, spruce trees precariously lean or have tipped into it, raking it with single strong limbs vibrating as if mischievous beavers were stirring them. Such "strainers" flip and drown boaters or damage hulls. "Sweepers" merely brush you from your seat. Less common "preachers" midstream, with roots snagged on the riverbed and angled trunks bobbing on the surface, suggest bowing ministers. My unease about trees reaffirmed, I give all these a wide berth.

Fretting, the Noatak has bared ice lenses in the banks under soil that drips and slumps here and there. Thawing permafrost chills the waters of tributaries, which could affect salmon populations. Perhaps now is the time to rename it "impermafrost." The center no longer holds.

The Kelly dumps barge loads of sediment into the Noatak, changing its steely complexion to a turbid tan. I watch private cabins, fish camps, and a huddle of neat Park Service cabins scroll upstream like scenery in one of those mid-nineteenth-century moving panoramas that toured the country before film was invented.

In the afternoon, the wind rallies. How could it not? The canoe's bottom must have sprung a leak. It sags, and at lunch and other breaks I bail an inch or two with my water bottle, since with bilge sloshing around, Blue Babe becomes heavy and sluggish, more mastodon or Paul Bunyan's ox. I wonder if the barrel could have rubbed through the floor, or if my anchor stones did. It takes me the longest time ever to locate a camp not too scarily brushy or rocky or windy, or with a bank too steep, or in some Inupiaq fisherman's yard.

Another twelve-hour shift on the bench, luckily unshackled, punctuated with breaks totaling less than an hour, has drained me. It's just not the kind of weather or landscape to dawdle and lounge in. The Brooks Range and upper Noatak spoiled me.

When I check more thoroughly, tiny bubbles pearl from a seam of the patch the manufacturer glued onto the floor to refurbish my craft. There's nothing I can do short of replacing the floor, which requires a heat gun and electric socket.

I am about twelve miles upstream from the village of Noatak, where I bowed out of my previous trip rather ungracefully, clad in a trash bag, due to the weather. Islands separate scores of channels in this upcoming stretch, with some sloughs potential dead ends even for shallow-draft boats.

THE COURAGE OF CRANES

DAY 57 / RIVER DAY 9 (24 MILES)
QUAD: NOATAK

The rain stops toward morning, so I pack up for another early start. Something inside me has got knocked loose and is tumbling downhill, something inevitable, like gravity, or irretrievable, like time.

Sheets of water slide dizzyingly every which way, a riverine Tilt-A-Whirl. In places, the boat is glued to the surface only to rocket forward seconds later. I check the shore sometimes, doubting even slight progress. I peer into sloughs, expecting moose immersed to their haunches browsing courtyards of willows. The Maiyumerak Mountains sink into the horizon behind me as fast as my memory of them fades. The water has risen several feet overnight, I estimate, and flushed out stout branches and root-balls. Noatak comes and goes, a huddle of red roofs in the wilderness. Choose an outside run or wipe rain from your eyes, and you'll miss it.

In 1908, the Quakers' California Yearly Meeting Friends Church established a federally supported mission school here; it rang in the erosion of shamanism, of spirits, taboos, and customs like facial tattoos, polygamy, and intertribal skirmishing in exchange for liquor and devastating diseases but also for store-bought goods and Western medicine and education, which could bring their own burdens. All of this altered subsistence patterns. Even in wildest Alaska, traditional costumes and customs yielded fast to foreign mores. By 1915 the upper Noatak basin lay largely abandoned except for sporadic visits by Inupiat who had largely moved into the village. Heavier spring rains and snowmelt have sped up erosion marching toward its runway as much as sixty feet annually.

Edward Sheriff Curtis remains Noatak's foremost visitor. After a cruise to Siberia with Muir and Dall, Curtis fell hard for a fledgling medium, photography;

this obsession inspired the Seattle citizen, former homesteader, and Klondike stampeder to compile *The North American Indian*, the most expensive and expansive book project by an individual and this country's largest ethnographic enterprise ever. Between 1906 and 1930, Curtis collected more than forty thousand images from roughly eighty tribes. The Alaska volume was the last to be finished. Fifteen hundred gelatin silver prints made the final cut for his magnum opus of oversize photogravure folios and twenty text volumes. The bound books alone fill five feet of shelf space. To his Indigenous subjects in this land of the midnight sun, Curtis was the Shadow Catcher, appropriately.

Curtis steamed north on *Victoria* in the summer of 1927 with his daughter Beth, who'd funded this venture, and the young ethnologist Stewart Eastwood. His mammoth installments, which at the time sold poorly, depleted Curtis financially, and he traveled on a tight budget. From Nome, the trio reembarked to visit seven Bering Strait settlements. Curtis had never been happier. Eskimo culture still appeared to be vibrant, and Alaska reminded him of youthful adventures in the Pacific Northwest.

Nome was a husk of its gold rush self. The population had shrunk from 20,000 to 750, most of them Inupiat. Stores, shops, hotels, and gambling dens housed only the wind. Boardwalks were gap-toothed or gone. Curtis bought the two-mast fishing schooner *Jewel Guard*, which came with a previous owner. Her skipper, Harry the Fish, a Swede, according to Beth hated liquor, tobacco, and women. The schooner, about forty feet long with a cabin and auxiliary engine, she deemed "not so bad." With some experience of seagoing vessels, Curtis thought her "an ideal craft for muskrat hunting in the swamps but certainly never designed for storms in the Arctic Ocean."

The locals warned him that launching so late in the season, he'd be pushing his luck. Foolhardy, perhaps, he insisted on one more adventure. Less than a week at sea, the travelers struck ice while a storm tossed them about. "The waves were ten times as great as our boat & we were shipping much water," Beth wrote. After nearly capsizing, *Jewel Guard* stranded on a sandbar, so Curtis waded away from the ship, set up his tripod, and snapped her portrait.

Storms again overtook them at Kotzebue, where a pilot Curtis had hired got them stuck, lost in the mudflats. The pilot later admitted that he knew everything there was to know about driving dog teams but not much about guiding big boats. A canoe excursion brought Curtis and Eastwood to Noatak, where for several days both worked hard at photography. Curtis still found time to praise the fine flavor of "Noatak salmon trout" (steelhead, or seagoing rainbow trout).

The company did not leave Kotzebue until September. The barometric pressure was falling. Days were getting short, and the locals putting boats up for the winter. Harry the Fish frothed at the gills because they had not sailed sooner. Vindicating him, a blizzard caught *Jewel Guard* on their run home. Assailed by ice, she was at risk of freezing in until spring. Then her hull sprang a leak, and the sea started pressing in. All hands shoveled snow off her wallowing bow and bailed a foot of water from the galley. Like a crippled seabird, she limped back to Nome, where her crew had been given up for dead. Curtis, however, was placid. "You either make it or you don't," he wrote in his journal. The main thing, he felt, were the images he had secured, the capstone of his career and some of his finest work.

The forest is starting to thin. I am approaching the tree line again. It marks off not only Alaska's northernmost margins but also its westernmost, the Seward Peninsula at the back of our hometown, Nome. This plant frontier should not be imagined as a defined edge but rather a forest-and-tundra puzzle with spruces growing ever more runty as conditions for them worsen. The ultimate holdout, *krummholz* ("crooked wood") forms gnarled, wind-battered, starved bushes rather than trees. The main limiting factor besides permafrost is summer temperature, which the bodies of the Beaufort and Bering Seas lower. Fairbanks and Nome share the same latitude two hundred miles shy of the Arctic Circle, but boreal forest encircles one while the other squats naked on tundra.

Tree-ring analysis or "dendrochronology" like young Bob Marshall employed in the Arctic furthers our understanding of climate change and the dating of archaeological sites, especially where the tree line shifts. Spruce ingrains longer summer growth spurts as broader rings, visible in core samples from driftwood, house remains, or living trees. Aligned with arboreal chronicles established elsewhere in high latitudes, these constitute a record of regional environmental conditions that spans centuries. Black or "bog" spruce rooting in poorly drained muskeg, however, often prove useless, with their rings distorted.

My appearance startles a gaggle of sandhill cranes convened on a gravel bar. They spring into flight directly, with a skip, pumping their primaries. It awes me still, after this many sightings, how birds so gawky on earth can assume pure grace in the air. Below a perched eagle some ravens harangue; a grizzly on hind legs, paws hanging by her side, stands among spruce. She is chocolate brown, darker than her tundra kin, a brunette to those blondes. But like most, she scents me, drops on all fours, and skedaddles. My odor cannot have improved.

The river's sped-up conveyor belt lets the miles fly by despite frequent lashings from wind. The only other boat on it is half in it, sunk and stranded midstream on a gravel bar. The current must have snatched it from moorings at Noatak. It has a nice outboard motor, worth salvaging. A cow moose and calf browse where the swollen channels conjoin. Cold rain stings my face and blots out the world beyond either bank. I am pulling my arms from their sockets on a fitness machine set up in limbo. Loons flap past with dagger bills and heads held below shoulder level, telltale, crucifix silhouettes. The black-and-white, boldly checkered backs and sweeping breast- and necklines of four of Alaska's five species suggest skeletons.

Loons were spirit helpers for shamans who underwent symbolic death and resurrection during conversion events. Initiates leaving their body might see their own skeleton or get devoured by a wolf or bear only to be reassembled afterward from their bones. Even more important, loons symbolized the shaman's journeying, movement between different worlds, as they dive from a lake's surface to the bottom. Their garnet stare was thought to pierce the murk of the afterlife, offering guidance. In a photo from the 1980s, ninety-year-old Elijah Kakinya, Simon Paneak's father-in-law, rumored to have been a shaman, wears a loon skin cap with the yellow bill pointing into the wind. A loon's and human skulls from a proto-Eskimo burial on Northwest Alaska's coast had jet-and-ivory eyeballs inserted in their sockets. On movie soundtracks, mournful loon calls connote mists and mystery even for modern sensibilities. Loons vanish magically: they flatten their feathers and exhale, dropping from sight without changing their posture, making you wonder if they were real.

Tired from rowing into the fists of the gale, I let it pummel me into a slough where it pins me. End of round seven. Time for a coffee break. I could even camp here and take a badly needed rest and maintenance day. With the Noatak gathering itself—himself? herself?—for the final run, I have plenty of food to spare. This site is attractive enough, a queer lumpy meadow of horsetails, Siberian asters, and Indian paintbrush. Ironically, given the randomness of my stranding, the ground is some of the best yet for tenting: firm and clean. (When did cleanliness start to concern me out here?) Joining the serpent at my back, even the clouds hurry now. The grass in the lee of some bushes does not move, while on the far side willows bow and sway like crazed penitents under the whip of an ethereal force.

After setting the tent up to let it dry, I blow up my camp chair. When I consult Magellan, I'm surprised to find I am only thirty miles from the coast and it's not even 1:00 p.m. This must be the brown snake god's doing. A driftwood knot submarining against the current catches my eye. It becomes a harbor seal's cannonball head. He eyes me curiously before sinking soundlessly, his ballast tanks blown, only a ring bespeaking his exit.

My Conoco vault has begun to rust inside, staining my gear orange. The bastards got in one more insult. I crack the barrel open and cook some Thai noodles. Then it's naptime. Afterward I decide to call this nook "home" for now and properly unload the canoe. I dry out my gear, brush sand from the inner tent and fly. I build a fire with sticks, the trip's first, more for ambience and company than for warmth. Voila. Stone Age TV.

Contemplating the flames, I suddenly realize: this adventure of a lifetime is almost over. I have not even started to process its myriad impressions. In my struggle to gain the coast I've forgotten that arrival means nothing. Well, not nothing. It means dry socks, a stocked fridge, and bugs only outside, with my sole hardship being Melissa hogging the duvet at night.

These days in their thrilling sameness now form the mold into which I pour my life, and it is hard to imagine any other. How did Alexander Selkirk, Defoe's model for *Robinson Crusoe*, feel upon reentry after more than four years as a castaway? Or Hiroo Onoda, the Japanese soldier who walked out of the Philippine jungle three decades after the end of World War II, having spent the last two years alone, finally conceding that it was over? Mine has been a splendid isolation, accented with rare human contact as well as plenty of trials and scares, though incomparable to theirs.

Narssuk pipes down some, and a motor skiff drones past my camp. They too must have hunkered down, waiting this out. If they can travel . . . could I?

Later that same day. The faint rumble of oars in their locks sets a rhythm that paces my strokes. I'm enjoying some of the journey's most serene rowing. The mood seems to affect even wildlife. A griz standing beside the river looks at it contemplatively, a hairier Diogenes, in no rush to do anything. A log cabin tilts on a crumbling bluff. The elements that polished its wood blinded its windows. The gloaming etches three backlit crosses high on the bank, near a conical structure of leaning wood poles, a smokehouse or fish drying rack perhaps. High clouds roll inland, an ethereal tide before salty ones. Golden light singles out a hill in the distance, bringing to mind the helmet of a man in a Rembrandt reproduction in my childhood home.

Sparsely timbered tundra country has returned. The river's skin is molten glass. I can see drip lines from the tips of my blades, which move of their own volition, cracking the mirror with every dip. The sky, reflected, becomes twice as vast. The green shoreline barely divides realities. In one, I soar among altocumulus marbled with blue. A loon yodels forlornly. One diving seal splashing rends the silence like a hand slap. Fins of salmon are breaching and wheeling as bodies rush toward death and decay but also new life. I could not think of a bigger contrast to Joe Creek, to the hours spent clasping a knife in my sleeping bag.

The Arctic will do this to you. Just when the time comes to leave, it takes your heart and squeezes it. This is what I want to remember: you give your soul to a place at the risk of getting it wounded. This will set me aglow when I tell friends and Melissa about it or when another winter howls at my door. This single day has made it all worthwhile.

Pterodactyl croaks from a trio of low-flying cranes echo. *Echo? There is no cliff, not a reflective surface in sight.* Then it hits me. *Their calls are bouncing off the still river.*

In my measured breathing at the oars, I partake of *sila*, "the great weather," our planet's vast, vital, and volatile atmosphere. The former environmental activist and Pulitzer Prize–winning Fairbanks composer John Luther Adams borrowed the concept for a piece for choir and orchestra. His intent is to school audiences in "ecological listening." Influenced by "winter silences and seasonal discords,"

Sila: Breath of the World was performed without a conductor, outdoors—once with musicians' sounds vibrating a pool's surface—as an aural analog to sculptural land art. The contemporary Inuit thinker Jaypeetee Arnakak defines *sila* as "an ever-moving and imminent force that surrounds and permeates Inuit life, and that is most often experienced with the weather."

The Iglulik Eskimo shaman Uvavnuk put it differently in a song Rasmussen recorded, in a way boaters, like I on this lambent night, can appreciate:

> The great sea has set me in motion,
> set me adrift,
> moving me like a weed in a river.
> The sky and the strong wind
> have moved the spirit inside me
> till I am carried away
> trembling with joy.

I imagine this arctic world from the cranes' point of view, their epic journey so different from that marked on my maps. Let their Brooks Range survey stand for mine here.

It is spring. Bound for the coastal plain south of the Beaufort Sea, a sandhill crane and her "siege" approach the Arctic National Wildlife Refuge, North America's last best place. Obeying the ancient urge, the cranes after rallying have loudly vacated staging grounds in Nebraska's Platte River Valley weeks earlier. They mostly travel by day, 350 miles on a good one, in family groups, using landmarks as beacons, soaring much of the way, riding thermal elevators, gaining altitude whenever possible, rationing fat reserves and their strength. They ripple past Arctic Village, and all villagers sense that once again time pivots in the roundelay of the seasons. Near the head of the Chandalar's East Fork, where knolls escalate into massifs and the boreal forest thins, they rise to meet what could be mirages, bunching together with hoarse, rattling calls.

Gar-r-r-r-o-o-o-a. Gar-r-r-r-o-o-o-a. Primaries splayed fingerlike push air for extra lift. Scores of bills point poleward, unwavering compass needles. With age, cranes become better navigators, setting straighter courses, cutting miles, saving calories. Their skills grow with practice, but young birds also learn from their elders, an example of culture transfer. Even without veteran fliers, first timers unfailingly launch, directed by genes, when spring alights. "Their annual return is the ticking of the geologic clock," Aldo Leopold wrote about sandhills. And: "Upon the place of their return they confer a peculiar distinction."

What are the lessons cranes teach? Grace. Exuberance. Determination. Mutuality that eases flights to imagined destinations. The importance of rooted-ness balanced by joy found in departure. Know-where-and-how spanning gener-ations. As members of a world population numbering three-quarters of a million, cranes are true cosmopolitans, reminders of the need for far-flung safe zones and corridors linking them.

The honking string trails over Guilbeau Pass, the Continental Divide, weaker birds in the lee of the strong, rested ones flying point; the hearts of those on the diagonals beat more slowly, and they flap less often. Strokes in a chain reaction skip down their line; each catches miniature updrafts from the wing pair ahead. This technique too is acquired, saving energy like a child postholing in snow in a parent's footprints. Some cranes prefer the arrow's left edge and others its right, yet all swap positions frequently in a lofty round of musical chairs. They glide exactly three feet behind and three feet to the side of a neighbor, in the aerodynamic sweet spot.

Snow and ice still choke the high country, though less than even a decade ago. Where the Rockies' hyperborean stretch crooks west, drainages also switch. South-slope runoff dilutes the Bering Sea, and north-face runoff the Arctic Ocean. On both sides of the flyway, spine upon rawboned spine thrusts up as if boosting the raucous V, peaking in Mount Isto and Mount Michelson in the Romanzofs and Mount Chamberlin, bold solitaire of the Franklins, the Brooks Range's grandest and most serene peak. Sir John Franklin named this segment of the snowy cordillera he sighted in 1826 during his initial attempts at the Northwest Passage, after a chancellor of the Russian tsar, a man fond of exploration and science. To the east, Esetuk, one of few remnant glaciers, has carved a swath through the mountains. With volume added from snowfields, it feeds Hulahula tributaries. Winter's release wafts up to the cranes as headwater susurrus. A gravel bar bush-plane strip, a few shacks on Inupiaq lots at sapphire grayling haunts, and the old USGS Peters Lake research station miniaturized by the summits are the sole hints of human agency in the birds' field of vision. Tern colonies and jack-in-the-box squirrel burrows are the refuge's most populous homes. The closest road, the Dalton Highway, lies a hundred miles to the west.

Before long, the range does run out—tectonic upheaval flatlines. Infinite space welcomes the cranes, a door flung wide open. From between foothills, the Hulahula River spills onto the coastal plain. It sways unfettered, lazily, postponing oblivion in a cobalt sea. Its dendritic flows and deposits at times recall capillaries. Aufeis in annual monthly growth rings encases channels and bars. The cranes' amber gaze beholds barrens come alive, a sight unchanged since lions and mammoths combed steppe here. The very hills seem to be moving as thousands of caribou zero in on their destination, tendrils of a single-bodied, single-minded rhizome with grizzlies and wolves following.

A flock of cranes is a "calamity" too, and on some level of their two-million-year-old consciousness, the relics that weathered prior extinctions may intuit trouble. From up high, they cannot distinguish the abundance of ground cover, a tangle of forbs, lichens, mosses, heather, and grasses. Soon, perennial bloom will ray about. River beauty will rouge cobbled flats. Moss campion will go pink in a burst, first on the sun-kissed half. Labrador tea pungent as smoke will scent the days.

When the wind stops stirring willows that foliate streambeds, the land exudes silence, not a void but the fount of its signature sounds: Loon laughter. Jaeger shrieks. Longspur jingles. The fluting of gold-mantled plovers. These fragments of meaning, baring nerve endings, forever touch lives.

Leaving behind the Sadlerochit Mountains, ramparts cleaved from the Brooks Range's bulk, the cranes are nearing the end of their journey. Permafrost beyond the Hulahula foothills has tessellated tussocks and soil polygons in buckskin-and-moss-green mosaics. Sunlight glints on melt ponds and on seepage in the frost fissures responsible for this strange symmetry. Scalloped from the horizon's blue, Camden Bay marks North America's line of surrender. Farther out still, flat as a griddle, floats Barter Island with Kaktovik, that Inupiaq outpost in no longer reliably ice-clad tides. Beaufort Lagoon, toward the Canada border, promises safety and sustenance. Flurries of shorebirds and geese will congregate there in July and August to refuel for their trip south.

In February, polar bears and their cubs crawl from birthing chambers dug into snowdrifts along this littoral, until recently the only 125 miles of Alaska's 6,500-mile arctic coast closed to oil drilling. With sea ice disappearing, more bears have started denning on shore, where they're vulnerable to pathogens, toxins, and home loss from seismic testing and construction. At last count, the Southern Beaufort Sea subpopulation numbered roughly nine hundred animals. Experts predict their demise by midcentury. A GPS-collared female with her yearling cub dog-paddled 426 miles across the Beaufort Sea. In search of an ice floe on which to haul out and rest, both spent nine days straight in barely-above-freezing water. The cub did not make it to land. Luckier bears slowly recover following marathon swims.

On turf still frozen, scarlet-browed crane pairs wearing gray engage in court-ship, shaking fannies, wings akimbo like crazed ballerinas. Cocks and hens trumpet in unison at their brightest during the mating ritual. While dances are performed year-round, they take center stage during the breeding season. The throaty duets and pas de deux weave tender bonds maintained for decades.

The late blow-ins, about to join the jubilee, prepare for arrival. Keeping their formation, they bank and then coast in at a low angle, eagerly trumpeting. At the last moment, one by one, they drop their landing gear, stall, fold up tired wings, and touch down, stilt legged, awkwardly, perhaps even a little surprised.

Their weeks at pasture pass in a frenzy of feeding and rearing their young. Before they decamp, slipping away in staggered files, filling the sky with calligraphy, life will begin again. Colts on their spindle shanks will scrounge bugs and berries. The ageless dance will continue.

If we can't save the land, it cannot save us. But apart from our requirements, wild landscapes and creatures exist with autonomy and their own right to thrive. We need an ethic reflective of this reality. In fact, we have such an ethic. The Muries, Bob Marshall, Aldo Leopold, and Rachel Carson laid it out for us. They're the elders who have shown us viable flight paths.

Posterity will not judge us by what we built or by what we amassed but by what we failed to do. Besides being flesh and blood, feathers and bones, sinew and spirit, cranes signify opportunities. They are bearers of hope, reminders that the worthiest journeys are journeys of daring. Do we dare to renounce one species' supremacy? Do we dare to meet nature on nature's terms? Can we leave some places alone? Can we, under epochal pressure, muster the courage of cranes?

Meanwhile, down on the Noatak, a blue speck mimicking the sandhills high above strokes and strokes through the old day and into the new. It's my last on the river, and I feel I could pull forever, right off the edge of the world.

PART V
STRAIT

Here we go . . . out of the sleep of the
mild people, into the wild rippling water.
—**JAMES DICKEY**, *Deliverance*

LOST AT SEA

DAY 58 / RIVER DAY 10
(NUMBER OF MILES UNCERTAIN)
QUAD: KOTZEBUE

What happened? Sitting in my spur-of-the-moment enforced camp downstream from Noatak yesterday, jazzed by late caffeine after a second dinner, I noticed the wind dying down. Half an hour later, I kept walking out to the point, eyeballing the river in its bed. Another half hour and I doused the fire, packed up my tent, stuffed the barrel, and loaded the boat. *Of course, it'll be howling beyond the first bend,* I inwardly groused. But worse was the thought of not taking advantage then and running into foul weather tomorrow—today. There was one way to find out. Move when conditions are favorable, I have learned in more than forty years of backcountry ventures. Damn all itineraries. And this time, I was richly rewarded.

This day after my all-nighter is a bit hazy, like scenery seen through wildfire smoke. Somewhere in Lower Noatak Canyon, I pull ashore at a homestead or fish camp to try and snatch a few zees. I manhandle the canoe up a slippery cutbank and tie her to alders, afraid that the wind will abduct her. The cabin porch is the one level spot where green does not riot, but it seems uncouth to roll out my sleeping bag here as a strange sort of welcome mat. Civilization is back and with it the frills of etiquette.

I launch again, but there is just nowhere a weary voyager might bed his head for an hour or two. Hunger and lack of sleep have sapped me. I'm a mineshaft ready to collapse. Onward I must go, onward. Westward I go, opposed only by the wind's force. After each curve's deflection, my bow swings back to find west unerringly, a pointer's muzzle aimed at fowl.

At some point, long before the first gull has winged in, the sea announces itself to me through a breeze redolent of sex. Seals follow or surface, puffing and bobbing near my bow, ogling this awkward creature. At Sakisalnak, the river knees Hugo Mountain and the Mulik Hills, Brooks Range blips a two-hour row from Hotham Inlet. The only forced break comes when a chair strap worn threadbare from thousands of push-pull sit-ups breaks and I sprawl in the stern after one mighty backstroke, hooting like a loon. Nothing a spare wouldn't fix.

Minutes or eternities later, the giant white fuel tanks on Kotzebue's dock flash when the sun illuminates them; but these beacons are drifting off portside, and Magellan hints that I'm moving farther away, toward Cape Krusenstern National Monument north of the delta. Did I take a wrong turn somehow? Have the laws of hydrology been suspended? The Noatak's mouth is a hydra, one last formidable foe to vanquish. I have a déjà vu of the missing corner near Lonely Lake, which makes me queasy. I should have landed and climbed Hugo Mountain to scout. This stream was supposed to deliver me.

I beach on mudflats wreathed with rank sea grass that rise barely half a foot from the water and stand on my tubes, disturbed and confounded. This is how the Eskimo blanket toss originated, to gain perspective in flatland (to spot whales). Perhaps I should overnight here and solve this problem tomorrow, clearheaded. But guck coating this plain shows that it will be land under, and I don't want to lie in the canoe like a dead Viking about to be shoved out to sea.

Continuing, I finally realize that the culprit is a mile-long meander. When it reverses, I approach the sea at long last. Screeches of unhinged gulls mixing with squeaks from my oarlocks taunt me. This is your mind on drugs, opiates the body produces and which the mind enjoys. *Get the keys, Bernadette.*

I call Melissa for an update before the crossing, letting her know I've reached the coast safely, early, and to send a cab my way the next day, a chauffeur to the airport, where yet another person would be in charge of transporting me. After almost two months of autonomous travel, it will be strange to give up the driver's seat, the vigilance and responsibility.

I am barely coherent. Melissa considered calling search and rescue, she told me afterward, when she heard that my oarlocks were speaking, as I had yet to cross Kotzebue Sound. Many Noatak travelers end their journey at the tideline and hail a prearranged water taxi. I was too cheap for that, and the friend who'd dropped me off at the Fairbanks airport, a veteran sea kayaker, said that on a mellow day paddling across those last seven miles would be smooth. I'd envisioned ice skating or buffing a mirror.

In a guidebook to Alaskan rivers a former boss of mine authored, she contrarily wrote, "Beware: high winds are notorious on the Sound and can capsize boats." And: "Do not attempt to cross except when conditions are very calm, early in the morning." And: "Crossing should be made only in a sleek boat, such as a folding kayak and *not* in a raft" [emphasis hers]. Extensive shoals from sediment the Noatak dumps into Kotzebue Sound make that sea treacherous, especially when wind and tide oppose each other. I can't check if the tide is incoming, outgoing, or slack because I did not bring a local tide table.

It *is* late in the day, and although my barge is shapely and sleek, it's not really seaworthy. Air balloons its tubes, which ride high on the water, creating a large profile, as a sail would. It has no rudder, no anchor. But the wind, offshore now, seems mild compared to the past days, force 3 on Beaufort's scale—a "gentle breeze" with large wavelets, and crests beginning to break with "foam of glassy appearance," and "leaves and small twigs in constant motion." I have no lightweight flag to see if the wind might extend it, another of Beaufort's markers.

I set out on the final leg unperturbed.

As soon as I leave the last bluff's lee, the beasts hereabouts called the "woollies" fall upon me with all might. White horse manes run along foot-high crests, spraying me. If I can slink from the delta past a point on the Baldwin Peninsula that guards a bay north of Kotzebue, I should be alright.

But the wind, having quartered perhaps, strikes from an angle to the rear and sideways, "aft and port" for people who know what they're doing, pushing me but not in the direction I would like to travel. I flail maniacally, struggling to keep my boat from turning broadside and then upside-down. One oar is flexing in troughs with my straining when the wind or crosscurrents don't wrench it away from me and pin it against the hull. Its twin every second stroke or so grabs air. Stupidly believing the crossing to be a cakewalk, I did not even don my life jacket. It's too late now; I cannot let go of the oars. My clawed hands have fused with the grips. For the same reason, I cannot retrieve my satellite phone and alert the Coast Guard. Plus, I'm too proud to be rescued this late in the trip.

Wish I had some olive oil to calm the sea.

When I dare to look away from the mayhem, Magellan, tucked in next to me in the camp-chair seat, shows town farther away than before. I'm getting blown or sucked out to sea, or both. Despite the fact that I've broken a sweat in my hip waders and raingear, the wind quickly chills me. I don't know how long I can last in this three-legged dog race.

Didn't Magellan die like this? Too many boaters do in Alaska each year. (He did not, I later read. A poison arrow in the right leg during a battle in the surf on the Philippine island of Mactan finished him off.)

A fata morgana or ice mirage parts distant whitecaps: a fishing boat, whose twin outboards plow a course tangential to mine, but a razor-straight furrow and in the opposite direction. I holler and wave with one arm, the oar grip tucked behind my knee to prevent losing the stick, while bracing the canoe with the other. I regret that I did not keep my flare handy either.

Lo and behold—the fishermen change their course, heading toward me. Three Inupiat seasoned by weather and brine pull alongside, and when I explain my predicament offer to take me to shore where they started.

Calloused hands lift first the Conoco barrel and then the canoe onto the deck. The outboards' speed, fumes, and roar are dizzying. The noise enveloping us makes conversation impossible, but I wouldn't know what to say anyway. I'm not capable of small talk at this point and neither ready to share details of my journey nor sure I could convey the essentials. We land on Kotzebue cobbles in fifteen minutes tops. This is Tent City, a jumble of wall tents and shacks people from upriver villages use as fish camps during the summer months, drying and smoking the season's catch, and socializing.

Embarrassed, ignorant even about where I keep my own wallet, I offer the captain my barrel instead as a Fort Knox camp cache after unloading from the bow. He accepts graciously before backing off the beach and gunning the blubbering engines to finally catch some fish.

There we both bask, the canoe and I, hauled-out seals, flaccid and spent. The Chukchi Sea laps at my feet innocent as a puppy. No fanfare has welcomed us, no drums as in the days of the trade fair. For these mariners, it's a regular workday. No one is paying attention to our arrival, which may be for the best.

My trust in Blue Babe, unlike that in my seafaring skills, never wavered. Like a loyal spouse, she buoyed me when I felt blue. She carried me where I wanted to go, where I was meant to be. She has been my wilderness home, my means of escape, a safeguard from danger and a goal badly needed. She buffered me in choppy waters, always low maintenance and even keeled. For days on end, my survival depended on her.

The drama of my arctic trip looped in beautiful symmetry with closing and opening acts steeped in terror, antipodes of the nearly disastrous. In a strange coincidence of caprice, I am falling short of the miles east from Joe Creek to the Yukon border and those covered in the powerboat ride that would have allowed me to brag about a full traverse. But full it has been. Perhaps I will return to finish one day, or on a different route. I might pull the old gal from storage, and unroll, patch up, and inflate her for one more adventure.

But for now, *it is done.* Zu Ende. Gwichìi làgwįį'aii. Pianiksimaruq.

An Alaska Airlines jet roars in—the iconic fur-framed Inupiaq face smiling on its tail—and with it, the demands of a faster, less patient world.

POSTSCRIPT:
HOME FROM THE RANGE

Home is the sailor, home from sea,
And the *hunted* home from the hill.
—Corrupted from **ROBERT LOUIS STEVENSON**, "Requiem"

Melissa saw me cross the tarmac in Nome the day after my maritime debacle, over-dressed in my blue puffy coat, bushy bearded, with a thousand-mile stare, a Käthe Kollwitz charcoal figure or refugee lost in a foreign country. I'd descended the ramp stairs without too much trouble. At the luggage claim I seemed displaced and to shrink into myself. "How do we return home without breaking these threads that bind us to life?" Terry Tempest Williams asked after a visit to the Arctic National Wildlife Refuge. How do we stretch them to intertwine home? The novelist Murray Lee suggested that "those who have gone through great personal pain to escape society do not tend to function well when confined back to it." Cultural disorientation upon reentry is real, lingering, and quite confounding, and the subject of many thru hikers' blogs. The inner glow lasts for weeks but dims inevitably, in inverse relation to pounds regained.

My girlfriend gasped when I undressed for my first shower in two months—and not in a smitten way. "Gulag survivor," she said, exaggerating, shocked perhaps. We had no bathroom scale, so I cannot provide a number, but when I sat down on the toilet it felt weird not just because of the flushing. There was no cushion-ing, no derriere there. I had not taken my clothes off in weeks, had slept in long underwear and not bathed; it had been cold and raining anyway and I alone and soaked much of the time, so hygiene never became an issue. When I glanced in the mirror, I scared myself. Melissa had prepared a big dinner, and I stuffed my face as I would a woodstove on a cold day. Long after midnight, she heard the fridge door open and close, not once, but repeatedly.

Blueberry picking at Glacier Creek the next day, I could barely walk uphill and languished in my camp chair, which against all odds had survived without a single puncture. Freshly groomed and fed, I felt invalided; it was too soon to tell if and how the experience had changed me besides in a physical way, an effect that was short-term anyway. I now longed for more off-trail thru hikes, the Grand Canyon on the Colorado River's north side, for instance.

In September, having recovered my strength, I did manage to squeeze in a Grand Canyon trip, rowing on a two-week commercial run, getting paid. I still had Noatak calluses, so my mitts and butt were fine. The year after, I walked a forty-day stint below the North Rim. Melissa, by then my wife, joined me for part of the way. We'd gotten married at the Nome courthouse, under the stare of a tusked walrus skull.

In late September, around the time I returned from the canyon, Thomas Seibold, a German trained survivalist and outdoor instructor on a five-month wilderness trip, was last seen at a fish camp thirty miles north of Ambler. Described as "a real nice guy" and "very capable," he had had prior experience camping in the North, having gone on reindeer hunts in interior Norway. A "midwinter guide," his boss and mentor called him. "If he's not injured or delirious," he said with Seibold two months overdue, "he will stay alive." A grizzly may have killed and cached Seibold, or he perhaps fell on glazed rocks or broke through newly forming river ice. This is a voracious land. Seibold, Guilbeau, McCunn, the unnamed thru hiker at Atigun, the plane crew in the upper Ivishak . . . on several occasions my name could have been added to that short, sad list. Such is the fragility of existence, the slim margin for error or misfortune, the edge between exhilaration and annihilation.

More than a decade later, that 990-mile summer remains the best outdoor season of my life. I learned that extended solitude does not break me and that fear will not keep me from doing the things that matter to me. I am glad not to have missed the window my aging body is closing. Had I never done anything else, these weeks of silence and distance alone would have made it all worthwhile.

I keep writing about the Arctic beyond these pages you've turned, speaking up on the refuge's anniversaries or when some idiocy threatens the Brooks Range. In part, my outspokenness reflects a wish to give back to the place that over the years allowed me to make a living. Bob Marshall, still overly stuck on northern Alaska's importance for humans, valued it for "the emotional values of the frontier," the sense of discovery, freedom, and self-sufficiency that it preserved. Modern developers embrace a materialistic slant of the same legacy: economic opportunity, weak government regulation, and prosperity for the ruthless few.

The Ambler Access Project ballyhooed by a State of Alaska public corporation entails a 211-mile road through the south side of Gates of the Arctic that would lead to the development of a massive copper mine, a "resource," in the official spin, "essential for . . . green energy products, and military effectiveness." This Haul Road spur would not only carve up and pollute an ecosystem that six wild and scenic rivers water but also harm wildlife, especially the Western Arctic caribou herd. Villagers, though not all, oppose this latter-day stampede the state labels a "path to opportunity."

After a lengthy permitting process, the scheme by 2022 had reached the phase of preparatory fieldwork when the Interior Department, believing the environmental analysis to be flawed, halted it. It will resume when the Washington pendulum swings to the right again.

Or even sooner. After ConocoPhillips posted record profits yet again and scientists announced that global heating would exceed 1.5° C, the Biden administration, breaking yet another pre-election promise, approved the Willow Project on the North Slope, one of the country's largest oil and gas developments, in its largest still untrammeled tract.

It's like a tragic, dirty *Groundhog Day.*

As Alaska's metaphorically challenged second and eighth governor, "Wally" Hickel, said, "Our goose that laid the golden egg, the North Slope oil, is running out, so we've got to build more geese." Aldo Leopold, by contrast, cautioned against building roads into lovely country in favor of building receptivity into still unlovely minds, minds deficient in moral fiber and grace. ("Spiritual beauty," he called it.)

News headlines break my heart over and over again. Worldwide, one of ten faunal species will be gone by 2100. Mere nostalgia has bled into solastalgia, the grieving for places irrevocably lost, lost not to creaky memory but to development and its apocalyptic horse- and henchmen.

The single most important insight from my quest is that in Nature's grand workshop, I am an expendable tool. We all are. Our misdeeds and monuments shall become dust, or rather, a toxic stratum to be superseded. In the long, geological view, our affluence and profligacy, our trials and technocrats' triumphs shall count for nothing—a thought that offers me some consolation.

On a positive note—I hear you must finish on one if you care to retain readers as nobody likes a downer—the Arctic refuge and Gates of the Arctic endure in much of their terrific splendor. Adaptation and evolution proceed, evidenced in recent grizzly–polar bear hybrids ("grolars" or "pizzlies") and in beavers engineering the tundra.

Still, an Arctic warming four times faster now than the rest of the globe breaks even the most sophisticated climate models. Trees growing ever farther north during longer summers shrink tundra habitat and may sentence some species to extinction. Like excessive snowfalls, forests insulate soils currently thawing, preventing refreezing in winter, which could cancel out the additional sequestering of carbon dioxide in the wood's biomass. A historical drop in trapping could swell the surge of northbound beavers, which in Northwest Alaska advance five miles per year on average. Already, their stick dams, easily counted on satellite photos, distend south-slope Brooks Range and Kotzebue-area creeks into wetlands, which speeds up permafrost decay by decades: a waist-deep pond can warm bottom muck fifty degrees Fahrenheit above the ambient air temperature. James Roth, a UAF ecologist, never expected beavers on the North Slope, yet he estimates that by the second half of this century, they'll be settling there. Fishes and insect larvae will live in ponds they create, which are deeper and do not freeze solid.

The author Jon Waterman, a former guide on the Noatak, in 2021 floated part of that river thirty-six years after his last visit. He faced August temperatures approaching 90 degrees for three days running and mosquitos "strangely thick." As he correctly observed, night frosts should have killed most by then. Throughout the range, meanwhile, some streams have turned cloudy, rust-orange, and so acidic they curdle powdered milk, tainted by degrading permafrost, scientists speculate.

In an encouraging unrelated trend, Brooks Range maps are being decolonized. The US Board on Geographic Names in 2016 restored Gwich'in names for the

Chandalar River system. "Chandalar" is a corruption of French "gens de large" or "nomadic people," the Hudson's Bay Company voyageurs' catchall for the region's original residents. While challenging speakers of English, Gwich'in names for the different forks—Teedriinjik ("Luminous Water River") and Ch'idriinjik ("Heart River")—must be considered improvements from a writer's and former anthropologist's perspective. The Alaska Historical Society voted against the name changes as being "too politically correct," worried about pronunciation problems and "all sorts of unwanted pushback" from still unlovely minds.

Unfortunately, since my traverse the range has become crowded in places. On a 2022 six-day jaunt from Anaktuvuk to a valley ringing with cascades leaping through garden-like terraces, Melissa and I met almost fifty people where before I would run into two to four, tops. I hear river runners nowadays race and queue for popular Noatak campsites while, to the bears' distress, overfishing the headwaters. To preserve cherished memories, I might stop visiting there altogether. Or I'll go in the spring, when only animals track snowy ground and mosquitos are absent.

Blogs, Instagram, backpacking magazines and apps, celebrity outfits, and perhaps COVID upticks in staycations and post-pandemic travel rebounds are to blame for this trend. I don't mind sharing the backcountry, just oversharing. Too many hikers diminish a place, as do oil wells or cows. To update Leopold, "What avail are forty freedoms without a *quiet* spot on the map?" Do we need a permit system next? The Zen-recluse poet Ryōkan supposedly said, "It is not that I dislike people. It is just that I am so very tired of them." Lacking Ryōkan's Zen mind, I dislike many and multitudes. I detest our time's fads, foremost how in quiet country, to quote Robert Frost, "way leads on to way." One trail breeds more. I've seen it happen. We are loving wildlands to death.

Civilization's mission creep in the high latitudes, the changed seasons and vegetation, the loss of species and silence, of clean water and contemplation, won't be outright clear to the next generation, which inherits all this. You could argue that I contributed through my writing and guiding and lifestyle, though the largest group I ever led numbered five—the High Peaks all-women trip that included Kate—and I remain child- and carless. We're all implicated in what happens in the Arctic and worldwide today, the main dilemma of our era, the Anthropocene. It is crucial that we curb our appetites, humbly make amends, and start to take drastic measures. And by "we," I mean primarily residents of the industrialized—and about-to-industrialize—world, and among those, the 10 percent of the wealthiest segment, who in the US account for close to half of our glutton's share in torching this wonderful ark.

Life will find a way to continue impoverished on a path forward, with or without us. I've paced out my songline and listened to fellow creatures, creatures big and small, fierce and flighty, and to the wind, rain, rivers, and mountains. They let me pass through their territories. Cleaving me open, baring my core, they made me vulnerable yet armed me for dark days ahead. I have practiced wonderment daily, celebrating minutiae. The pleasure and mystery found in a flower or oddly shaped cloud have served me well in the strife of city life. I'll continue to walk on this feverish planet to stave off despair, staying connected to what is good, whole, worth preserving.

ACKNOWLEDGMENTS

Creating a book from the seed of an idea to the pages you hold resembles a long wilderness walk—except that it is the polar opposite as far as the involvement of people goes. Rosemary Alles got my heart churning during that Hulahula trip grounded at East Patak Creek when she inquired about our pet projects. She is now saving wild elephants, and I wish her luck.

Writing this book reanimated two intense months, and the passage of time revealed aspects I did not see then. In the research phase, Jennifer Runyon of the US Board on Geographic Names helped me solve place-name and map mysteries. Keith Nyitray, still managing Sitka's food co-op, shared his *National Geographic* article and recollections of his traverse with me.

Caltech Archives and Special Collections reference archivist Loma Karklins promptly sent the intriguing Guilbeau materials. Electronic Resources Librarian Amy Guy at East Los Angeles College equally shone by feeding me online articles. Jeff Rasic of the National Park Service enlightened me about Agiak Lake's archaeological record and Anaktuvuk's last caribou drive. Assistant Professor Hishinlai' Peter at the Alaska Native Language Center answered questions about Gwich'in linguistics and culture for me, as Larry Kaplan, a retired director of the center, did for Inupiaq.

Jane Billinghurst read my draft during a vacation ferry trip from Juneau to Bellingham and gave early encouragement. Bruce "Buck" Nelson generously agreed to let me use images and his fine documentary *Alone Across Alaska: 1,000 Miles of Wilderness* in promoting this book, which is most welcome since I did not take any photos.

Emily White, the manuscript's first champion at Mountaineers Books, shepherded it through initial development. Having turned down my proposal for an essay collection, she'd softened the blow by asking me to contact her if I ever decided to write about my traverse, which spurred me into doing it. Forgotten memories consequently spiraled off ones I had safely stored, vortexes following oar blades. For these, I am especially grateful. Laura Shauger and Lorraine Anderson helped this project across its finish line with substantially more grace than I showed at mine in Kotzebue Sound. Lorraine exceeded the call of duty by also double- and triple-checking some facts.

Because of the trip's nature, the list of people I thank for assistance—besides Dave Marsh on the Sheenjek, the anonymous worker at the Chandalar Shelf DOT, and the Kotzebue rescue boat's crew—is very short. Kirk Sweetsir of Yukon Air Service provided excellent support by placing my caches (and giving background information about the Sheenjek grave); over the years I have flown with him, he has always shortened the time with stimulating conversation. He is the antithesis of the cliché Arctic bush pilot, the Brian Dennehy character in *Never Cry Wolf*.

Bernie Kremer offered his place as a staging area and saw me off at the Fairbanks airport when I embarked upon my adventure. My Kaktovik friend Robert Thompson loaned me his satellite phone; I wish it had worked better, but I could never have afforded a rental, and it proved to be a lifesaver psychologically and logistically. My thanks also go to all the bears who spared me.

I owe utmost gratitude to the writers whose words and thoughts I've pilfered. We all stand on the shoulders of others, which out on the tundra helps you to chart a course. The most recent person in this lofty line has been Robert Moor, who suggested a better ending.

Last but far from least, Melissa Guy: without her care package to Anaktuvuk, her words of comfort, and her cartographic sleuthing during my liminal crisis of "the missing corner," I could not have finished. She was the home at the end of my thousand-mile journey and has been before and since.

NOTES

These notes describe people and works that informed my writing and otherwise influenced me. Many of them deserve to be more widely known.

PROLOGUE: GEOGRAPHY OF DESIRE

p. 11 **Thoreau counseled:** Quoted from his lecture "Walking," first published in the *Atlantic Monthly* in 1862 and sometimes referred to as "The Wild."

p. 12 **US Geological Survey quadrangles:** A USGS topographic quadrangle or "quad," like the ones I carried, at the 1:250,000 scale flattens a swath of terrain roughly 68 by 70 miles, bound by a latitude-longitude grid and shrunk impossibly to fit in a backpack's top pocket. This scale shows a larger area but with fewer details than other commercially available maps. I wanted the bigger picture to better gauge the flow of the range rather than dozens of 1:24,000 sheets (each mapping an area 7 by 8.5 miles), which I would have had to piece together on uneven tundra and weigh down with rocks, often in the wind or rain.

A WARM WELCOME

p. 21 **Breakup:** Like any tribe worth its salt, Alaskans have coined a slew of regionalisms that confound Outsiders. Here, "breakup" is not a relationship term, and "snowmachines" aren't creating film special effects. With countless citations of prior usages, *Dictionary of Alaskan English* by Russell Tabbert is the go-to source for word nerds but unfortunately out of print.

p. 23 **The safety margin:** Sales of personal locator beacons and similar devices have jumped 10 percent annually since 2016 and the number of individuals rescued in recent Alaska summers by 20 percent, according to Zachariah Hughes in the *Anchorage Daily News*, 2022.

p. 23 **inReach:** Readers interested in the effects of communication devices on wilderness experiences can find much to ponder (and mourn) in Ted Kerasote's *Out There: In the Wild in a Wired Age*—his account of clashing philosophies on a four-hundred-mile canoe trip in Canada's Northwest Territories—and in *Sierra* magazine editor Jason Mark's *Satellites in the High Country: Searching for the Wild in the Age of Man*, a broader look at facets of the Anthropocene including oyster farms, microchipped wolves, and light pollution in night skies.

p. 23 **"Why should a man be scorned":** Tolkien was also an essayist, and this quote is from "On Fairy-Stories," first published in 1947 and included in his collection *Tree and Leaf* (1964).

DIVIDING THE INDIVISIBLE

p. 25 **The boundary:** Lewis Green's hard-to-find *The Boundary Hunters: Surveying the 141st Meridian and the Alaska Panhandle* is much more fun to read than its title suggests. Besides incorporating firsthand reports of the surveyors whom the rough terrain challenged, Green delves into the line's political history, starting with its inception in the Anglo-Russian Treaty of 1825. Tim Ingold in *Lines: A Brief History* takes the opposite approach to the linear, including Australian Aboriginal songlines, comparing the line's cross-cultural, interconnecting role in weaving, observing, storytelling, singing, drawing, writing, and walking.

p. 26 **Dreads the day:** Chris Allan's *A Line in the Wilderness: Alaska-Canada Border* is only a National Park Service flyer but has some good historical photos.

p. 26 **65 million years ago:** The Brooks Range, peaking and subsiding like a wave, in its current configuration is only about twenty million years old. The Alaska Range of the Interior, culminating in

Denali, is the true "baby range." It formed very recently *in the big picture*, within the last five million years. You are not alone if these figures make your brain woozy, and one could argue that that is a raison d'être of geology.

p. 27 **1:250,000 Demarcation Point map:** I learned about this late lacuna from Christopher Norment, *In the Memory of the Map: A Cartographic Memoir*. Norment, a former Outward Bound instructor and ornithologist with field experience in the Canadian Arctic (described in his excellent *Return to Warden's Grove: Science, Desire, and the Lives of Sparrows*), built this memoir around his fascination with maps—a fascination I obviously share. His *In the North of Our Lives: A Year in the Wilderness of Northern Canada* is equally enjoyable and valuable for its insights into personal dynamics and the psychology of longer trips, in this case a Yukon-to-Hudson Bay canoe traverse.

p. 28 **Charles Evans on Kangchenjunga:** Charles Evans's *Kangchenjunga, the Untrodden Peak*, an account of the first ascent by the expedition leader, is unfortunately out of print. The team had agreed beforehand that they would not set foot on the summit if they reached the top, because of its religious importance to the local people. George Band and Joe Brown stopped about twenty feet shy of the summit.

ORIGINS

p. 29 **Two northern shrikes:** A whole book could be (and should be) written about the nature, history, and importance of field guides. The relevant ones on my shelf include Robert H. Armstrong's *Guide to the Birds of Alaska*, which is basic but shows how common species are in different seasons and regions throughout the state. He's also the coauthor, with John Hudson, of *Dragonflies of Alaska*—chasing dragons has become a popular pastime much like bird-watching. The multi-author *Arctic Wings: Birds of the Arctic National Wildlife*, edited by Stephen C. Brown, while not a guidebook, is a thoroughly researched anthology about groups of birds by people with on-the-ground experience. It features Alaska Native voices and a CD of birdcalls from the Arctic National Wildlife Refuge. For tomes on pan-Arctic fauna, it would be hard to do better than Richard Sale's *A Complete Guide to Arctic Wildlife* and Sharon Chester's *The Arctic Guide: Wildlife of the Far North*. The latter impresses with artistic renditions of the species and a wealth of information about trees, flowers, insects, mushrooms, mosses, even dog breeds and reindeer, all in one handy package that, however, most people will find too heavy to carry while backpacking. *A Naturalist's Guide to the Arctic* by E. C. Pielou has interesting bits about topography and meteorological phenomena, even if its exclusively black-and-white drawings are uninspired. Last, there's Alex Huryn and John Hobbie, *Land of Extremes: A Natural History of the Arctic North Slope of Alaska*. These ecologist researchers involved with the Toolik Field Station included a chapter about the region's human prehistory and an appendix for a self-guided Haul Road trip from Atigun Pass to Deadhorse, presenting mile-by-mile features of interest.

p. 32 **Thad Ziolkowski:** Thad Ziolkowski's *The Drop: How the Most Addictive Sport Can Help Us Understand Addiction and Recovery* is a memoir that can illuminate other habit-forming outdoor activities, such as long-distance hiking. (I prefer the term over the more popular "thru-hiking," which marks off chunks of terrain as something on the way to somewhere else, not a place worth dwelling in and on.) This is for surfing fans mostly; William Finnegan's *Barbarian Days: A Surfing Life*, reeling in even non-acolytes, surpasses it.

p. 34 **Keystone XL:** This was a proposed extension of "the safest pipeline ever built," which caused three major spills within five years. See theguardian.com/environment/2022/dec/21/oil-spills-keystone-pipeline-seem-worse-kansas.

p. 34 **In 1959:** The most accessible overviews of the history of the refuge and designation of public lands in northern Alaska remain Debbie Miller's *Midnight Wilderness: Journeys in Alaska's Arctic*

National Wildlife Refuge and Jonathan Waterman's *Where Mountains Are Nameless: Passion and Politics in the Arctic National Wildlife Refuge,* with the second highlighting the Muries' role. *Arctic Voices: Resistance at the Tipping Point,* edited by the photographer Subhankar Banerjee, updates the political issues in a polyphony of perspectives—all pro-refuge, naturally—but can feel a tad repetitive and lacking depth. Still, distributed to members of Congress, it was an impassioned plea and rallying cry badly needed. Banerjee's career-defining photos in *Arctic National Wildlife Refuge: Seasons of Life and Land* add power to the words of its co-contributors for people unable or unwilling to walk this hallowed land.

p. 36 **Grant Spearman:** Spearman is quoted in *In a Hungry Country: Essays by Simon Paneak,* edited by John Campbell.

VETERAN WALKERS

p. 42 **Getting up in the winter:** There's nothing wrong, really, with darkness. I imbibe it star dusted and moon faced, and value the relief it brings in the desert; and skiing or hiking or floating at night can be magic. (Don't even get me going on auroras.) Increasingly rare outside of Alaska, truly black nights buttress wildlife and human mental and physical health. Like noise pollution, a surfeit of light at the wrong time in the wrong place remains an underappreciated problem. Two thoughtful books on the subject are Paul Bogard's *The End of Night: Searching for Natural Darkness in an Age of Artificial Light* and *Let There Be Night: Testimony on Behalf of the Dark,* an anthology edited by the same author.

p. 42 **Gwich'in neighbors in Arctic Village:** Much has been written about the Gwich'in in journalistic reports, and in ethnographies now severely outdated. Much less has been heard in book form from the people themselves. Velma Wallis's *Raising Ourselves: A Gwich'in Coming of Age Story from the Yukon River* details lives on the brink between the past and modernity. Drawing on deep storytelling and bush-craft traditions, her epic *Two Old Women: An Alaska Legend of Betrayal, Courage and Survival,* the next best thing to time travel, has justly become a classic. A cinematic, feature film bookend to *Raising Ourselves* is worth tracking down: *The Sun at Midnight.* It sprang from seven years of collaboration with the Fort McPherson (Canada) Gwich'in and depicts the realities of cultural alienation. A hunter reluctantly mentors a teenager raised in the south who is sent north to stay with family after the death of her mother. In the documentary short *The Sacred Place Where Life Begins,* which toured the US, Gwich'in women speak out against oil development in voices heard too seldom. Among anthropological texts, Cornelius Osgood's *Contributions to the Ethnography of the Kutchin* deserves a browse for nuggets of lore, customs, and beliefs largely forgotten. If also now dated, Richard Nelson's *Hunters of the Northern Forest: Designs for Survival Among the Alaskan Kutchin* is a good summary of subsistence practices. In *Gwichya Gwich'in Googwandak: The History and Stories of the Gwichya Gwich'in,* Ingrid Kritsch and the elders of Fort McPherson provide a Canadian insider perspective.

p. 43 **Karsten Heuer:** Karsten Heuer, *Being Caribou: Five Months on Foot with an Arctic Herd.* For people tired of reading or more susceptible to visuals, I suggest the documentary with the same title, by his spouse, Leanne Allison, and Diana Wilson. (My favorite scene shows them after their trek, taking to Washington, DC, the George Bush doll that accompanied them.) In *Walking the Big Wild: From Yellowstone to Yukon on the Grizzly Bear's Trail,* Heuer chronicles a wilderness trip to promote wildlife migration corridors and the preserves they link.

p. 44 **The Arctic's only horned ungulate:** If you read only one book about northern sheep, make it Valerius Geist's *Mountain Sheep and Man in the Northern Wilds.* Geist was a Ukrainian-Canadian pioneer in large-mammal field studies with a sideline of Neanderthal research. If this book whets your appetite, move on to Ellen Meloy's *Eating Stone: Imagination and the Loss of the Wild*, a meditation on the Dall's Canyon Country bighorn kin leavened with humor and heartbreak.

p. 44 **One former president:** Theodore Roosevelt, in case you wonder. Ranking among the most literate of all US presidents—a progressive and wordsmith confined by bloodlust, saber rattling, antipredator sentiments, and machismo—he knew Great Plains winters with cold similar to the Arctic's. "All the land is like granite," he wrote in *Ranch Life and the Hunting-Trail* (1896), and "the great rivers stand still in their beds, as if turned to frosted steel." While he arbitrated in the US-Canada dispute that launched the boundary survey, Teddy Roosevelt, like William McKinley, the assassinated president he succeeded (and for whom Denali was renamed), never visited Alaska, which is surprising given his proclivities. He never managed to add a polar bear to his trophy hunting collection.

p. 44 **A handful of adventurers:** The literature of recent Brooks Range traverses is scant. The only other book I know is David J. Cooper's *Brooks Range Passage*. Cooper, a botanist, finished his 36-day, 280-mile trip with an Alatna float on a log raft. Keith Nyitray wrote about his quest in "Alone Across the Arctic Crown" (*National Geographic*, April 1993), and his article makes me sentimental about the time in the not-too-distant past when magazines still commissioned original art for illustrations. Sections in Kaylene Johnson's *Canyons and Ice: The Wilderness Travels of Dick Griffith* also paint a vivid picture of early traversers who tried living off the land. A great low-budget video production is Bruce "Buck" Nelson's *Alone Across Alaska: 1000 Miles of Wilderness*. Nelson, a former smokejumper and long distance hound living near Fairbanks, traversed the range on a route similar to mine. For an overview of miners and surveying parties ranging throughout the Brooks Range before recreationists, see *The History of the Central Brooks Range: Gaunt Beauty, Tenuous Life*. The book's author, William E. "Wild Bill" Brown, was an official Gates of the Arctic park historian and helped prepare the ANILCA legislation.

p. 47 **We puny humans:** For an excellent paper on "anthropophobia" in bears, see Stephen F. Stringham and Lynn L. Rogers, "Fear of Humans by Bears and Other Animals" in *Journal of Behavior*, July 11, 2017, bearstudy.org/images/stories/Publications/Is_Fear_of_Humans_Natural.pdf.

p. 48 **Robert Perkins:** The book by Perkins I carried was *Into the Great Solitude: An Arctic Journey*. Perkins deserves acknowledgment here for the thoughts his writing inspired in me during the hike. It was almost like having an invisible companion. (That was before the hallucinations started.)

p. 50 **In Indigenous minds:** *The Sacred Paw: The Bear in Nature, Myth, and Literature* by Paul Shepard and Barry Sanders, and Bernd Brunner's *Bears: A Brief History* did for ursine species what Barry Lopez did for wolves: a cross-cultural examination of what binds us to bears, a spell that does not seem to weaken over time but merely shifts in its emphasis. Shepard draws on Native American cultures outside of Alaska, but the themes and manifestations have resounded in the Arctic and Subarctic since the Neolithic age in what anthropologists call the Eurasian bear cult or, less awe inspiring, "arctolatry," which is not "worship of the Arctic." For an academic take on the subject, see Alfred Irving Hallowell's *Bear Ceremonialism in the Northern Hemisphere*, a text I devoured as a graduate student. Tooting my own horn, I refer interested readers to several chapters in *Ice Bear: The Cultural History of an Arctic Icon*.

KING OF THE KONG

p. 55 **"Gather at the River":** Part of Abbey's collection *Beyond the Wall*. His other Alaska river essay, "Notes from a Cold River," about his Tatshenshini trip, appropriately is in *Down the River*. Like me at Joe Creek, Ed lay in his tent with his knife unsheathed, though not for defense but rather, self-mockingly, to slash his way quickly out the back if "Lord Grizzly should come nosing around the entrance."

p. 55 **Singing cultures:** For details about the origins of animal voices and natural soundscapes, many of which are fast changing under human influences, see David George Haskell's *Sounds Wild and Broken: Sonic Marvels, Evolution's Creativity, and the Crisis of Sensory Extinction*, as well as Gordon Hempton's road trip science memoir *One Square Inch of Silence: One Man's Quest to Preserve Quiet*.

FLOWERS FOR THE AGES

p. 57 **"brotherhood of the butterfly net":** See Jennie Erin Smith, "Brotherhood of the Butterfly Net" in the *Wall Street Journal*, February 4, 2012, wsj.com/articles/SB1000142405297020457370457 7187081491942546. Linnaeus and the apostles streamlined biological nomenclature to overcome regional variations in species names. While this was useful and I appreciate their efforts, the lover of language in me frets at this Latin globalization. Over time, it might make obsolete many folksy yet precious regional terms.

THE FAT OF THE LAND

p. 63 **Philosopher-clown Ellen Meloy:** These words by Ellen are from *The Anthropology of Turquoise*.

p. 63 **Biologists like E. O. Wilson:** In my opinion, the best fleshing-out of Wilson's idea is Stephen R. Kellert's *Kinship to Mastery: Biophilia in Human Evolution and Development*. Another, related, Paul Shepard favorite is *The Others: How Animals Made Us Human*.

p. 63 **Prognostic myopia:** The term is Justin Gregg's. He lays it out next to other flaws in *If Nietzsche Were a Narwhal*, a book pithily subtitled: *What Animal Intelligence Reveals About Human Stupidity*.

p. 64 **John M. Kauffmann:** Kauffmann's *Alaska's Brooks Range: The Ultimate Mountains*, a good introduction to the range, contains chapters on geology, human history, and conservation, plus a literature overview. Similar in style and scope is *Earth and the Great Weather: The Brooks Range* by Kenneth Brower, son of the conservation icon Dave Brower, but unfortunately it is out of print.

BONES ON THE BLOSSOMING ARCTIC SPINE

p. 65 **Sweep of bull caribou antlers:** David Petersen's *Racks: A Natural History of Antlers and the Animals That Wear Them* is a hunter-naturalist's take on the headgear of North American deer species plus that of the truly impressive extinct Irish elk. Petersen is best known as the editor of Abbey's journals and letters. His no-nonsense, funny *Writing Naturally: A Down-to-Earth Guide to Nature Writing* brims with tips and encouragement for fledgling Thoreaus. Sumner MacLeish's beautiful antler image came from *Seven Words for Wind: Essays and Field Notes from Alaska's Pribilof Islands*. *On Trails: An Exploration*, by the Appalachian trail hiker Robert Moor, fed my ruminations on caribou and human pathways. His polished prose, bridging biology, history, and philosophy, broaches topics like neural networks, interstates, and the internet.

p. 67 **Father Christmas's beard:** Fitting into your back pocket, Gavin Pretor-Pinney's *The Cloud Collector's Handbook* makes an excellent gift for weather buffs. It has slots for recording personal sightings and awards points for different cloud types depending on their rareness.

p. 68 **"There's an art of attending":** This lovely, so-true statement is from Solnit's *A Field Guide to Getting Lost*, a meditation in autobiographical essays on uncertainty, trust, loss, memory, place, and desire. On the river trip to which I refer, through the Grand Canyon, I rowed and set up the toilet and listened while Rebecca read from her writings and spoke about our craft and on occasion also tried her skills on the oars.

p. 68 ***Helicoprion* roamed Permian Seas:** *Helicoprion* is a poignant reminder of the "Great Dying," the largest of five previous mass extinctions, in which spiking carbon dioxide levels killed 90 percent of Earth's life.

p. 69 **Alaska moss campion:** Northern plant guides I own and frequently consult include Jim Pojar and Andy MacKinnon, *Alpine Plants of the Northwest: Wyoming to Alaska*, and their equally extensive companion *Plants of the Pacific Northwest Coast: Washington, Oregon, British Columbia and Alaska*; Verna E. Pratt, *Field Guide to Alaskan Wildflowers: A Roadside Guide*; John G. Trelawny, *Wild Flowers of the Yukon, Alaska and Northwestern Canada*; and for foragers, Anore Jones, *Plants That We Eat: Nauriat Niġiñaqtuat*, a compendium of Inupiaq elders' botanical knowledge.

THE ONLY GOOD BEAR IS A DEAD BEAR

p. 77 **Bears in close combat:** Among the best of a handful of books about the nature of bears (black, brown, and/or polar), their conservation status, and their often-contentious relationship with Alaskans are Bjorn Dihle's *A Shape in the Dark: Living and Dying with Brown Bears* and Sherry Simpson's *Dominion of Bears: Living with Wildlife in Alaska*. For polar bears specifically, I recommend Ian Stirling, *Polar Bears: A Natural History of a Threatened Species*; Nikita Ovsyanikov, *Polar Bears: Living with the White Bear*; and Andrew E. Derocher, *Polar Bears: A Complete Guide to Their Biology and Behavior*. (It seems that the species' magnetism is enough of a hook in any main title.)

IN THE FOOTSTEPS OF ANCESTORS

p. 82 **The first White man:** Samuel B. McLenegan arrived on the US revenue cutter *Corwin* and made his way up the Noaktak River, a journey he recounts in *Report of the Cruise of the Revenue Marine Steamer Corwin in the Arctic Ocean in the Year 1885*, lead author Michael A. Healy. Such cutters, including the famous steam-assisted three-master USS *Bear*, were an early police presence in the lawless new US territory of Alaska, intercepting poachers, smugglers, and unscrupulous traders of liquor and firearms. The US Revenue Cutter Service, which evolved into the Coast Guard, also partook in humanitarian efforts like rescues of Arctic explorers and introduction of Siberian reindeer for Inupiaq herding.

p. 82 **Swarms at their worst:** Alaskan mosquito info is as scattered as the bugs themselves on a good day. A lovely starting point is Richard Jones's *Mosquito* in Reaktion Books' Animal series. Each volume examines the cultural-biological interface of a charismatic species with humanity throughout history.

p. 84 **Margaret "Mardy" Murie:** The prime source for the couple's life together and their explorations and plan for an Arctic refuge is Margaret E. Murie's *Two in the Far North: A Conservation Champion's Story of Life, Love, and Adventure in the Wilderness*. The Bonnie Krepps documentary *Arctic Dance: The Mardy Murie Story* is worth watching for the archival material and cameos of current conservation figures.

p. 84 **It would cheer her to hear:** The debate around the rights of nature intensified after *Should Trees Have Standing? Toward Legal Rights for Natural Objects* by American law professor Christopher D. Stone was published in 1972. New Zealand was the first to recognize a river as a living entity and has also acknowledged the legal standing of Mount Taranaki and a region, Te Urewera. See Patrick Barkham, "Should Rivers Have the Same Rights as People?" in the *Guardian*, July 2, 2021, theguardian.com/environment/2021/jul/25/rivers-around-the-world-rivers-are-gaining-the-same-legal-rights-as-people.

p. 87 **Hanshan:** Hanshan's poetry has appeared in numerous collections and translations. Many consider Red Pine's annotated, bilingual *The Collected Songs of Cold Mountain* to be the definitive edition, with images of the cave that was the hermit's home.

BROTHER AND SISTER BEAR

p. 92 **"Very tasty and nutritious":** Archives and Special Collections in the library at Guilbeau's alma mater, Caltech, holds his unpublished journal. The materials that archivist Loma Karklins sent to me included newspaper articles concerning the search-and-rescue operation; correspondence between Guilbeau's parents and the school; photos of the journal pages; and a patchy transcript of the youth's final journal entries, patchy because his worm-track words had been hard to decipher. The ultimate cause of his death remains a mystery.

p. 94 **Alaska's Koyukon Athabaskans:** Richard Nelson was the anthropologist most closely affiliated with this group. *Make Prayers to the Raven: A Koyukon View of the Northern Forest* and the five-part documentary with the same title are a justly acclaimed treasure trove of beliefs, practices, and taboos for a world that is animated, always watchful. Abandoning anthropology, Nelson became first a nature writer—authoring *The Island Within* and *Heart and Blood: Living with Deer in Alaska*—and later a radio host and natural-sound collector. Hank Lentfer's *Raven's Witness: The Alaska Life of Richard K. Nelson* does justice to the man who was a role model for me as an anthropologist and as a writer. More translated stories are in *As My Grandfather Told It (Sitsiy Yugh Noholnik Ts'in): Traditional Stories from the Koyukuk* by Koyukon oral historian Catherine Attla.

p. 97 **Athabaskan-Inupiat relations:** The works of ethnohistorian Ernest "Tiger" S. Burch Jr. offer the most in-depth information about Northwest Alaska's Inupiaq societies and their relations with neighbors, from warfare to trading. Among his publications are *Caribou Herds of Northwest Alaska, 1850–2000; Alliance and Conflict: The World System of the Iñupiaq Eskimos*; and the delightful paper "The Nonempirical Environment of the Arctic Alaskan Eskimos" in the *Southwestern Journal of Anthropology*, Summer 1971, journals.uchicago.edu/doi/10.1086/soutjanth.27.2.3629237, which discusses Inupiaq beliefs about ghosts, dragons, and giant birds.

p. 98 **In an interview:** The interview with Amundsen was recapped by Chris Zdeb in his article "May 19, 1927: Arctic explorer Roald Amundsen speaks in Edmonton" in the *Edmonton Journal*, May 19, 2015.

THE ELUSIVE RED SHEEP

p. 100 **Mark Cocker:** In Mark Cocker and David Tipling's *Birds and People*. This engaging doorstopper of a book about a fraught relationship gathers stories and anecdotes as well as cultural practices from hundreds of contributors.

p. 100 **Laurence Irving:** Laurence Irving, *Birds of Anaktuvuk Pass, Kobuk, and Old Crow: A Study in Arctic Adaptation*. Irving's observations on distribution, arrival date, and behavior, as well as Inupiaq names he gathered for birds, drew heavily on informants like Simon Paneak at Anaktuvuk Pass. The book is similar in style to Joseph Grinnell's *Birds of the Kotzebue Sound Region, Alaska*, and is based on Grinnell's field notes during the Nome and Kobuk River gold rushes.

A ROBIN BY ANY OTHER NAME

p. 103 **The names of things:** David Lukas's *Language Making Nature: A Handbook for Writers, Artists, and Thinkers* is a professional naturalist's tour de force on the complexities of biological taxonomy. Lukas encourages linguistic creativity—for instance, the coining of new species names—in people like you and me. Don't let the fact that this book was self-published fool you. It's important, provocative stuff.

p. 104 **We outnumber:** Partners in Flight (partnersinflight.org) estimates Alaska's raven population at 430,000. Its human population in 2020 was 736,000.

p. 106 **Ellen Meloy's mulling:** This quote is from Meloy's *Eating Stone: Imagination and the Loss of the Wild*.

p. 106 **Nietzsche wrote:** This dictum popular among canyoneers is from Nietzsche's *Beyond Good and Evil: Prelude to a Philosophy of the Future.* He wrote this in 1885, three years before his mental collapse.

THE LONGEST DAY

p. 108 **Rika Mouw:** Some of the artwork described can be seen at earthisland.org/journal/index.php /magazine/entry/seeds_of_hope/.

p. 110 **Out of Eden Walk:** Salopek's project resulted in a series of *National Geographic* articles at nationalgeographic.org/projects/out-of-eden-walk/#section-1.

p. 111 **"Panda bears of the insect world":** While the phrase has been making the rounds and has also been applied to the monarch and the golden-spotted beaked phoenix butterfly, in the context of arctic buzzers I've traced it to University of California Riverside assistant professor of entomology Hollis Woodard, quoted by Sean Nealon in "The Search for the Arctic Bumblebee," *UCR* magazine, Fall 2016, magazinearchive.ucr.edu/5269.

p. 112 **Circumpolar *Bombus polaris*:** According to Paul H. Williams et al. in *Bumble Bees of North America: An Identification Guide.* For an Alaska species list and basic information, see nps.gov /articles/000/alaska-bees.htm.

p. 112 **"As long as we have lots of energy":** University of Alaska Museum insect curator Derek Sikes is quoted in Anne Sutton's "The Brief Busy Life of the Arctic Bumblebee," *Alaska Fish and Wildlife News,* June 2012, adfg.alaska.gov/index.cfm?adfg=wildlifenews.view_article&articles_id=558.

BARREL IN A HAYSTACK

p. 117 *Vox clamantis in deserto*: This biblical reference in Isaiah 40:3 is also the title of a book of Edward Abbey musings and aphorisms, *A Voice Crying in the Wilderness.* Then there's the Eric Temple documentary *Edward Abbey: A Voice in the Wilderness* with cameos by friends and activists. Did this guy have a monopoly on shouting out loud where nobody hears you?

POST-SOLSTICE BLUES

p. 119 **Inflating car tires:** Although it's hard to nail down who said it first, the same claim has been made for the oil to be found in offshore drilling. For a discussion of the measure's effectiveness, see Michael Grunwald, "The Tire-Gauge Solution: No Joke," *Time* magazine, August 4, 2008. The direct comparison seems to have been made in the public's (or this writer's) mind. Originally, inflating tires properly was proposed as one of a bundle of energy-saving measures to prevent the need for drilling the refuge. The fact is, if all Americans kept their tires properly inflated, our nation would cut its gasoline use by 2 percent. So said Daniel Lashof, senior scientist with the Natural Resources Defense Council, before the House Committee on Energy and Commerce in his statement "On Hurricane Katrina and Gasoline Prices," September 7, 2005.

MEMORIES OF THE CORPUSCLES

p. 121 **George Schaller wrote:** Schaller kept a journal of his trip to the upper Sheenjek River with the Muries during the summer of 1956 and wrote it up as *Arctic Valley: A Report on the 1956 Murie Brooks Range, Alaska Expedition.* The trip is also documented in Roger Kaye's *Last Great Wilderness: The Campaign to Establish the Arctic National Wildlife Refuge.*

ONE BUNTING A SUMMER MAKES

p. 125 **"I never tire of the snow buntings":** Not much Olaus Murie wrote is easily accessible. Some watercolors are in *The Alaskan Bird Sketches of Olaus Murie: With Excerpts from His Field Notes,* which Mardy edited and from which I lifted this quote. His *Animal Tracks*, a Peterson Field Guide, abounds with track profiles and first-person anecdotes.

p. 126 **In a wayfinding feat:** Readers interested in more details about Inuit orienteering skills can find those in my Terrain.org article "Arctic Wayfinders: Inuit Mental and Physical Maps," March 14, 2019, at terrain.org/2019/nonfiction/arctic-wayfinders/.

p. 127 **Amelia Edwards** and **Edward "Uncle Bill" Wilson:** For a multifaceted, richly illustrated behind-the-scenes peek at explorers as artists and diarists, including the often-neglected contributions of women, I cannot recommend highly enough Huw Lewis-Jones and Kari Herbert, *Explorers' Sketchbooks: The Art of Discovery and Adventure*.

THINKING ON YOUR FEET

p. 128 **I do some of my best thinking:** Another stimulating read is *Walking: One Step at a Time* by the Norwegian polar explorer—philosopher Erling Kagge. His *Silence: In the Age of Noise* is also worth seeking out.

TWO TRAGEDIES

p. 133 **McCunn wrote:** Excerpts of his journals were published in an article entitled "Tragedy in Frozen North: Victim Writes Own Death Diary" in the Palm Springs, California, *Desert Sun* newspaper, December 16, 1982.

CARIBOU MINDS

p. 144 **Aleut hunters killed whales:** An eccentric little book by David E. Jones, *Poison Arrows: North American Indian Hunting and Warfare*, has information about early biological warfare as well as (speculative) instructions for how to bring down a woolly mammoth.

FAREWELL TO A REFUGE

p. 150 **Audubon noted:** In *The Birds of America: From Drawings Made in the United States and Their Territories, Volume 5*.

TROUBLE AND COFFEE CAKE AT THE DOT

p. 160 **Ned Rozell:** That book is *Walking My Dog, Jane: From Valdez to Prudhoe Bay Along the Trans-Alaska Pipeline*.

INTO THE GLORIOUS UNKNOWN AGAIN

p. 168 **The father of boreal ecology:** This quotation is from Pruitt's *Wild Harmony: The Cycle of Life in the Northern Forest*. Pruitt was not your typical scientist. He learned outdoor skills from local hunters and trappers. UAF fired the field biologist when he refused to tone down his report on the environmental consequences of Project Chariot—a Cold War scheme to blast out a deep-water harbor servicing future mining enterprises in Northwest Alaska with up to six nuclear bombs. He ended up teaching at the University of Manitoba and became a Canadian citizen. Pruitt's microscopic portrayal of wildlife has narrative flair without anthropomorphizing. Plus he's good on snow, employing Inupiaq and Chipewyan (Canadian Athabaskan) terminology.

p. 169 **Anglos, conversely, employed the possessive:** My go-to for Alaska toponyms, besides the USGS, is Donald J. Orth's *Dictionary of Alaska Place Names*, which now fortunately is available online: digital.library.unt.edu/ark:/67531/metadc303962/. Also online is an interactive atlas of Gwich'in place-names in the eastern Brooks Range with notes on some names' origins: eloka-arctic.org/communities/gwichin/atlas/index.html?module=module.gwichin.links.

p. 170 **Simon Schama:** From his book *Landscape and Memory*.

p. 170 **Mountains without tollbooths or handrails:** I borrowed part of this phrase from *Mountains Without Handrails: Reflections on the National Parks*, published when ANILCA was finalized. In it, the environmental law professor Joseph L. Sax convincingly argues for minimal management of at least some public lands or, putting it differently, for management that minimizes visitor impact. With mass tourism, the dual Park Service mandate of preserving while promoting the use and enjoyment of parks often damages them ecologically. Instead of catering to public demands, Sax reasons, parks should shape the taste for outdoor recreation. It's the sedate version of Abbey's anti-car ranting to "get out of the goddamn contraption and walk" so that you may learn something.

p. 170 **We owe much:** *Alaska Wilderness: Exploring the Central Brooks Range* is Marshall's classic account of rambles in what would become Gates of the Arctic National Park. His *Arctic Village* is notable for vivid character sketches of Anglo miners and Alaska Natives at Wiseman in the 1930s and of the social life there. A good biography, the only biography, is James M. Glover, *A Wilderness Original: The Life of Bob Marshall*, with details about Marshall's support of socialism and civil liberties.

TO THE ITKILLIK

p. 173 **Nunamiut hunters:** Like the Southwest's Pueblo Indians, the Nunamiut have attracted their share of ethnographers, which overall have been a rather competent and considerate bunch. Helge Ingstad, a Norwegian explorer, novelist, and playwright who in 1960 discovered L'Anse aux Meadows with a hunch and an ancient map, thereby proving Norse settlement in North America, taught Anaktuvuk kids how to ski. Upon his return to Norway, the author of *Nunamiut: Among Alaska's Inland Eskimos* sent them twelve pairs of skis and poles. Another is Margaret B. Blackman, who, drawing on twenty years of field seasons, infused her writing in *Upside Down: Seasons Among the Nunamiut* with observations of change that affected this community, as well as of changes in her health and marriage. It's Margaret Mead in the Arctic, if you will. Last in this trio is Nicholas Gubser (*The Nunamiut Eskimos: Hunters of Caribou*), an anthropologist-mountaineer with Denali and summits in the Andes and Himalayas to his credit. Anthropologists have not always been respectful toward this community. In the late 1950s, John Campbell excavated the remains of a Nunamiut man buried around the 1800s, which he shipped to the Yale Peabody Museum of Natural History in Connecticut. Only in 2022 did this ancestor return to Anaktuvuk Pass in a carry-on suitcase, accompanied by three elders and a teenager.

WHERE MOUNTAINS AREN'T NAMELESS

p. 175 **Mammoth bones:** For mammoth holdouts and climate change, see my brief *Alaska* magazine article "The Last Mammoth in Alaska," February 23, 2021, alaskamagazine.com/authentic-alaska /wildlife-nature/the-last-mammoth-in-alaska/.

p. 177 **Fashion statements:** For millinery as a catalyst in American conservation (and some absurd photos), see Linton Weeks, "Hats Off to Women Who Saved the Birds," npr.org/sections/npr -history-dept/2015/07/15/422860307/hats-off-to-women-who-saved-the-birds.

BOB'S COUNTRY

p. 178 **"So-called exploring expeditions":** This quotation is from US Geological Survey Circular 991, "Field Surveying and Topographic Mapping in Alaska 1947–83," published by the US Government Printing Office in 1984.

p. 180 **"A strikingly unflowerlike flower":** This comes from an ecologist no less, though a statistical one, E. C. Pielou in *A Naturalist's Guide to the Arctic*. But why did Evelyn Chrystalla hide her mellifluous name behind those initials?

p. 180 **Ruined the planet:** Eighty-five percent of all fossil fuels burned in history have been burned since World War II ended, and more than 50 percent since *Seinfeld* premiered in 1989, the year I moved to Alaska, according to David Wallace-Wells in *The Uninhabitable Earth: Life After Warming*. The American Psychological Association officially recognizes eco-stress, defined as "a chronic fear of environmental doom." Needless to say, it afflicts some of the guilty—us boomers—as well. See Susan Clayton et al., *Mental Health and Our Changing Climate: Impacts, Implications, and Guidance*; and Jason Plautz, "The Environmental Burden of Generation Z," in the *Washington Post*, February 3, 2020. In recent surveys, every other American teenager reported anger and/or anxiety about the climate crisis. Some act on it. The environmental journalist George Monbiot defends young anti-oil activists defacing classic art in "Do We Really Care More About van Gogh's Sunflowers than Real Ones?" in the *Guardian*, October 19, 2022, theguardian.com/commentisfree /2022/oct/19/van-gogh-sunflowers-just-stop-oil-tactics.

A CLOSE ENCOUNTER OF THE STRANGE KIND

p. 182 **"A forest of knee-high black pillars":** This phrase occurs in Chelsea Wald's article "For Global Warming, Tundra Fires' Effects May Be Skin Deep," *Science*, June 25, 2010, science.org/content /article/global-warming-tundra-fires-effects-may-be-skin-deep.

p. 183 *Whose dog is this? About Looking* is Berger's fantastic anthology; the chapter relevant here is "Why Look at Animals?" Of related interest is Jon Mooallem's *Wild Ones: A Sometimes Dismaying, Weirdly Reassuring Story About Looking at People Looking at Animals in America*. Barry Lopez's *Of Wolves and Men* needs no introduction; neither does *Arctic Dreams*, into which I dip frequently for inspiration. Less well known is a reference work Lopez and his wife, Debra Gwartney, edited. For *Home Ground: Language for an American Landscape*, dozens of poets and writers penned vignettes about rare or obsolete regional landscape terms. Use them or lose them.

p. 184 **Their push out of Beringia:** The latest in New World human migration theory and data, combining archaeology and paleogenetics, is Jennifer Raff's *Origin: A Genetic History of the Americas*.

FINDINGS

p. 186 **"They are better behaved than white men":** Raymond Barnett in "John Muir: Racist or Admirer of Native Americans?" partakes of some long-overdue housecleaning within the White middle-class conservation movement. Find it online at vault.sierraclub.org/john_muir_exhibit/life /racist-or-admirer-of-native-americans-raymond-bennett.aspx.

THE PLACE OF CARIBOU DROPPINGS

p. 191 **A Harvard philosophy graduate:** Most of my information about Jeffries Wyman and his Anaktuvuk Pass sojourn stems from a slim, lovely, hard-to-track-down book that also showcases some of his watercolors: his *Alaska Journal 1951*.

p. 192 **Simon Paneak:** Unfortunately, no biography yet exists about the prolific local historian-naturalist. However, some of his writings, drawings, and plant and animal lists are in *In a Hungry Country: Essays by Simon Paneak*, edited by John Campbell, and in Campbell's *North Alaska Chronicle: Notes from the End of Time*.

WEAKEST MEMBER OF THE HERD

p. 195 **Sir John Franklin:** More territory was probably explored in the search-and-rescue efforts for his last, doomed expedition than he himself covered. In 1825, Franklin left for his second Canadian and third arctic probe, the Mackenzie River expedition, as part of the effort of piecing together the Northwest Passage. Sailing west as far as Return Reef, 150 miles short of Point Barrow, he turned back in 1826. Along the way, he named a distantly visible range the Rocky Mountains (later to be called the Brooks Range) and a sub-range the Romanzof Mountains. His account can be found in his *Narrative of a Second Expedition to the Shores of the Polar Sea, 1825, 1826, and 1827.*

p. 195 **We drank tea:** The menu is from Fergus Fleming's *Barrow's Boys.* The Second Secretary to the Admiralty, John Barrow—for whom Barrow, Alaska, was named—launched a series of missions that drew on British naval officers idle after the Napoleonic wars.

p. 195 **Peter Freuchen:** How does eating your boots rank compared to this on the toughness scale? This and other outrageous feats (including the famous shitsicle episode and his escape from a Gestapo prison, where they took his prosthetic away) are in his smashingly titled *Vagrant Viking: My Life and Adventures.* If you read one autobiography this year, read this one!

p. 195 **Mobility itself may be enough:** The English anthropologist of the Arctic Tim Ingold has thought much more widely and deeply than I about nomadic elan or "life as a process of wayfaring" made coherent by storytelling. He presents his results in *Being Alive: Essays on Movement, Knowledge, and Description.*

HELL IS A PLACE WITH TUSSOCKS

p. 200 **Rock tripe:** Punchy little essays about eating lichen, seal eye, and ptarmigan droppings spice up *The Last Speaker of Bear: My Encounters in the North* by adventure-gourmet and mycologist Lawrence Millman. *Mosses, Lichens and Ferns of Northwest North America* by Dale Vitt and Janet Marsh emancipates cryptic life forms easily overlooked for the showier flowers. And while Ann Zwinger's *Land Above the Trees: A Guide to the American Alpine Tundra* focuses on high-elevation Rocky Mountain regions, much of it applies to Alaska's arctic latitudes. (In North America, vegetation changes observed with each thousand feet of climbing roughly equal those of driving three hundred miles north, as the temperature drops by about five degrees Fahrenheit in these increments.)

THE MOTHER OF WOLVES

p. 207 **Maps can be rabbit holes:** Peter Turchi's *Maps of the Imagination: The Writer as Cartographer* surveys the history of mapping and similarities with the literary creative process.

p. 207 **The daughter of a Protestant minister:** I fear that similar to the compassionate, well-researched northern wildlife portraits of Sally Carrighar's *Icebound Summer,* Fred Bodsworth's *Last of the Curlews,* and Henry Williamson's *Salar the Salmon,* Lois Crisler's books, *Arctic Wild* and *Captive Wild,* are no longer widely read.

p. 209 **Hundreds of stone** *inuksuit***:** For more on these markers, see Norman Hallendy's *Inuksuit: Silent Messengers of the Arctic.* For an overview of other forms, from the Bronze Age to Franklin's expeditions and beyond, see the crackling *Cairns: Messengers in Stone* by David B. Williams.

PROFESSOR COLD

p. 214 **Noah's Ark:** This quotation is from zoologist William R. Dawson's obituary for Irving, "Laurence Irving: An Appreciation," *Invited Perspectives in Physiological and Biochemical Zoology,* December 1, 2006.

CONDITIONS CANNOT BE IGNORED

p. 221 **John Luther Adams's:** These words are from Adams's book *Winter Music: Composing the North.* Another good example of this composer's lyrical prose is his memoir *Silences So Deep: Music, Solitude, Alaska,* which also addresses his leaving the rapidly heating state after forty-four years there, "for new topographies and sources of inspiration."

p. 222 **When Olaus and Adolph ran out:** Most of the information in this section comes from Olaus's unpublished field notes in the Alaska and Polar Regions Collections and Archives at UAF's Elmer E. Rasmuson Library. A good summary of his time in various parts of the territory is James M. Glover's "Sweet Days of a Naturalist: Olaus Murie in Alaska, 1920–26" in *Forest and Conservation History*, July 1992, jstor.org/stable/3983796.

I SHALL GATHER BY THE RIVER

p. 224 **A phony rush on the Kobuk:** Chris Allan's *Fortune's Distant Shores: A History of the Kotzebue Sound Gold Stampede in Alaska's Arctic* is downloadable for free as a National Park Service publication at npshistory.com/publications/gaar/fortunes-distant-shores.pdf. My favorite among the excellent accompanying photos is one of the Prussian Carl von Knobelsdorff, "The Flying Dutchman," who delivered mail to the miners on *ice-skates*.

p. 226 **McLenegan:** Quoted sentences are from *Report of the Cruise of the Revenue Marine Steamer Corwin in the Arctic Ocean in the Year 1885*, lead author Michael A. Healy.

TEEKKONA

p. 234 **The human geographer Andreas Malm:** For the Prussian general Carl von Clausewitz, war was "simply the continuation of political intercourse with the addition of other means." So is Andreas Malm's *How to Blow Up a Pipeline*, a sequel of sorts to Naomi Klein's *This Changes Everything: Capitalism vs. The Climate*. Don't let its title or a glowering bookseller intimidate you. Unlike William Powell in *The Anarchist Cookbook*, Malm offers no how-to advice but rather a timely discussion and moral justification of militant resistance for averting the worst. Climate researchers endorse direct action in Damien Gayle, "Scientists Call on Colleagues to Protest Climate Crisis with Civil Disobedience," in the *Guardian*, August 29, 2022, theguardian.com/environment/2022 /aug/29/scientists-call-on-colleagues-to-protest-climate-crisis-with-civil-disobedience.

SMOOTH SAILING

p. 240 **In Inuit myths:** In *The Eskimo Storyteller: Folk Tales from Noatak, Alaska* the Yale archaeologist Edwin S. Hall Jr. assembled two hundred regional stories that perfectly capture the Inupiat's earthy humor and their relations with nature and each other.

IN THE ZONE

p. 249 **To a Park Service biologist:** Marci Johnson, quoted in Suzanna Caldwell, "Rash of Bear Break-ins Hits Northwest Alaska Cabins," *Alaska Dispatch News*, August 21, 2014.

p. 250 **An attentiveness:** The seminal work by Mihaly Csikszentmihalyi is 1990's *Flow: The Psychology of Optimal Experience*.

A STRONG BROWN GOD

p. 254 **In a stunning discovery:** The archaeologists Mike Kunz and Robin Mills detail the find in the January 20, 2021, *American Antiquity* article "A Precolumbian Presence of Venetian Glass Trade Beads in Arctic Alaska," cambridge.org/core/journals/american-antiquity/article /precolumbian-presence-of-venetian-glass-trade-beads-in-arctic-alaska /3465746929B31ADBC6E1D1A23D09A2CD.

THE COURAGE OF CRANES

p. 257 **Edward Sheriff Curtis:** The best biography is Timothy Egan, *Short Nights of the Shadow Catcher: The Epic Life and Immortal Photographs of Edward Curtis*. More than two hundred of his Alaska photos not previously known were found in 2018 as described in the Isis Davis-Marks article "Trove of Unseen Photos Documents Indigenous Culture in 1920s Alaska" in *Smithsonian*, September 20, 2021, smithsonianmag.com/smart-news/trove-of-unseen-photos -documents-indigenous-culture-in-1920s-alaska-180978713/. Of these spoiled negatives, one hundred, repaired with Photoshop, are available (if pricey) in the limited edition *Edward S. Curtis: Unpublished Alaska*, edited by one of his great-grandsons, John E. Graybill, and John's wife, Coleen. Villagers love to identify relatives—or themselves—in historical photos. One of Curtis's subjects, the Inupiaq girl Anna Nashoalook Ellis, was still alive in 2021, aged ninety-seven. A bonus is the personal journals of Edward and his daughter Beth from the 1927 field season, also previously unpublished in their full length.

p. 262 **John Luther Adams:** In another composition, Gwich'in and Inupiaq voices and instruments joined the orchestra. For Inuit influences on Adams's work, see the excellent article by Dianne Chisholm, "Shaping an Ear for Climate Change," *Environmental Humanities*, August 2016, read.dukeupress.edu/environmental-humanities/article/8/2/172/8117/Shaping-an-Ear-for -Climate-ChangeThe.

p. 263 **A song Rasmussen recorded:** Rasmussen translated the song from the original Inuktitut into Danish, and his Danish account was first translated into English by William John Alexander Worster as *Intellectual Culture of the Iglulik Eskimos*. Many alternative translations are floating around but the heart of the message remains the same.

p. 264 **Aldo Leopold wrote about sandhills:** In his classic *A Sand County Almanac: With Essays on Conservation from Round River*. I reread the almanac almost every year, especially its paradigm-shifting chapter, "The Land Ethic."

LOST AT SEA

p. 272 **Wish I had some olive oil:** For documentation of this ancient practice, see Andrea Deri, "Oil, Storms and Knowing Part 1," British Library, December 4, 2019, blogs.bl.uk/science/2019/12 /seafarers-calm-waves-with-oil.html. And for scientific evidence, Peter Behroozi, "The Calming Effect of Oil on Water," *American Journal of Physics*, April 10, 2007, aapt.scitation.org/doi /10.1119/1.2710482.

POSTSCRIPT: HOME FROM THE RANGE

p. 275 **Terry Tempest Williams:** Quoted from her *The Open Space of Democracy*. I briefly met Terry at the Murie Ranch in Wyoming, when her husband, Brooke Williams, was the Murie Center director and Melissa interned as a designer. The ranch sees guests from all over the world. In my favorite anecdote (related to me by my wife), Terry was worried where on a ranch not set up for livestock they'd put the llamas Brooke had announced—they actually were Tibetan lamas.

p. 276 **Murray Lee:** Lee's *Compass* is a sendup of exploration literature by a doctor who practiced in the Far North. A publisher blurb describes it as "Part *Life of Pi*, part *Into the Wild*." It's a hoot; take it from someone who doesn't read much fiction anymore.

p. 276 **"If he's not injured or delirious":** The outdoor school's founder, Tamarack Song, quoted in Joshua Gardener, "Man Missing in Alaska Wilderness Since September," *ABC News*, November 19, 2012.

p. 278 **Warming four times faster:** Igor Krupnik and Dyanna Jolly synthesized an invaluable Indigenous perspective on the climate crisis in *The Earth Is Faster Now: Indigenous Observations of Arctic Environmental Change*, described at arcus.org/publications/eifn.

BIBLIOGRAPHY

Abbey, Edward. *Beyond the Wall: Essays from the Outside*. New York: Henry Holt, 1984.
———. *Down the River*. New York: Plume, 1991.
———. *A Voice Crying in the Wilderness: Notes from a Secret Journal*. New York: St. Martin's Press, 1990.
Adams, John Luther. *Silences So Deep: Music, Solitude, Alaska*. New York: Picador, 2021.
———. *Winter Music: Composing the North*. Middletown, CT: Wesleyan University Press, 2004.
Armstrong, Robert H. *Guide to the Birds of Alaska*. Anchorage: Alaska Northwest Books, 2000.
Armstrong, Robert H., and John Hudson. *Dragonflies of Alaska*. Juneau: Nature Alaska Images, 2010.
Atkinson, Brooks, ed. *Walden and Other Writings*. New York: Random House, 2000.
Attla, Catherine. *As My Grandfather Told It (Sitsiy Yugh Noholnik Ts'in): Traditional Stories from the Koyukuk*. Fairbanks: Yukon-Koyukuk School District, 1991.
Audubon, John James. *The Birds of America: From Drawings Made in the United States and Their Territories, Volume 5*. New York: V. G. Audubon, 1856.
Banerjee, Subhankar. *Arctic National Wildlife Refuge: Seasons of Life and Land*. Seattle: Braided River, 2003.
———, ed. *Arctic Voices: Resistance at the Tipping Point*. New York: Seven Stories Press, 2013.
Berger, John. *About Looking*. New York: Vintage, 1992.
Blackman, Margaret B. *Upside Down: Seasons Among the Nunamiut*. Lincoln: University of Nebraska Press, 2004.
Bodsworth, Fred. *Last of the Curlews*. Berkeley: Counterpoint Press, 2011.
Bogard, Paul. *The End of Night: Searching for Natural Darkness in an Age of Artificial Light*. New York: Back Bay Books, 2014.
———, ed. *Let There Be Night: Testimony on Behalf of the Dark*. Reno: University of Nevada Press, 2008.
Brower, Kenneth. *Earth and the Great Weather: The Brooks Range*. New York: Seabury Press, 1971.
Brown, Stephen C., ed. *Arctic Wings: Birds of the Arctic National Wildlife*. Seattle: Braided River, 2006.
Brown, William E. *The History of the Central Brooks Range: Gaunt Beauty, Tenuous Life*. Anchorage: University of Alaska Press, 2007.
Brunner, Bernd. *Bears: A Brief History*. New Haven, CT: Yale University Press, 2007.
Burch, Ernest S. Jr. *Alliance and Conflict: The World System of the Iñupiaq Eskimos*. Lincoln: University of Nebraska Press, 2005.
———. *Caribou Herds of Northwest Alaska, 1850–2000*. Anchorage: University of Alaska Press, 2012.
Campbell, John Martin, ed. *In a Hungry Country: Essays by Simon Paneak*. Anchorage: University of Alaska Press, 2004.
———. *North Alaska Chronicle: Notes from the End of Time*. Santa Fe: Museum of New Mexico Press, 1998.
Carrighar, Sally. *Icebound Summer*. New York: Ballantine Books, 1971.
Carthew, Kirsten. *The Sun at Midnight*. Jill and Jackfish Productions, 2016.
Chatwin, Bruce. *Songlines*. New York: Viking, 1987.
Chester, Sharon. *The Arctic Guide: Wildlife of the Far North*. Princeton, NJ: Princeton University Press, 2016.

Clayton, Susan, et al. *Mental Health and Our Changing Climate: Impacts, Implications, and Guidance*. ecoAmerica and the American Psychological Association, 2017.

Cocker, Mark, and David Tipling. *Birds and People*. London: Jonathan Cape, 2013.

Cooper, David J. *Brooks Range Passage*. Seattle: Mountaineers Books, 1982.

Crisler, Lois. *Arctic Wild*. New York: Harper, 1958.

———. *Captive Wild*. New York: Harper Collins, 1968.

Csikszentmihalyi, Mihaly. *Flow: The Psychology of Optimal Experience*. New York: Harper Perennial Modern Classics, 2008.

Derocher, Andrew E. *Polar Bears: A Complete Guide to Their Biology and Behavior*. Baltimore, MD: Johns Hopkins University Press, 2012.

Dihle, Bjorn. *A Shape in the Dark: Living and Dying with Brown Bears*. Seattle: Mountaineers Books, 2021.

Egan, Timothy. *Short Nights of the Shadow Catcher: The Epic Life and Immortal Photographs of Edward Curtis*. Boston: Mariner Books, 2013.

Engelhard, Michael. *Ice Bear: The Cultural History of an Arctic Icon*. Seattle: University of Washington Press, 2016.

Evans, Charles. *Kangchenjunga, the Untrodden Peak*. London: Hodder and Stoughton, 1956.

Fleming, Fergus. *Barrow's Boys: A Stirring Story of Daring, Fortitude, and Outright Lunacy*. New York: Grove Press, 2001.

Franklin, John. *Narrative of a Second Expedition to the Shores of the Polar Sea, 1825, 1826, and 1827*. Philadelphia: Carey, Lea, and Carey, 1828.

Freuchen, Peter. *Vagrant Viking: My Life and Adventures*. New York: Julian Messner, 1953.

Geist, Valerius. *Mountain Sheep and Man in the Northern Wilds*. Caldwell, NJ: Blackburn Press, 2002.

Glover, James M. *A Wilderness Original: The Life of Bob Marshall*. Seattle: Mountaineers Books, 1986.

Graybill, Coleen, and John Graybill, eds. *Edward S. Curtis: Unpublished Alaska*. Indianapolis: Vedere Press, 2021.

Green, Lewis. *The Boundary Hunters: Surveying the 141st Meridian and the Alaska Panhandle*. Vancouver: University of British Columbia Press, 1982.

Gregg, Justin. *If Nietzsche Were a Narwhal: What Animal Intelligence Reveals About Human Stupidity*. New York: Little, Brown, 2022.

Grinnell, Joseph. *Birds of the Kotzebue Sound Region, Alaska*. Santa Clara: Cooper Ornithological Club of California, 1900.

Gubser, Nicholas. *The Nunamiut Eskimos: Hunters of Caribou*. New Haven, CT: Yale University Press, 1965.

Haines, John. *The Stars, the Snow, the Fire*. Saint Paul, MN: Graywolf Press, 2000.

Hall, Edwin S. Jr. *The Eskimo Storyteller: Folk Tales from Noatak, Alaska*. Knoxville: University of Tennessee Press, 1975.

Hallendy, Norman. *Inuksuit: Silent Messengers of the Arctic*. Vancouver: Douglas and McIntyre, 2001.

Hallowell, Alfred Irving. *Bear Ceremonialism in the Northern Hemisphere*. Philadelphia: University of Pennsylvania, 1926.

Hanshan. *The Collected Songs of Cold Mountain*. Translated by Red Pine. Port Townsend, WA: Copper Canyon Press, 2000.

Haskell, David George. *Sounds Wild and Broken: Sonic Marvels, Evolution's Creativity, and the Crisis of Sensory Extinction*. New York: Viking, 2022.

Hay, John. *The Bird of Light*. New York: Norton, 1991.

Healy, Michael A. *Report of the Cruise of the Revenue Marine Steamer Corwin in the Arctic Ocean in the Year 1885*. US Government Printing Office, 1887.

Heinrich, Bernd. *Bumblebee Economics*. Cambridge, MA: Harvard University Press, 1979.

Hempton, Gordon. *One Square Inch of Silence: One Man's Quest to Preserve Quiet*. New York: Artia, 2010.

Heuer, Karsten. *Being Caribou: Five Months on Foot with an Arctic Herd*. Minneapolis, MN: Milkweed Editions, 2008.

———. *Walking the Big Wild: From Yellowstone to Yukon on the Grizzly Bear's Trail*. Seattle: Braided River, 2004.

Huryn, Alex, and John Hobbie. *Land of Extremes: A Natural History of the Arctic North Slope of Alaska*. Anchorage: University of Alaska Press, 2012.

Ingold, Tim. *Being Alive: Essays on Movement, Knowledge, and Description*. London: Routledge, 2021.

———. *Lines: A Brief History*. London: Routledge, 2016.

Ingstad, Helge. *Nunamiut: Among Alaska's Inland Eskimos*. Woodstock, VT: Countryman Press, 2006.

Irving, Laurence. *Birds of Anaktuvuk Pass, Kobuk, and Old Crow: A Study in Arctic Adaptation*. Washington, DC: Smithsonian Institution, 1960.

Johnson, Kaylene. *Canyons and Ice: The Wilderness Travels of Dick Griffith*. Eagle River, AK: Ember Press, 2013.

Jones, Anore. *Plants That We Eat: Nauriat Niġiñaqtuat*. Anchorage: University of Alaska Press, 2010.

Jones, David E. *Poison Arrows: North American Indian Hunting and Warfare*. Austin: University of Texas Press, 2022.

Jones, Richard. *Mosquito*. London: Reaktion Books, 2012.

Jonsson, Erik. *Inner Navigation: Why We Get Lost and How We Find Our Way*. New York: Scribner, 2002.

Kagge, Erling. *Silence: In the Age of Noise*. New York: Vintage, 2018.

———. *Walking: One Step at a Time*. New York: Vintage, 2020.

Kauffmann, John M. *Alaska's Brooks Range: The Ultimate Mountains*. Seattle: Mountaineers Books, 2005.

Kaye, Roger. *Last Great Wilderness: The Campaign to Establish the Arctic National Wildlife Refuge*. Anchorage: University of Alaska Press, 2006.

Kellert, Stephen R. *Kinship to Mastery: Biophilia in Human Evolution and Development*. Washington, DC: Island Press, 1997.

Kerasote, Ted. *Out There: In the Wild in a Wired Age*. Stillwater, MN: Voyageur Press, 2004.

Klein, Naomi. *This Changes Everything: Capitalism vs. the Climate*. New York: Simon and Schuster, 2015.

Kreps, Bonnie. *Arctic Dance: The Mardy Murie Story* (documentary). Craighead Environmental Research Institute, 2001.

Kreps, Bonnie, and Charles Craighead. *Arctic Dance: The Mardy Murie Story*. Portland, OR: Graphic Arts Books, 2002.

Kritsch, Ingrid, and the elders of Fort McPherson. *Gwichya Gwich'in Googwandak: The History and Stories of the Gwichya Gwich'in*. Tsiigehtsik and Fort McPherson, Northwest Territories: Gwich'in Social and Cultural Institute, 2007.

Krupnik, Igor, and Dyanna Jolly, eds. *The Earth Is Faster Now: Indigenous Observations of Arctic Environmental Change*. Fairbanks, Alaska: Arctic Research Consortium of the United States, 2002.

Leclerc, George-Louis, Comte de Buffon. *Histoire Naturelle de Buffon, vol. 5*. Paris: Hacquart, 1801.

Lee, Murray. *Compass*. Portland, ME: Publerati, 2022.

Lentfer, Hank. *Raven's Witness: The Alaska Life of Richard K. Nelson*. Seattle: Mountaineers Books, 2020.

Leopold, Aldo. *A Sand County Almanac: With Essays on Conservation from Round River*. New York: Ballantine Books, 1986.

Lewis-Jones, Huw, and Kari Herbert. *Explorers' Sketchbooks: The Art of Discovery and Adventure*. San Francisco: Chronicle Books, 2017.

Lopez, Barry. *Arctic Dreams*. New York: Vintage, 2001.

———. *Of Wolves and Men*. New York: Simon and Schuster, 1979.

Lopez, Barry, and Debra Gwartney, eds. *Home Ground: Language for an American Landscape*. San Antonio: Trinity University Press, 2013.

Lukas, David. *Language Making Nature: A Handbook for Writers, Artists, and Thinkers*. Big Oak Flat: Lukas Guides, 2015.

Malm, Andreas. *How to Blow Up a Pipeline*. London: Verso, 2021.

Mark, Jason. *Satellites in the High Country: Searching for the Wild in the Age of Man*. Washington, DC: Island Press, 2015.

Marshall, Bob. *Alaska Wilderness: Exploring the Central Brooks Range*. Berkeley: University of California Press, 1970.

———. *Arctic Village*. Anchorage: University of Alaska Press, 1991.

Meloy, Ellen. *The Anthropology of Turquoise: Reflections on Desert, Sea, Stone, and Sky*. New York: Vintage Books, 2003.

———. *Eating Stone: Imagination and the Loss of the Wild*. New York: Vintage Books, 2006.

Miller, Debbie. *Midnight Wilderness: Journeys in Alaska's Arctic National Wildlife Refuge*. Seattle: Braided River, 2011.

Millman, Lawrence. *The Last Speaker of Bear: My Encounters in the North*. San Antonio: Trinity University Press, 2022.

Mooallem, Jon. *Wild Ones: A Sometimes Dismaying, Weirdly Reassuring Story About Looking at People Looking at Animals in America*. New York: Penguin, 2014.

Moor, Robert. *On Trails: An Exploration*. New York: Simon and Schuster, 2017.

Murie, Margaret E., ed. *The Alaskan Bird Sketches of Olaus Murie: With Excerpts from His Field Notes*. Portland, OR: Alaska Northwest Books, 1979.

———. *Two in the Far North: A Conservation Champion's Story of Life, Love, and Adventure in the Wilderness*. Portland, OR: Alaska Northwest Books, 2020.

Murie, Olaus. *Animal Tracks*. New York: Chapters Pub Limited, 1998.

Nelson, Bruce T. *Alone Across Alaska: 1,000 Miles of Wilderness* (documentary). Fairbanks: Buck Publishing, 2008.

Nelson, Richard. *Heart and Blood: Living with Deer in Alaska*. New York: Vintage, 1997.

———. *Hunters of the Northern Forest: Designs for Survival Among the Alaskan Kutchin*. Chicago: University of Chicago Press, 1969.

———. *The Island Within*. New York: Vintage, 1991.

———. *Make Prayers to the Raven: A Koyukon View of the Northern Forest*. Chicago: University of Chicago Press, 1986.

Norment, Christopher. *In the Memory of the Map: A Cartographic Memoir*. Iowa City: University of Iowa Press, 2012.

———. *In the North of Our Lives: A Year in the Wilderness of Northern Canada*. Camden, ME: Down East Books, 1989.

————. *Return to Warden's Grove: Science, Desire, and the Lives of Sparrows*. Iowa City: University of Iowa Press, 2007.

Orth, Donald J. *Dictionary of Alaska Place Names*. Washington, DC: US Government Printing Office, 1971.

Osgood, Cornelius. *Contributions to the Ethnography of the Kutchin*. New Haven, CT: Yale University Publications in Anthropology, 1936.

Ovsyanikov, Nikita. *Polar Bears: Living with the White Bear*. Stillwater, MN: Voyageur Press, 1996.

Perkins, Robert. *Into the Great Solitude: An Arctic Journey*. New York: Henry Holt, 1991.

Petersen, David. *Racks: A Natural History of Antlers and the Animals That Wear Them*. Santa Barbara: Capra Press, 2010.

————. *Writing Naturally: A Down-to-Earth Guide to Nature Writing*. Durango, CO: Raven's Eye Press, 2014.

Pielou, E. C. *A Naturalist's Guide to the Arctic*. Chicago: University of Chicago Press, 1994.

Pojar, Jim, and Andy MacKinnon. *Alpine Plants of the Northwest: Wyoming to Alaska*. Edmonton, Alberta: Lone Pine Publishing, 2013.

————. *Plants of the Pacific Northwest Coast: Washington, Oregon, British Columbia and Alaska*. Edmonton, Alberta: Lone Pine Publishing, 2016.

Pratt, Verna E. *Field Guide to Alaskan Wildflowers: A Roadside Guide*. Anchorage: Alaskakrafts, 1989.

Pretor-Pinney, Gavin. *The Cloud Collector's Handbook*. San Francisco: Chronicle Books, 2011.

Pruitt, William O., Jr. *Wild Harmony: The Cycle of Life in the Northern Forest*. New York: Nick Lyons Books, 1988.

Raff, Jennifer. *Origin: A Genetic History of the Americas*. New York City: Twelve, 2022.

Rasmussen, Knud. *Intellectual Culture of the Iglulik Eskimos*. Translated by W. Worster. New York: AMS Press, 1976.

Rozell, Ned. *Walking My Dog, Jane: From Valdez to Prudhoe Bay Along the Trans-Alaska Pipeline*. Pittsburgh: Duquesne University Press, 2000.

Sale, Richard. *A Complete Guide to Arctic Wildlife*. Richmond Hill, Ontario: Firefly Books, 2012.

Sax, Joseph L. *Mountains Without Handrails: Reflections on the National Parks*. Ann Arbor: University of Michigan Press, 2018.

Schaller, George. *Arctic Valley: A Report on the 1956 Murie Brooks Range, Alaska Expedition*. Unpublished, 1957.

Schama, Simon. *Landscape and Memory*. New York: Vintage, 1996.

Shepard, Paul. *The Others: How Animals Made Us Human*. Washington, DC: Island Press, 1995.

Shepard, Paul, Barry Sanders, et al. *The Sacred Paw: The Bear in Nature, Myth, and Literature*. New York: Viking, 1985.

Simpson, Sherry. *Dominion of Bears: Living with Wildlife in Alaska*. Lawrence: University Press of Kansas, 2013.

Solnit, Rebecca. *A Field Guide to Getting Lost*. New York: Penguin Books, 2006.

Stirling, Ian. *Polar Bears: A Natural History of a Threatened Species*. Markham, Ontario: Fitzhenry and Whiteside, 2011.

Stone, Christopher D. *Should Trees Have Standing? Toward Legal Rights for Natural Objects*. New York: Oxford University Press, 2010.

Tabbert, Russell. *Dictionary of Alaskan English*. Juneau: Denali Press, 1991.

Temple, Eric. *Edward Abbey: A Voice in the Wilderness* (documentary). Highway 89 Media, 2010.

Trelawny, John G. *Wild Flowers of the Yukon, Alaska and Northwestern Canada*. Winlaw, British Columbia: Sono Nis Press, 1988.

Tuan, Yi-Fu. *Topophilia: A Study of Environmental Perception, Attitudes, and Values*. New York: Columbia University Press, 1990.

Turchi, Peter. *Maps of the Imagination: The Writer as Cartographer*. San Antonio: Trinity University Press, 2007.

Vitt, Dale, and Janet Marsh. *Mosses, Lichens and Ferns of Northwest North America*. Edmonton, Alberta: Lone Pine Publishing, 1988.

Wallace-Wells, David. *The Uninhabitable Earth: Life After Warming*. New York: Tim Duggan Books, 2019.

Wallis, Velma. *Raising Ourselves: A Gwich'in Coming of Age Story from the Yukon River*. Fairbanks: Epicenter Press, 2003.

———. *Two Old Women: An Alaska Legend of Betrayal, Courage and Survival*. New York: Harper Perennial, 2013.

Waterman, Jonathan. *Where Mountains Are Nameless: Passion and Politics in the Arctic National Wildlife Refuge*. New York: W. W. Norton, 2005.

Williams, David B. *Cairns: Messengers in Stone*. Seattle: Mountaineers Books, 2012.

Williams, Paul H., et al. *Bumble Bees of North America: An Identification Guide*. Princeton, NJ: Princeton University Press, 2014.

Williams, Terry Tempest. *The Open Space of Democracy*. Eugene, OR: Wipf and Stock Publishers, 2010.

Williamson, Henry. *Salar the Salmon*. New York: Penguin, 1994.

Wrigley, Robert. *Moon in a Mason Jar*. Chicago: University of Illinois Press, 1986.

Wyman, Jeffries. *Alaska Journal 1951*. Rockport, MA: Protean Press, 2010.

Ziolkowski, Thad. *The Drop: How the Most Addictive Sport Can Help Us Understand Addiction and Recovery*. New York: Harper Wave, 2021.

Zwinger, Ann. *Land Above the Trees: A Guide to the American Alpine Tundra*. New York: Harper Collins, 1972.

Melissa Guy

ABOUT THE AUTHOR

Michael Engelhard worked for twenty-five years as an outdoor instructor and wilderness guide in Alaska and the Canyon Country. He moved north at age thirty to study subarctic cultures and follow the call of the wild. Engelhard received a master's degree in cultural anthropology from the University of Alaska Fairbanks, where he also taught very briefly; indoor classrooms just weren't his thing. A fence sitter and migrant by training and inclination, he moves wherever his needs are best met, just like the animals he admires.

Engelhard is the recipient of a Rasmuson Foundation Individual Artist Award, a *Foreword* INDIES and Independent Publisher Book Award, and three Alaska Press Club Awards. His books include *Ice Bear: The Cultural History of an Arctic Icon*; and the forthcoming essay collections *No Walk in the Park*; and *What the River Knows.*

recreation · lifestyle · conservation

MOUNTAINEERS BOOKS, including its two imprints, Skipstone and Braided River, is a leading publisher of quality outdoor recreation, sustainability, and conservation titles. As a 501(c)(3) nonprofit, we are committed to supporting the environmental and educational goals of our organization by providing expert information on human-powered adventure, sustainable practices at home and on the trail, and preservation of wilderness.

Our publications are made possible through the generosity of donors, and through sales of 700 titles on outdoor recreation, sustainable lifestyle, and conservation. To donate, purchase books, or learn more, visit us online:

MOUNTAINEERS BOOKS

1001 SW Klickitat Way, Suite 201 • Seattle, WA 98134

800-553-4453 • mbooks@mountaineersbooks.org • www.mountaineersbooks.org

An independent nonprofit publisher since 1960

YOU MAY ALSO LIKE: